Futilitarianism

Futilitarianism

Neoliberalism and the Production of Uselessness

Neil Vallelly

Goldsmiths Press

Copyright © 2021 Goldsmiths Press
First published in 2021 by Goldsmiths Press
Goldsmiths, University of London, New Cross
London SE14 6NW

Printed and bound by Versa Press
Distribution by the MIT Press
Cambridge, Massachusetts, and London, England

Copyright © 2021 Neil Vallelly

The right of Neil Vallelly to be identified as the author of this work has been asserted by him in accordance with sections 77 and 78 in the Copyright, Designs and Patents Act 1988. Every effort has been made to trace copyright holders and to obtain their permission for the use of copyright material. The publisher apologises for any errors or omissions and would be grateful if notified of any corrections that should be incorporated in future reprints or editions of this book.

All Rights Reserved. No part of this publication may be reproduced, distributed or transmitted in any form or by any means whatsoever without prior written permission of the publisher, except in the case of brief quotations in critical articles and review and certain non-commercial uses permitted by copyright law.

A CIP record for this book is available from the British Library

ISBN 978-1-912685-90-5 (hbk)
ISBN 978-1-912685-89-9 (ebk)

www.gold.ac.uk/goldsmiths-press

In memory of Mum and Nellie

Contents

Acknowledgements ix

   Introduction 1
1 The Futilitarian Condition 23
2 The Rise of *Homo futilitus* 53
3 Useless Responsibility 79
4 Semio-Futility and Symbolic Indigestion 105
5 The Politics of Futility 127
6 Futilitarianism in the Age of Covid-19 151
   Conclusion: The Becoming-Common of the Futilitariat 173

Notes 185
Index 227

Acknowledgements

The idea for this book emerged in 2016 during a wave of job cuts in the humanities division at the University of Otago, Aotearoa New Zealand. It started with the question, "Why are the humanities deemed so useless?" and grew into a wide-ranging study of the relationship between uselessness and neoliberalism. I am grateful to those academics, students, and activists who protested and, in some cases, resisted the job cuts. I wrote this book in-between various casual teaching contracts in the Schools of Arts and Social Sciences at Otago, and I stand in solidarity with the huge number of teaching staff in similar precarious roles in universities across the globe. The concept of futility will certainly not be alien to many of them.

I am indebted to my PhD supervisor Evelyn Tribble for giving me the opportunity to move from Northern Ireland to Aotearoa New Zealand to pursue my PhD research at Otago in 2012. This opportunity has been transformative both academically and personally. This may not be the book you imagined I would write, but your unmatched curiosity and integrity have served as models for my own research career.

The book evolved through discussions with friends and colleagues in the last few years, and I can only thank the many who gave me the encouragement to persevere with the project, especially Catherine Dale, Simone Drichel, Rhian Gallagher, and Sonja Mitchell. Rhian's suggestions for the book proposal were immensely helpful and profoundly appreciated. I would also like to thank Mark Seymour for acting as a mentor in recent years, and my colleagues at Economic and Social Research Aotearoa and the Centre for Global Migrations at

Otago for their continual stimulation. My research and life have also been made much richer by discussions with Jean Hogan, whose intellect always inspired me – she is greatly missed.

Parts of this book have appeared as articles in journals and magazines, and I thank these publications for the kind permission to reprint these in the book. Sections of Chapter 3 appeared in "The Self-Help Myth," published in *New Internationalist* 525 (April 2020): 56–59. Portions of Chapter 6 were published under the title "Counting the Costs: Covid-19 and the Crisis of Utilitarianism," in a *Rethinking Marxism* special dossier, "Pandemic and the Crisis of Capitalism" (Summer 2020): 215–223.

The staff at Goldsmiths Press have been reassuring, flexible, and conscientious, and I especially thank Susan Kelly, Ellen Parnavelas, and Guy Sewell for all their help. I extend my deep gratitude to Will Davies, the editor of the Political Economy Research Centre (PERC) series, for his initial interest in pursuing the project and his comments throughout the drafting and reviewing process. My thanks go to the reviewers of the proposal and manuscript for their constructive feedback, and I am grateful to Wendy Brown, Jessica Whyte, Adam Kotsko, and Richard Seymour for reading the manuscript and providing generous endorsements.

This book is dedicated to the memory of my mother and grandmother, who died within a month of one another at the end of 2015. Their love, compassion, and humour will always live with me, and I miss them dearly. I am likewise fortunate to have the constant support of my family and my partner's family.

Finally, this book would not have been remotely possible without the love, companionship, laughs, and piercing intellect of Lynley Edmeades. The book took shape through hours of conversations with her and every page bears her imprint. Not only has she read and commented on drafts throughout the book's development; she has also remained resolute in her belief in the project, even when everything pointed to the contrary. She always garners optimism when futility seems all-encompassing. We have added another to our midst, our son Molloy, who brings unbridled joy and perspective. Every day, he provides the reason to fight against futility.

The useful could only become a value after it had been sanctified.
Maurice Merleau-Ponty

Introduction

For centuries, economists and philosophers have theorised the value of utility, and how it shapes the division of labour, influences consumer choice, and contributes to conceptions of the good life or common good. Utilitarian philosophers told us that maximising utility was the magical ingredient to happiness. Economists, from classical to neoclassical to neoliberal, have invented terms such as "ordinal utility," "cardinal utility," "utility function," "total utility," "expected utility," and "marginal utility" to describe the behaviour of individuals and consumers, who themselves are conceived as rational "utility-maximisers." Karl Marx reminded us that "nothing can be a value without first being an object of utility."[1] While these thinkers may differ on how utility should be maximised, and who reaps the rewards of this process, few have disagreed that the maximisation of utility is in and of itself a good thing. After all, where would human society be without utility?

But utility is not something that naturally exists; it is not a neutral or objective concept. Utility is always an effect of social relationships, constructed politically, and deeply enmeshed in the power structures of a society. The question, then, is not so much "what is useful?" Rather, it is "how does something become defined as useful and who gets to judge it as such?" Utilitarianism provides a good example of the importance of this question. For utilitarians, the morality of an action rests on its potential to maximise usefulness, often understood as producing the most pleasure and least pain, for the greatest number of people. But in order to be maximised, utility must first be identified in certain materials and social practices, and this is where the question of who gets to judge utility becomes crucial. If capitalists hold power in a society, then it is easy to see how utilitarianism overlaps with discourses of productivity and accumulation, because processes like economic growth, trade, and wealth generation will be politically constructed as the most useful courses of action for both individual and social happiness. But if utility were defined in other ways, such as strong social bonds, universal welfare, non-hierarchical political forms, and environmental protection, then the maximisation of utility would look very different. For this reason, utility can never be conceived exclusively as an economic or philosophical concept. Instead, utility is always representative of a certain understanding of *political economy*, of the relationships between forms of production, labour, and trade and the mechanisms of government, power, and, ultimately, capitalism. This fact is most evident in the work of Jeremy Bentham, the founder of utilitarianism, who could only find one credible measure for utility: *money*. "The Thermometer is the instrument for measuring the heat of the weather," he wrote, "the Barometer the instrument for measuring the pressure of the Air... Money is the instrument for measuring the quantity of pain and pleasure."[2] Under such logic, the most moral society is the one in which individuals pursue the accumulation of money, under the ethical dictate that not only will this lead to individual happiness but also greater collective wellbeing. The perceived symbiosis between utility maximisation and the accumulation of wealth has been a dominant mantra of capitalist societies, where political power routinely ensures that utility is defined as money, and where a utilitarian ethics is continually invoked as justification for the exploitations and inequalities involved in the accumulation of capital.

The utilitarian fantasy of a world of utility-maximisers, rationally pursuing the accumulation of money and contributing to a secure and healthy common good, has predictably not materialised. Instead, especially with the neoliberal mutation of capitalism, a society of atomistic individuals has emerged, who view utility maximisation as a competitive endeavour, one that attempts to alleviate any responsibility towards the common good. The practice of utility maximisation, far from pushing us towards a more egalitarian society, has ultimately trapped us in a destructive relationship with capital.

Utilitarianism has flipped into futilitarianism. We get into debt in order to gain qualifications, only to discover that employment is increasingly sparse, casualised, and precarious; we wash out our plastic jam pots for recycling as fossil fuel companies destroy our seas and corporations raid rainforests at unprecedented rates; and, as a deadly virus brings the world to a standstill, we find that global efforts at utility maximisation have not rewarded the majority of the world's population with greater social and financial security. In fact, many of us maximise utility to ends that are useless to the greater wellbeing of society, often just to secure some semblance of individual survival. I describe this entrapment throughout this book as *the futilitarian condition*.[3]

The genesis of the futilitarian condition emerged precisely at the point where utility became sanctified under capitalism, because at that moment futility took on an essential dialectical value. Quite simply, for something to be useful, its opposite must be deemed useless. And the negative value of uselessness enhances the positive value of usefulness. It seems logical to focus on and critique what any given society values as useful, but the practices, behaviours, things, and ideas that are deemed useless can tell us a lot about the political and social conditions of any time period. Yet futility has rarely featured in any comprehensive way in the study of capitalism, aside from Richard Sennett's "spectre of uselessness" thesis.[4] Perhaps this is because futility appears to be a side-effect of capitalist production and its social relations, something that is not intrinsic to the functionality of capitalism. The aim of this book is to illustrate, on the contrary, that the concept of futility deserves more attention in critical examinations of capitalism, especially because futility is central to the development, implementation, and longevity of neoliberal capitalism in the early twenty-first century.

The example of the contemporary university can help contextualise the concept of the futilitarian condition. The university is now dependent on a vast army of casual and adjunct teaching staff, mostly postgraduate students or post-PhD gig workers, without whom the university would collapse.[5] Yet these staff are routinely treated with contempt by university hierarchies and exploited on short-term contracts that rarely cover the entirety of the hours they actually work. But in order to get a full-time academic job – which are increasingly rare in some disciplines, especially the humanities – these workers are required not only to gain as much teaching experience as possible, but also to relentlessly publish their research, which is of course done in their own time (and often without access to university libraries). In other words, they are forced to maximise their utility as much as possible, with the faint hope that this might lead to a secure job in the future. For a very select few, this full-time job becomes a reality. But for the vast majority, the desire to make themselves useful traps them in a cycle of short-term contracts that pay very little and ultimately lead nowhere. The university knows that this intellectual precariat has little choice but to maximise utility, so it can exploit their acts by paying less and less for the labour of teaching, while still maintaining the influx of students and fees. It is clear, therefore, that the practice of utility maximisation on the part of this intellectual precariat might on a few occasions lead to individual wellbeing in the form of a permanent position, but it also entrenches the conditions that make the wellbeing of the vast majority of the precariat impossible.

The university is by far not the only example of the logic of the futilitarian condition, as will become evident in the subsequent pages of this book. In fact, we will find that neoliberal capitalism seems to work better when many of us are rendered useless, not only because we are incapable of challenging its hegemony, but also because, in our desperation to maximise utility to improve our individual social and economic conditions, we simultaneously internalise the rationalities of self-sufficiency, personal responsibility, and competition that dismantle social solidarities. Moreover, maximising utility often generates debt, which has become the prime commodity of a predatory financialised capital.[6]

Increasingly, use value is unrelated to our conscious attempts at utility maximisation. For many corporations, we are at our most useful in our leisure time, when we are shopping online, posting on social media, scrolling through the news on our phones, wearing Fitbits, or simply turning on Alexa as we wander around the house.[7] When we do so, we generate information for a vast technological infrastructure that generates capital through sharing this information with other corporations and advertisers. This is not to mention the existential futility of neoliberal life, where we are confronted by such vast social, political, and environmental inequalities and catastrophes, that it is almost impossible not to feel useless in confronting these issues. The complexity of these issues and their amorphous, decentralised nature also mean that most of us do not understand, for example, how the financial system works, how data is collected, stored, and used, or the microbiology of viruses, and therefore we do not know who or what exactly is responsible for financial crises, privacy breaches, or pandemics. It is much easier to blame immigrants, elites, or even postmodernism.

Neoliberal capitalism feeds on our futility and, at the same time, as a normative governing reason – in the Foucauldian sense of "the conduct of conduct"[8] – neoliberalism pushes us to behave as if our individual acts of utility maximisation will secure our wellbeing, and even at times affect substantive social change. By always translating the social through the lens of the individual, neoliberalism reduces questions of social justice and transformation to little more than forms of marketisation and consumer choice. Throughout this book, I will provide several examples of how neoliberal reason manifests itself in a series of useless social and political endeavours, from self-marketing to ethical consumerism, which often see themselves as radical alternatives to the status quo but in practice only reinforce it. Futility masked as utility is the essence of neoliberalism's transformation of everyday life, and this book seeks to identify and extrapolate the rationalities, tactics, experiences, and politics of futility that dominate life in the early twenty-first century.

Neoliberalism was born in the minds of European philosophers and economists in the 1920s and 1930s, turned into a "movement" by the members of the Mont Pèlerin Society in the late 1940s, promoted by the public intellectuals of the Chicago School of Economics in the mid-twentieth century, energised by the economic and political crises of the 1970s, embraced by the New Right (and Left in Australia and Aotearoa New Zealand) of the 1980s, transformed into a technocratic project by the New Democrats and New Labour of the 1990s, and fortified in the aftermath of the 2008 global financial crisis. Throughout this evolution, it has organised an attack on the very foundations of social life by, to quote Wendy Brown, "dismantling and disparaging the social state in the name of free, responsibilised individuals."[9] Margaret Thatcher's infamous claim in the late 1980s that "there is no such thing as society" symbolised the political victory of the neoliberal reimagining of the social. Brown notes that this reimagining has "produced massive disorientation" on the Left. "If there is no such thing as society," she writes, "but only individuals and families oriented by markets and morals, there is no such thing as social power generating hierarchies, exclusion, and violence, let alone subjectivity at the sites of class, gender, or race."[10] This disorientation was compounded by the ascent of leftist governments in parts of the Global North that effectively agreed with Thatcher's assessment of society, prioritising personal responsibility, entrepreneurialism, and competition between citizens over economic intervention, welfare, and social security.

This is not to say that the term "social" disappears in "actually existing neoliberalism."[11] William Davies points out that the "rhetoric of the social" permeates so much of contemporary governance and policy, from "social enterprise" and "social indicators" to "social impact bonds" and "social neuroscience." But rather than representing "neoliberalism in retreat," these invocations of the social are "brought back as a way of providing support, such that individuals can continue to live self-reliant, risk-aware, healthy lifestyles that neoliberalism requires of them." Neoliberalism, in this sense, has effectively colonised the social in ways that consolidate neoliberal rationality, using state infrastructure to do so. "The new form of sociality that is emerging," Davies writes, "may not represent a buffer *between* the coercive state and the spontaneous economic individual. Instead, it may be that this is precisely how the two are most firmly cemented together."[12] When the state uses the social to demand neoliberal conformity from its citizens, then the fruits of utility maximisation no longer find an avenue for collective expression. This reinvention of the social has enabled neoliberalism to undercut most democratic values, not by eradicating democracy *per se*, but by hollowing out the essence of democratic institutions so that all that is left is a mirage.[13] Without a functioning democratic framework, dependent on strong social bonds and institutions, utility maximisation aims not at an aggregation of prosperity, where democratic decisions and institutions ensure that the majority of people are better off, but at an entirely individualistic result, where each citizen rates her or his utility against others.

Davies lays out this logic of competition in detail in his book *The Limits of Neoliberalism*, where he notes that neoliberalism pursues the "deconstruction of the language of the 'common good' or the 'public,' which is accused of a potentially dangerous mysticism."[14] This deconstruction is clear in the ideas of one of the most influential neoliberal thinkers of the twentieth century, Friedrich Hayek, who contended that competition "is the only method by which our activities can be adjusted to each other without coercive or arbitrary invention of authority." He continued: "one of the main arguments in favour of competition is that it dispenses with the need for 'conscious social control' and that it gives the individuals a chance to decide whether the prospects of a particular occupation are sufficient to compensate for the disadvantages and risks connected with it."[15] Under this model, economic rationality and market-based calculations replace politically contracted concepts of "common good" or the "public," which effectively entail "*the disenchantment of politics by economics.*"[16] By subsuming the political into the economic, the neoliberal state situates economic experts and technocrats at the heart of the state apparatus, rendering almost all policy decisions to cut-throat cost and benefit calculation.

To say that neoliberalism has led to the "disenchantment of politics by economics," however, does not mean that neoliberals have taken a backseat in the world of politics. In his extensive history of what he calls the Geneva school of neoliberalism, Quinn Slobodian makes the point that "neoliberalism emerged in the 1930s less as an economic project than as a project of politics and law. The search was on for models of governance, at scales from the local to the global, that would best encase and protect the world economy."[17] The early neoliberals realised that the kind of world economy they envisaged – a borderless market aggressively protected by global legal infrastructures and regulatory bodies – could not become a reality without first of all capturing political imaginations and laying legal infrastructure. Far from absent, the state had a critical role to play in this project. Ludwig von Mises, Hayek's mentor, outlined the state's role in blunt terms: "The state, the social apparatus of coercion and compulsion, does not interfere with the market and with the citizens' activities directed by the market. It employs its power to beat people into submission solely for the prevention of actions destructive to the preservation and the smooth operation of the market economy."[18] To this end, the neoliberals were, on the whole, ferociously antidemocratic and bitterly opposed to a politics that protected national or collective interests, which had become the dominant political and economic model with the Keynesian-inspired social democratic state in the aftermath of the Great Depression and Second World War. As Slobodian puts it, "[the neoliberal project] was not a minimalist but an activist vision of statecraft mobilised to push back against the incipient power of democratically elected masses and those special interests, including unions and cartels, who sought to obstruct the free movement of competition and the international division of labour."[19] It is clear, therefore, that neoliberalism has always been, and continues to be, a political project, where, somewhat paradoxically, the rights of private property and capital are protected from the activity of politics and democracy by state or global institutions and legislation.

The antidemocratic and globalist vision of the neoliberals would not gain serious political traction until the economic crises of the 1970s. But when it took hold in the Global North, especially with the emergence of the New Right in the US and UK, it radically transformed the nature of utility and how it should be maximised. A new human has emerged in the ensuing decades, whose subjectivity must always be sanctioned by its market relevance. *Can this part of myself be sold to others?* This has become the ontological question of our times. We are less human beings and more *human capital*, defined not by our social bonds but by our individual market value, skills, and capacity to contribute to production. Our relationship to other humans is constructed as one of antagonism because human capital does not see a world shared with others but a world of other living and breathing goods and services against which each piece of human capital must compete. The real battleground today is not between capitalists and workers, or governments and citizens, but between one's self and the image of one's self, how one appeals to consumers in the market of human relations. The vast systemic inequalities of the early twenty-first century are reconceptualised as personal deficiencies, failures in our ability to effectively accumulate human capital. Futility flourishes under such conditions.

For some, the term neoliberalism has come to embody a certain lack of imagination within current critical theory, one that has outlived its helpfulness in understanding the febrile political environment of the early twenty-first century.[20] Kean Birch and Simon Springer note that "neoliberalism has become a word thrown around with much abandon to mean almost anything academics of a certain political persuasion do not like."[21] Undoubtedly, neoliberalism is an often misused term, one that can foreclose rather than open critical debate. But its misuse does not mean that neoliberalism is a redundant critical concept, any more than misuses of the term capitalism or socialism render these terms worthless. I agree with Slobodian and Dieter Plehwe that to revoke the term neoliberalism is a form of "self-defeating denialism." They continue: "Marxism, liberalism, and conservatism have experienced kaleidoscopic refraction, splintering, and recombination over the decades. We see no reason why neoliberalism would not exhibit the same diversity."[22] In fact, the misuses of the term might require us to find new ways of extrapolating the particularities of neoliberalism, which is precisely the aim of this book. To this end, I coin a number of new theoretical concepts, from "the futilitarian condition" and "*Homo futilitus*" to "semio-futility" and "symbolic indigestion." Far from adding a new register of denunciation of neoliberalism, this book proposes that these new theoretical concepts can invigorate the study of neoliberalism, avoiding the kind of impotence that Birch and Springer worry has come to infect the critical literature.

To be clear, I am not proposing a new definition of neoliberalism, but a novel angle to its study. I do not see understandings of neoliberalism as a political project to restore class power, an economic and political rationality that governs human behaviour and organises social life, or a distinct and evolving intellectual tradition as mutually exclusive.[23] Rather, I envisage futility as adding a new dimension to each of these strands of critical approaches to neoliberalism. I also conceive of neoliberalism as describing both a period of time – the early

1970s until the present day – and a distinct but not immutable development of capitalism. I do not deny that neoliberalism has manifested itself in different times and ways across the globe, or that neoliberalism might not be appropriate to describe some contemporary manifestations of capitalism. But I certainly propose that neoliberalism has instilled a widespread rationality that has transformed what it means to be human in the twenty-first century. I agree with Pierre Dardot and Christian Laval's description of neoliberalism as "a political rationality that has become global, which consists in government imposing the *logic of capital* in the economy, but also in society and the state itself, to the point of making it the form of subjectivity and the norm of existence."[24] Likewise, I share Brown's opinion that "neoliberalism is semiotically loose, but designates something very specific. It represents a distinctive kind of valorisation and liberation of capital. It makes economics the model of everything, [including the] *economisation* of democracy in particular and politics more generally. It has brought a libertarian inflection of freedom to every sphere, even, strangely, the sphere of morality."[25] The concept of futility is my contribution to understanding neoliberalism's transformation of subjectivity and norms of existence.

I combine my account of neoliberalism with a vision of anticapitalist politics, furnished by the ideas of the likes of Jodi Dean, Mark Fisher, David Graeber, and many others. I do so because while neoliberalism might have widely instituted the futilitarian condition, futility does not begin and end with neoliberalism. For, as Birch and Springer note, "there is a concern that arises from the notion that by criticising neoliberalism, we leave significant space for ostensibly 'good' versions of capitalism."[26] Neoliberalism liberates capital in particularly destructive ways, but capitalism itself is always on the path to destruction, no matter which course it takes.

Those who call for a return to a Keynesian-esque version of capitalism or a progressive capitalism[27] often ignore the fact that, as one commentator puts it, "perpetual growth on a finite planet leads inexorably to environmental calamity."[28] Even the idea of "green growth," in which economic growth is decoupled from the use of natural resources, has been shown to be a practical impossibility. By drawing on empirical evidence on resource use and carbon emissions, Jason Hickel and Giorgos Kallis illustrate that while there have been examples of relative decoupling of GDP growth and resource use in the short term, the "absolute decoupling of GDP from resource use ... is not feasible on a global scale ... [and] is physically impossible to maintain in the longer term."[29] In other words, the pursuit of economic growth can never redress the ecological balance that has been destroyed by centuries of the expropriation of natural resources in the aim of generating profit. The futilitarian condition and capitalism are now inextricably conjoined in the decaying environment. If we are to counter futility, we must do so by dismantling capitalism.

Despite claims of its demise in the wake of the 2008 financial crisis, neoliberalism persists today in a more aggressive and parasitic form than ever before. Dardot and Laval write that "the 2008 crisis, which for many should have ushered in a *post-neoliberal moderation*, facilitated a *neoliberal radicalisation*."[30] The 2008 crisis made it clear that neoliberalism is a system destined to endless crises, and yet the vast majority of states and supranational organisations around the world have doubled down on policies of austerity, tax cuts for the rich, greater financialisation, outsourcing and casualisation of labour, privatisation of public services, and so on. This wave of aggressive austerity and extreme wealth inequality heralded the age of "new neoliberalism," which Dardot and Laval note "openly adopted the paradigm of war *against the population*."[31] By waging this war, governments around the world have pushed the responsibility of the post-crisis clean-up onto those citizens who were most severely affected, while absolving blame for those actually responsible for the financial meltdown.

After (or even during) any serious global event in recent decades – most notably, the 2008 crisis, the election of Donald Trump, and now the Covid-19 pandemic – commentators line up to declare the death of neoliberalism, only to fall silent when it appears that reports of its death have been very much exaggerated.[32] This endurance mostly produces two scholarly responses. One is to view neoliberalism as a zombie or a ghost ship, delegitimised but still sailing the global seas, unrestrained and unrepentant.[33] The second response – and the more productive one, I believe – is to map the restructuring, multitudinous, and mutative qualities of neoliberalism as a living political rationality and economic system.[34] William Callison and Zachary Manfredi outline the contours of this second response by introducing the metaphor of the mutant, contra the zombie. The mutant metaphor allows us to imagine neoliberalism as an evolutionary process, where "within the 'species' of neoliberalism, new variants are emerging that are distinct but nevertheless members of the same cast."[35] These contrasting metaphors are particularly important when it comes to analysing the recurring crises of neoliberal capitalism. Callison and Manfredi note that "unlike the image of an undead zombie, mutants are new life forms seeking to survive within changing environments."[36] Whereas the zombie assumes the continuation of a previous life form, the mutant accounts for the adaption of that life form to the shifting environment, and its evolution into a potentially stronger and more dominant version of the species. In doing so, the mutant metaphor permits us to examine what neoliberalism currently is, rather than merely asking why it still exists. A mutant version of neoliberalism also allows us to more effectively adjust politically to its evolving dynamics.

In the spirit of the mutant metaphor, this book views futility as an evolving process within neoliberalism, one that requires a critique on those terms. The futility of neoliberal life is abundantly clear on a daily basis, whether one works in hyper-bureaucratic institutions, trudges through pointless jobs, jumps through hoops to obtain welfare support, pays sky-high fees to get a university degree only to find a precarious job market, lives on land that will soon be under water, or simply stands in a seemingly endless queue as only one checkout counter is open. And crucially, the everydayness of this futility is on the rise, especially as the Covid-19 pandemic locks us in isolated bubbles, distant from others. Of course, it is also essential to note that these experiences of futility are differentially distributed across the social sphere, depending on a host of identifiers such as class, gender, race, ethnicity, and sexuality. But what I hope to show in this book are some common features of futility across social and cultural divides. These commonalities include entrapment in a series of labour tasks or behaviours that only reinforce capitalist exploitation, complete responsibility for one's wellbeing in an economic and social system that dominates and exploits individual utility, inability to counter the rapid destabilisation of the natural environment, failure to use language in a way that might be heard or has meaning beyond its information value, increasing isolation from social life, reduction of the political to consumer choice, and incapacity to imagine anything other than the present state of affairs. This book illustrates that these features of futility do not represent a defect in our characters, but are instead effects of the operating principles of neoliberal capitalism and our internalisation of neoliberal rationality.

It is certainly true, however, that many people do not care about whether utilitarianism has flipped into futilitarianism, or whether their acts of utility maximisation are exploited by neoliberalism to dismantle the notion of society. In fact, in the Global North, lots of people are relatively secure and settled, especially if they are white, middle-aged to elderly, and have citizenship, a house (or several), a regular income or pension, and access to decent (increasingly private) healthcare. They might not care that the income gap between the Global North and the Global South has nearly quadrupled since the 1960s, or that economic and social inequalities have sharply risen since the 1980s, because everyone on their street seems to be doing fine.[37] And even some of those who are not secure are rarely directly angry with capitalism, but rather with urban elites, immigrants, or benefit cheats. But in this respect we are witnessing an important inter-generational divide between the old and the young, the baby-boomers and the millennials.[38] The naysayers, dissenters, and anticapitalists across the globe are increasingly emerging from the younger generations, the very ones who were born into neoliberalism and have known nothing else. Millennials often get a bad rap as the narcissistic, lazy, technology-dependent, avocado-smash generation who wouldn't know a day's work if it hit them in the face.[39] What is willfully overlooked in these criticisms is the fact that this generation have been thrown into a world where education is extortionately expensive, debt is unavoidable, work is scarce and precarious, wages are depressed, social services are diminished, the planet is on fire, and the future is seemingly non-existent. For many of them, the lived experience of neoliberalism – or whatever term they choose to use – is grim. From the US and the UK to Hong Kong and Chile, we are witnessing large pockets of anticapitalistic resistance led by these so-called lazy millennials. These are the desperate shouts of a generation rejecting the futility of neoliberal life.

Futility is not nihilism. Certainly, nihilism is a prominent feature of neoliberalism.[40] Mark Fisher even went as far as to describe it as "nihiliberalism."[41] Brown also argues that "nihilism intersects neoliberalism," creating a strange confluence of "ethical destitution" and "religious righteousness or conservative melancholy for a phantasmatic past."[42] This confluence of nihilism and neoliberalism, sewn together by governments on the Right and Left in the last four decades, has given rise to a reactionary politics that revels in simultaneously not caring about the welfare of the most destitute – exemplified by Melania Trump's "I really don't care do U" jacket, worn on the way to meet immigrant children imprisoned at the US–Mexico border – but also exclaims that the world is going to hell in a handbasket because of the loss of traditional conservative values.[43]

This nihilistic outlook has been developing throughout the neoliberal decades. Earlier this century, in the wake of 9/11, Simon Critchley identified a "motivational deficit" at the heart of Western liberal democracy, which created what he defined as "passive" and "active" nihilism. "The passive nihilist," he wrote, "looks at the world from a certain distance, and finds it meaningless ... In a world that is all too rapidly blowing itself to pieces, the passive nihilist closes his eyes and makes himself into an island." The active nihilist, however, "also finds everything meaningless, but instead of sitting back and contemplating, he tries to destroy this world and bring another into being."[44] As a result, the world is a split between extreme inertia and spectacular violence, between the mindfulness guru and the terrorist.[45] In recent years, the trend towards active nihilism has rapidly accelerated, especially with the election of antidemocratic and increasingly neofascist leaders. Moreover, the embeddedness of communicative media at the heart of social life facilitates instantaneous and ubiquitous expressions of anger and, on occasions, encourages terrorist attacks, exemplified by those conducted by members of the Incel (involuntary celibate) community, which constitutes a blending of toxic masculinity and celebratory violence.[46]

The concept of futility, however, makes room for another dimension in the meaningless of neoliberal life. In this dimension, meaninglessness is neither something that is passively instituted nor actively embraced, but something that emerges in people's lives without their consent or even knowledge, whether this be in their job, education, social circumstances, economic situation, or legal status. Where nihilism entails taking up a certain outlook on the world, futility is much more insidious and internalised. After all, many of us might believe we are contributing to society in a meaningful way – ask any PR consultant. Futility is instead a form of entrapment in the pursuit of meaningfulness, where we are forced to repeat a series of daily behaviours that ensnare us deeper into the pure logic of competition and individualism that negates any development of common bonds and collective welfare. By focusing on futility rather than nihilism, this book extrapolates not only the experience of meaninglessness that comes with neoliberalism, but the construction of that meaninglessness in contemporary social and political practices. *Futilitarianism* brings the futility of everyday life in the neoliberal period to the fore, with the hope of generating ideas of how to counter meaninglessness that do not end up in nihilism. Nihilism is an end in itself; an increased awareness and understanding of futility can be the starting point of something meaningful.

While this is certainly a book about neoliberalism, it is so in a way that differs to any other book in the growing critical literature. For one, it is not an intellectual history of neoliberalism nor is it solely an exercise in political theory or philosophy, although it certainly engages with these approaches. Instead, the book emerges at the intersections of political economy, social philosophy, critical theory, and cultural studies, excavating the philosophical history of capitalism and utility maximisation, examining the transformations of notions of utility and futility by neoliberal theory and policy, and detailing manifestations of futility in the labour, linguistic, social, and political spheres of the present. It draws on several concrete examples of futility from contemporary media, literature, politics, and popular culture to accompany the theoretical impetus of the overall argument. It is, in many ways, a *critique of everyday neoliberal life*.

The opening chapter lays the philosophical foundations of the book by examining the historical relationship between capitalism and utilitarianism, illustrating how the works of utilitarian philosophers in the eighteenth and nineteenth centuries came to influence classical and neoclassical economics. The 1929 Wall Street Crash led to a re-evaluation of utilitarianism's relationship to economics, which brought about two contrasting responses: Keynesian-inspired social democracy and Hayekian-infused neoliberalism. The former dominated in the mid-twentieth century, but the latter won the day by transforming the notion of utility in the late twentieth century.

Triumphant neoliberalism bought into existence *the futilitarian condition*, and the subjectivity of this condition is the focus of Chapter 2. In particular, the theory of human capital and logic of self-branding have come to re-shape human behaviour and relationality, leading to the evolution of the rational utility maximiser *Homo economicus* into the figure of

Homo futilitus, which maximises its own utility in a way that is largely pointless. To exemplify this metamorphosis, I focus on the contemporary world of work, in which many of us work harder and longer than ever but at tasks that have little, if no, social utility.

Chapter 3 shifts emphasis onto one the more pernicious aspects of neoliberalism: the ideology of personal responsibility. This ideology has been cemented in everyday life by a series of governments, employers, and corporations, which tie personal responsibility to ideas of individual liberty. In particular, the magical power of personal responsibility has been juxtaposed with the supposedly mortifying condition of dependency, which governments have used to justify the assault on the welfare state throughout the neoliberal decades. Ultimately, I contend, it is useless to have responsibility under neoliberalism because to take on greater personal responsibility only perpetuates the social conditions that require further acts of personal responsibility.

The flipside of personal responsibility is utter isolation, which is augmented by the communication landscape of the twenty-first century. Chapter 4 examines how the hyper-acceleration of language production by technology affects the use of language in digital communication. This hyper-acceleration transforms meaning – which requires the inter-relation of human bodies – into mere information. I call this phenomenon *semio-futility*, in which language is unable to be used to create the meaning intended in the act of enunciation. To accompany the phenomenon of semio-futility, I develop a theory of *symbolic indigestion*, where the hyper-production of language in digital communication is vastly disproportionate to the deceleration required to digest language and make meaning. Semio-futility and symbolic indigestion severely limit political debate and democratic participation because without the ability to make meaning or digest language, the political dissolves into simple binaries between good and bad.

Building on the concepts of semio-futility and symbolic indigestion, Chapter 5 maps the intersections of the political and futilitarianism, where political engagement and participation routinely serve to reinforce the operating principles of neoliberal capitalism and the pervasiveness of neoliberal rationality, even in political expressions that set themselves up against the status quo. Here, I look at examples of political consumerism, such as "buycotting" and "voting with your dollar," and forms of environmentalism that prioritise individual autonomy and personal responsibility. These forms of activism fall under the umbrella of what I define as "the politics of futility," in which political participation negates any real antagonism by entering the political on the terms presented by neoliberalism.

While this book was mostly written in the years preceding the Covid-19 pandemic, the book's central claims have been confirmed by the consequences of and responses to the pandemic. To this end, the final chapter reflects on how the logic of futilitarianism has been exposed by the Covid-19 pandemic, but, nonetheless, futilitarianism has been further cemented by governmental responses to the pandemic. To exemplify this point, I focus on two distinct governmental policies – the Coronavirus Aid, Relief, and Economic Security (CARES) Act in the US and the Australian higher-education reforms – displaying how a blending of utilitarianism and neoliberalism has enabled governments to shore up neoliberal hegemony. I finish by imagining what these developments might tell us about the post-pandemic future.

Ultimately, this book is a hopeful endeavour, if at times the content appears pessimistic. Futility is an experience that many of us share to varying degrees and, as such, it can also be the foundation of a *becoming-common*, where seemingly disparate lives are bound together by a shared relationality under the name of the *futilitariat*. This process of becoming-common can be the starting point for an emancipatory politics that refuses to accept the imposition of futility on our collective lives. This book contends that a different future is possible, but only if we confront futility head-on. *Futilitarianism* does so by developing a series of theoretical tools to navigate a way out of the non-future presented to us by the destructive forces of neoliberalism.

1
The Futilitarian Condition

In an eviscerating footnote to volume one of *Capital*, Karl Marx describes the utilitarian philosopher Jeremy Bentham as a "purely English phenomenon," claiming that "in no time and in no country has the most homespun manufacturer of commonplaces ever strutted about in so self-satisfied a way." Marx continues: "with the driest naiveté he [Bentham] assumes that the modern petty bourgeoise, especially the English petty bourgeoise, is the normal man. Whatever is useful to this peculiar kind of normal man, and to his world, is useful in and of itself. He applies this yardstick to the past, present, and future ... This is the kind of rubbish with which the brave fellow ... has piled up mountains of books." He finishes: "I should call Mr. Jeremy a genius in the way of bourgeois stupidity."[1] It hardly gets any better in the main body of the text, where Bentham appears as "the arch-philistine ... that soberly pedantic and heavy-footed oracle of the 'common sense' of the nineteenth-century bourgeoisie."[2] What is it about Bentham and his ideas that rile Marx so much? Utility is an important component of both of their worldviews, central to processes of production and social life. But utility for Marx means something very different to Bentham. For Marx, utility is an immanent concept, historically contingent and developed through concrete social and labour relations. In this sense, it is always evolving. For Bentham, utility is an immutable fact of nature that can accessed through rational thought and calculation. Where Marx's version of utility can potentially present obstacles to capitalism – if social relations begin to define utility in a way that does not aid capital accumulation – Bentham's version of utility is much more amenable and malleable to the capitalist class. Benthamite utilitarianism enables utility to be constructed by those in positions of power – or, as is increasingly the case in the neoliberal decades, by unelected technocrats – and then used to govern social life. In doing so, citizens pursue a form of utility that is not developed through their relationships with other social beings, and thus mediated by their collective needs, but rather assists the needs of the capitalist class. This might be a form of "bourgeois stupidity," but it is one that has served capitalism very well.

Few philosophical traditions have had a more direct impact on the discipline of economic science than utilitarianism, a consequentialist ethics that places utility maximisation at the heart of moral reasoning. Broadly speaking, utilitarianism distinguishes itself from antecedent ethical theories by focusing on the consequences of an action rather than the character of the actor involved. It views the most moral action as the one that maximises good or utility for the most amount of people. Furthermore, utilitarianism is committed to agent-neutrality, in which the morality of an action is not judged according to a particular agent's perspective or response but is evaluated via a generalised and supposedly impartial view of what is good or useful. In theory, no specific individual's happiness is prioritised above another's. It is possible, according to utilitarian logic, for an action to cause pain to some individuals and still be considered moral if its consequences maximise good or utility for the greatest amount of people, even if that utility only reveals itself a long way down the track – a logic that is still used to justify the rampant inequalities of capitalism.

We see such justification in the "progressive humanism" of the popular psychologist Steven Pinker, who argues in *Enlightenment Now* that "understanding inequality in the context of human progress is to recognise that income inequality is not a fundamental component of wellbeing."[3] Pinker shares this view with the neoliberals of the twentieth century. As the Austrian neoliberal Ludwig von Mises argued, "Men are altogether unequal," and "inequality of wealth and incomes is an essential feature of the market economy."[4] Pinker follows in these footsteps by telling us that we are wrong to equate inequality with unfairness because some basic psychological experiments have shown that "people are content with economic inequality as long as they feel that the country is meritocratic."[5] What's more, we need not worry about the data that illustrates that between 1979 and 2014 "the rich got richer faster than the poor and middle class got richer [because] everyone (on average) got richer."[6] The neoliberal world order, in Pinker's analysis, is one giant orgy of human progress, in which utility maximisation over the last few centuries has steadily brought about a global society where the majority of people are better off than in the disease-ridden societies of the past. He does not deny that there are still those whose daily lives are a struggle, but overall he concludes that, to quote Peter Fleming's reading of Pinker, "we should all lighten up."[7] It is no surprise that Pinker's *there's-nothing-to-see-here* philosophy has been enthusiastically embraced by the capitalist elite, because he provides them with a pseudo-intellectual justification to link individual wealth accumulation to human progress, even if such wealth accumulation creates greater economic inequality.[8] Boris Johnson certainly agrees with Pinker. In the 2013 Annual Margaret Thatcher Lecture at the neoliberal thinktank Centre for Policy Studies, he claimed it was "futile" to confront inequality. Instead, he claimed, "some measure of inequality is essential for the spirit of envy and keeping up with the Joneses that is, like greed, a valuable spur to economic activity."[9] As will be evident in due course, Pinker's theory of human progress and Johnson's Gordon Gecko impersonation bear much resemblance to Bentham's contributions to the discipline of political economy in the late eighteenth century – a sign that we have not progressed too far at all.

Utilitarianism has always been a flawed system of ethics, one that not only sanctioned the accumulation of wealth in the hands of the few, but also helped justify the atrocities of colonial expansion in the nineteenth century and beyond. In the hands of the capitalist class, utilitarianism has provided the pretext for endless capital accumulation by spuriously associating this accumulation with concepts of social wellbeing and human progress. But there is no intrinsic reason for capitalism to ensure the wellbeing of the majority. Its only operating logic is to enhance the conditions for the production and circulation of capital. Utilitarianism might have provided capitalism with an ethical impetus, but this did not mean that capitalism legitimised utilitarianism. When conditions changed, as they did with the economic stagnation and political crises of the 1970s, capitalism mutated beyond utilitarianism to embrace the ethos of individual autonomy that had come to permeate both sides of the political divide. This shift enabled capitalism to demand one key utilitarian principle (utility maximisation) without having to supply another (the greatest-happiness principle). Neoliberalism precipitated the separation of the practice of utility maximisation from social utility, which has instituted what I call *the futilitarian condition*: where the practice of utility maximisation actively worsens collective social and economic conditions.

This chapter provides the historical context for the emergence of the futilitarian condition by mapping the interrelation of utilitarianism, economic science, and political economy in the last three centuries. I do this primarily by turning to the work of Bentham, illustrating how his notion of "the principle of utility" – the maximisation of pleasure and minimisation of pain – overlaps with the ethos of capital accumulation, a link that Bentham himself develops in his economic writings. I then consider the evolution of utilitarianism in the mid- to late nineteenth century in the works of John Stuart Mill and Henry Sidgwick, explicating the latter's influence on the field of neoclassical economics. The financial collapse of the late 1920s led to a re-evaluation of the expediency of utilitarianism for economic theory, which instigated a form of anti-utilitarianism, encapsulated in the vastly contrasting theories of John Maynard Keynes and Friedrich Hayek. Both Keynes and Hayek were extremely critical of utilitarianism as a philosophical doctrine – particularly the Benthamite tradition – and yet both retained utilitarian aspects in their economic theories – majoritarian ethics (Keynes) and individual autonomy in a community (Hayek). The shift from post-Depression Keynesian consensus to a Hayekian-infused neoliberal economics from the mid-1970s onwards marked a change in emphasis from majoritarian to individualistic, or macro to micro, economic policies and initiatives, which, somewhat paradoxically, overlapped with a demand for individual autonomy in the anti-capitalist politics of the same period. Futilitarianism in turn became the new moral philosophy of neoliberal capitalism, and the futilitarian condition the dominant mode of being-in-the-world for the greatest majority.

The Principle of Utility

The "principle of utility" is central to Bentham's utilitarianism, which he defines as the "principle which approves or disapproves of every action whatsoever, according to the tendency which it appears to have to augment or diminish the happiness of the party whose interest is in question." The definition of "utility" is key here:

By utility is meant that property in any object, whereby it tends to produce benefit, advantage, pleasure, good, or happiness (all this in the present case comes to the same thing), or (what comes again to the same thing) to prevent the happening of mischief, pain, evil, or unhappiness to the party whose interest is considered.[10]

To maximise utility, according to Bentham's ethics, is to expand the conditions of pleasure concurrently with the contraction of the conditions that produce pain.[11] To make this point, Bentham contrasts the principle of utility with that of "asceticism," which he attributes to a certain set of moralists and religionists who, "having perceived, or fancied, that certain pleasures, when reaped in certain circumstances, have, at the long run, been attended with pains more than equivalent to them, took occasion to quarrel with every thing that offered itself under the name of pleasure."[12] He implies here that some philosophical and religious orders have sacrificed pleasure in fear of future pain, even to the point where they "think it meritorious to fall in love with pain" in an attempt to control its effects.[13]

Alongside asceticism, Bentham places "sympathy" and "antipathy" against the principle of utility. Sympathy and antipathy are character judgements, he notes, in which one "approves or disapproves of certain actions, not on account of their tending to augment the happiness, nor yet on account of their tending to diminish the happiness of the party whose interest is in question, but merely because a man finds himself disposed to approve or disapprove of them."[14] There is no moral justification, according to Benthamite utilitarianism, for the abandonment or condemnation of actions according to one's personal opinion. "The only right ground of action that can possibly subsist," Bentham concludes, "is, after all, the consideration of utility, which, if it is a right principle of action, and of approbation, in any one case, is so in every other."[15] One might act out of sympathy or antipathy, Bentham suggests, and that action might lead to the augmentation of pleasure and the reduction of pain, but the morality of that action cannot be attributed to the principles of sympathy or antipathy. For one might act out of antipathy or sympathy in the future and it might lead to the augmentation of pain and the reduction of pleasure. Rather, the only moral barometer of an action is its utility, which means that an action is judged moral if it maximises pleasure and minimises pain, irrespective of whether one acts out of sympathy or antipathy.

It is important to note that the principle of utility does not sanction any cruelty in the pursuit of utility maximisation – although, we could argue that settler colonialism, the War on Terror, border prisons, and refugee camps exemplify a utilitarian logic in which such cruelty is deemed moral because it maximises the happiness of the greatest amount of people (who overwhelmingly live in the wealthiest states). Utilitarians have always been wary of the potential for utilitarianism to be used to justify immoral acts, and they established a series of rules and procedures that aim to nullify this potential. Benthamite utilitarianism insists on measures for calculating utility maximisation that have come to be known as the *felicific calculus*. Bentham names these measures: "intensity" of pleasure or pain; "duration" of pleasure or pain; "certainty or uncertainty" over whether an action will cause pleasure or pain; "propinquity" or remoteness to the occurrence of pleasure or pain; "fecundity," or the genesis of further pleasure or pain; "purity" of the pleasure or pain, and whether the one mixes with the other; and "extent" of those affected by pleasure or pain.[16] This ideal scenario was summed up in a "mnemonic doggerel," which reads:

Intense, long, certain, speedy, fruitful, pure –
Such marks in pleasures and in pains endure.
Such pleasures seek if private be thy end:
If it be public, wide let them extend
Such pains avoid, whichever be thy view:
If pains must come, let them extend to few.[17]

Bentham's *felicific calculus* attempts to offset the use of utilitarianism for immoral ends by instituting some ethical safeguards. He argues that we cannot simply judge an action moral if it generates, for instance, short-term benefits but long-term ills, an argument that has long since disappeared in the era of neoliberal economics.

More importantly, however, Bentham paves the way for individual experiences of utility to precede collective or social experiences. "It is vain to talk of the interest of the community," he writes, "without understanding what is the interest of the individual." For Bentham, pleasure and pain are initially calculated on an individual level and then this experience can be extended towards the public sphere by aggregating the experience of other individuals. "The community is a fictitious *body*," he argues, "composed of the individual persons who are considered as constituting as it were its *members*. The interest of the community then is, what? – the sum of the interests of the several members who compose it."[18] Bentham viewed himself as a social reformer, but these words are clearly anti-communal or anti-social. Utilitarianism, at least according to Bentham's logic, conceives of the social as an aggregate of individuals, foreclosing the establishment of a collective body that can universalise the plurality of individual acts of utility maximisation. For him, the ultimate aim of utilitarianism was to inform social policy and legislation, but not to create a body that could be called "society" – this suspicion of the social is certainly something that Bentham shares with the neoliberal thinkers of the twentieth century.

Utilitarianism and the Fetishisation of Money

By removing the principle of utility from the realm of philosophical reflection, utilitarianism became attractive to economists because it provided them with a calculable entity that could be used as a model for governing economic life. This separation of morality from philosophical reflection had a huge impact on the discipline of economic science from the nineteenth century onwards, because, as Luc Boltanski and Ève Chiapello observe in their book *The New Spirit of Capitalism*, it became "possible to impart substance to the belief that the economy is an autonomous sphere, independent of ideology and morality, which obeys positive laws." In doing so, those in charge of national economies and capitalist institutions ringfenced the rational economic sphere from the unpredictable fluctuations of human life, allowing them to detach capital accumulation from notions of justice, social cohesion, and morality. "This separation between morality and economics," write Boltanski and Chiapello, "and the incorporation into economics in the same gesture of a consequentialist ethics, based upon the calculation of utilities, made it possible to supply a moral sanction for economic activities solely by dint of the fact that they are profitable."[19] Boltanski and Chiapello pinpoint this epistemic shift at the beginning of the nineteenth century because the development of economic science overlaps symbiotically with the emergence of utilitarianism as an ethical discourse.

While utilitarianism might ultimately aim at collective wellbeing, it encourages the subjugation of collective interests to that of the individual in order to reach this end goal, which, when incorporated into the discipline of economic science, situates individual wealth creation at the heart of any economic model. Boltanski and Chiapello write:

> [Utilitarianism] regards it as self-evident that the specific – but not readily calculable – moral cost (devotion to the passion for material gain) of establishing an acquisitive society (a cost that still preoccupied Adam Smith) is amply offset by the quantifiable benefits of accumulation (material goods, health, etc.). It also allows it to be argued that the overall increase in wealth, regardless of the beneficiary, is a criterion of the common good, as it is attested on a daily basis by the presentation of the health of a country's firms, measured by their profit rate, their level of activity and growth, as a criterion for measuring social wellbeing. This enormous social labour, performed in order to establish individual material advancement as a – if not the – criterion of social well-being, has allowed capitalism to wrest unprecedented legitimacy, for its designs and mainspring were thus legitimised simultaneously.[20]

It is not difficult to see here, in the amalgamation of utilitarianism and economic science, the intellectual shoots of Pinker's progressive humanism, where "the overall increase in wealth, regardless of the beneficiary, is a criterion of the common good." It is clear, therefore, that capitalism has been aided and abetted by a utilitarian ethical code, which has ensconced an ethos of hyper-productivity and unbridled individualism at the heart of democratic societies. If a healthy society is one that produces the most utility, as proponents of utilitarianism argue, then that society is compelled to facilitate the labour and social conditions for the maximisation of utility. And with the economy as a seemingly unideological indicator of the health of a society, as the discipline of economic science attests, then the aim of utility maximisation is to stimulate the economy, creating growth and profit primarily through the aggregation of individual wealth.

Boltanski and Chiapello's hypothesis holds up to scrutiny when we consider Bentham's contributions to the field of political economy. In *Defence of Usury* (1787), Bentham lays out a simple proposition:

> That no man of ripe years and of sound mind, acting freely, and with his eyes open, ought to be hindered, with a view to his advantage, from making such bargain, in the way of obtaining money, as he thinks fit: nor, (what is a necessary consequence) any body hindered from supplying him, upon any terms he thinks proper to accede to.[21]

To defend this proposition, albeit not in its entirety, Bentham – contra Adam Smith, who thought liberal laws and certain government intervention would curb the practice of usury – argues that there is no utilitarian justification for the restriction of interest rates because to do so would inhibit the maximisation of utility.[22] Instead, Bentham envisages a culture of adventure and risk in which individuals should be free to enter a market at their choosing without government intervention. Moreover, he argues that the practice of usury encourages innovation and technological development, and so to regulate interest rates is antithetical to notions of human progress. Again, the positing of the government as antithetical to freedom is also a fundamental feature of neoliberal theory.

Bentham draws a direct relationship between the principle of utility and the accumulation of wealth throughout *Defence of Usury*, a relationship that provides the ethical foundations for a laissez-faire form of capitalism. He writes that "to get money is what most men have a mind to do: because he who has money gets, as far as it goes, most other things that he has a mind for."[23] The fetishisation of money – and its centrality to the principle of utility – leads Bentham to conclude that the accumulation of money is the primary measurement of an individual's happiness, to the point that those who already have money are compelled, according to the principle of utility, to continually seek the accumulation of more money. In such a world, greed is not only justifiable at the level of ethics, but actively encouraged at the level of governance and social relations. And, crucially, the market would facilitate this imperative as the mechanism through which the accumulation of wealth and happiness could be judged. Consequently, the role of government becomes to safeguard the freedom of the market. As William Davies writes, "by putting out there the idea that money might have some privileged relationship to our inner experience, beyond the capabilities of nearly any other measuring instrument, Bentham set the stage for the entangling of psychological research and capitalism that would shape the business practices of the twentieth century."[24]

While Bentham certainly accepts and promotes a view of the human as self-interested and the government as antagonistic towards individual freedom, it is worth noting that utilitarianism is still aimed at a form of wellbeing that extends beyond the individual. Utilitarianism, after all, intends to maximise utility for the greatest amount of people, with, theoretically, no individual's happiness prioritised over another's. But the insistence on the egoic individual as the *prima facie* utilitarian subject undercuts any ethical imperative towards the social, because the principle of utility operates initially at the level of the individual. The onus is on the individual to share his or her experience with others in order to calculate utility on a social level. Under the conditions of capitalism, it is equally, if not more, likely that the individual will maximise his or her own utility *as if* it represents the needs of others.

Utilitarianism and the Mathematics of Morality

In the mid-twentieth century, the sociological economist and editor of Bentham's collected works, Werner Stark, laid out in detail the entirety of Bentham's economic thought and its impact on nineteenth-century economics. He illustrated, for instance, the influence of Bentham on the classical economist David Ricardo. Stark argued that Bentham and Ricardo were "flesh of one flesh and blood of one blood" because they "shared the belief that man is essentially a selfish animal; that it is useless to fight that selfishness, and unnecessary at the same time, because, where freedom is guaranteed, a conflict between personal and public welfare is precluded by the admirable mechanism of modern market relations; that this mechanism must not be clogged by governmental interference; and that it will work for the better, the more equality there is in society, because the free play of equal forces will lead to the most sound and satisfactory equilibrium."[25] This view of the relationship between the economy and society, which Bentham and Ricardo shared, raises several questions. For one, if the human is fundamentally a selfish animal, then how can the flourishing of individual freedom avoid a conflict with the notion of public welfare? Furthermore, if government intervention is opposed to individual freedom, then what overarching system can ensure the kind of social equality that benefits the "mechanism of modern market relations"? For Bentham, while the state should not place any unnecessary obstacles in the way of individual freedom and the accumulation of wealth, he viewed certain social liberties as of higher importance than economic freedom. In *Principles of the Civil Code* (1780), he writes that "the pain of death, which would finally fall upon the neglected indigent, will always be a greater evil than the pain of disappointed expectation, which falls upon the rich when a limited portion of his superfluity is taken from him."[26] Given the likelihood of such a scenario, Bentham argues for provisions of basic social care and welfare. Nonetheless, a utilitarian ethics can in no way guarantee social welfare. It can only intimate towards it, because it views society only as a collection of individuals and not as a whole. In a utilitarian political economy, the provision of social welfare requires an aggregation of individual desires towards that end. But if each individual is conceived as fundamentally selfish, then it is easy to see how social welfare can fall by the wayside under the conditions of capitalism.

The value of utilitarianism for economic science is evident not only in Ricardo's work but also in a number of other nineteenth-century economists, including the early neoclassical economist William Stanley Jevons, who posited the principle of utility as the main problem of economics.[27] Davies argues that "Jevons's landmark contribution was to plant [the utilitarian] vision of a calculating hedonist firmly in the marketplace. Bentham was seeking mainly to reform government policy and punitive institutions, which acted on the public in general. But Jevons converted utilitarianism into a theory of rational consumer choice."[28] Rational choice theory deeply influenced the neoliberal economists of the Chicago School of Economics, especially the Nobel Prize-winner Gary Becker, who made it the cornerstone of his "economic approach to human behaviour."[29] Rational choice theory, based on the adventures of the utility-maximising individual, illustrates the extent to which utilitarianism enabled economics to become a discipline that theorised the entirety of human life and not simply those aspects that directly engaged in economic affairs.

Benthamite utilitarianism also evolved through the work of subsequent utilitarian and liberal philosophers, most notably Mill and Sidgwick. Mill largely agreed with Bentham that the human is a pleasure-seeking animal, but he took issue with Bentham's insistence that the goal of utilitarianism was to increase the quantity of pleasures rather than the quality. Mill argued that certain pleasures are of greater value than others, affording higher value to bourgeois endeavours of the intellect and moral reflection. Mill might have opened the door for a kind of moral relativism to enter utilitarian ethics, one that prioritised certain pleasures over others, but he was still committed, like Bentham, to utilitarianism as a form of social reform, as his writings against women's oppression and in favour of women's suffrage exemplify. He argued that "it is an injustice to the individuals [denied freedom of choice], and a detriment to society, to place barriers in the way of their using their faculties for their own benefit and for that of others."[30] Again, the freedom of the individual, central to any utilitarian ethics, was the driving force of Mill's political economy, but this individual freedom was still aimed towards a larger sense of social betterment. Like Bentham, he viewed equality as the optimal social conditions for the maximisation of utility, and he created the space for a "pluralistic utilitarian doctrine" that better correlated to the "liberal system of weighty rights and duties" in the late nineteenth century.[31]

The Victorian utilitarian philosopher Henry Sidgwick developed and diverted from Bentham and Mill, and we could argue that his work had the most direct impact on the discipline of economic science, particularly the Oxford and Cambridge schools of economics of the same period.[32] He shared with Bentham, contra Mill, a belief in the quantitative nature of utilities, which he combined with a strong emphasis on rational decision-making and prediction. In the preface to *The Methods of Ethics* (1884), Sidgwick sums up his approach: "I have wished to put aside temporarily the urgent need which we all feel of finding and adopting the true method of determining what we ought to do; and to consider simply what conclusions will be rationally reached if we start with certain ethical premises, and with what degree of certainty and precision."[33] A concept that distinguished Sidgwick from his utilitarian predecessors was the notion of "the dualism of practical reason," which encapsulates a tension at the heart of utilitarian ethics between the pursuit of individual happiness and the sacrifice of one's own happiness for the happiness of others. Sidgwick notes that "even if a man admits the self-evidence of the principle of Rational Benevolence, he may still hold that his own happiness is an end which it is irrational for him to sacrifice to any other."[34] In other words, the principles of self-interest and social welfare are not mutually exclusive and, most importantly, they need not co-exist for a utilitarian ethics to function. Again, as I suggested above, it is easy to see how one principle, primarily self-interest, might be privileged above another in capitalist social relations.

Utilitarianism's promise of a value-free and calculable morality provided the discipline of economic science with a viable ethics.[35] No longer did ethics constitute abstract notions of right or wrong, which might present obstacles to some economic actions, but rather ethics could be calculated according to the consequences of an action. Economic science was therefore able to reframe questions of what constitutes social wellbeing by pointing to indicators such as economic growth, technological development, and productive output – much in the same way that Pinker and the like rely on data on life expectancy, income distribution, and poverty to supposedly prove human progress. As Jonathan Riley notes, "early neoclassical economists, especially [Francis] Edgeworth, answered

[Sidgwick's] call and used the tools of mathematical calculus to formulate the ideal versions of quantitative hedonistic utilitarianism."[36] These versions veered away from individual judgements of utility, which were the basis of Bentham's *felicific calculus*, towards increasingly complex mathematical equations of utility that could transcend individual experience. Riley notes, as a result, "a utilitarian calculus is thus no longer necessarily linked to majoritarian aggregation procedures as it was with Bentham and Mill. Indeed, an authoritarian elite might perform and enforce the utilitarian calculations." Neoclassical economists encouraged the establishment of such an "authoritarian elite" by employing mathematical models to illustrate that "utilitarianism does not necessarily imply equal distribution of the 'means of pleasure' or of the work required to produce the means." Riley also observes that neoclassical economists "found more or less ingenious ways to overcome Sidgwick's 'dualism of practical reason' " in which they "imported the idea of an evolutionary process as they understood it, whereby ignorant and selfish individuals might eventually evolve into intelligent and virtuous ones through cultural and ... even biological transmission of the relevant concepts and dispositions."[37]

The spurious claims of virtuous evolution on the part of wealth holders and their offspring, which predictably have not come to pass, did not so much overcome the dualism of practical reason as sidestep it. Despite their insistence on the precision of mathematical calculation, neoclassical economists – similar to the colonisers of their era – relied on myth in order to implement their doctrine: the myth of human progress and future prosperity. By incorporating aspects of utilitarianism into economic science, neoclassical economists found the ethical justification for the accumulation of capital at one end of the social spectrum without the need to link this accumulation to individuals at the other end of the spectrum. The free market replaced the *felicific calculus* as the measurement of the principle of utility, backed up by a turn to rational choice theory as the most accurate reflection of human behaviour.

The Anti-Benthamites: Keynes and Hayek

The utilitarian vision of the neoclassical economists came to a head with the Great Depression of the late 1920s, when economic activity stalled then collapsed, and unemployment went through the roof. The relationship between utilitarianism and economic science had to be re-evaluated, which was captured in the emergence of a predominantly anti-utilitarian discourse from both sides of the economic fraternity. This re-evaluation is most evident in the works of Keynes and Hayek, who both significantly impacted the direction of the twentieth century, albeit in wildly contrasting ways. While both were anti-utilitarian, again in conflicting ways, they built on concepts that had been thoroughly elaborated by utilitarians: the need for the welfare of the majority (Keynes) and the freedom of the individual (Hayek) in the economy.

It is not my intention to outline the entirety of Keynesian economic theory here, as more qualified scholars have done so in great detail.[38] Instead, I want to focus specifically on Keynes's engagement with utilitarianism. Keynes was belligerently anti-utilitarian.[39] In his essay "My Early Beliefs," which discusses his time at Cambridge in the early twentieth century, Keynes writes that "we were amongst the first of our generation, perhaps alone amongst our generation, to escape from the Benthamite tradition," which he describes as "the worm which has been gnawing at the insides of modern civilisation and is responsible for its present moral decay." He was particularly scathing of Bentham's "over-valuation of the economic criterion," which reduced all value decisions to monetary consequences.[40] Peter V. Mini clarifies Keynes's view of classical utilitarianism: "Popular Benthamism, the overvaluation of economic factors, the calculating mentality, the philosophy of money-making, these are all synonymous terms in Keynes's writings for a major disease of the spirit to which capitalist countries have succumbed."[41] For Keynes, the figure of *Homo economicus* was far too rational and self-interested to accurately reflect the illogical fluctuations of the market economy.

In criticising utilitarianism's excessive individualism and reduction of social relations to monetary transactions, Keynes places a strong emphasis on notions of the social and communal. Where Bentham saw the community as an aggregate of individual desires, Keynes views the individual as constitutive of its community, and thus a healthy community lays the social foundations for the welfare of its individuals. Keynes is at his most poetic when discussing the effects of utilitarianism on the community in his essay "Art and State," in which he writes that "the utilitarian and economic ... ideal, as the sole, respectable purpose of the community as a whole [is] the most dreadful heresy, perhaps, which has ever gained the ear of a civilised people. Bread and nothing but bread, and not even bread, and bread accumulating at compound interest until it has turned into a stone."[42] For Keynes, utilitarianism fossilises human life by reducing all that is living to merely its monetary value. To overcome this petrification, he inverts the principle of utility. A utilitarian ethics, particularly after its confluence with neoclassical economics, encourages individuals to seek economic betterment as the barometer of the moral health of a society. Keynes insists, on the contrary – and more in line with Marx – that ridding individuals of their economic burden frees them to create healthy communities that ensure each individual's wellbeing.

The Keynesian emphasis on the welfare of the majority became the basis of New Deal capitalism from the 1930s until the 1970s. But while Keynesian economists were working on a series of interventionist economic strategies that would ensure social wellbeing, Hayek was busy organising the first meeting of the Mont Pèlerin Society (MPS) in April 1947 at the lavish Swiss resort from which the society took its name.[43] The Society's founding statement reads in stark contrast to economic philosophy of Keynes. "The central values of civilisation are in danger," it states, where "the position of the individual and the voluntary group are progressively undermined by extensions of arbitrary power." In particular, the MPS pinpointed "a decline of belief in private property and the competitive market" as one of the primary reasons for the endangerment of civilisation, "for without the diffused power and initiative associated with these institutions it is difficult to imagine a society in which freedom may be effectively preserved."[44] The MPS saw interventionist economic strategies as antithetical to freedom, but at the same time it called for a strong legislative system to guarantee the freedom of individuals and voluntary groups in the market economy. David Harvey identifies a number of contradictions in the theoretical structure of the MPS doctrine. "The scientific rigour of its neoclassical economics," he suggests, "does not sit easily with its political commitment to ideas of individual freedom, nor does its supposed distrust of all state power fit with the need for a strong and if necessary coercive state that will defend the rights of private property, individual liberties, and entrepreneurial freedom."[45] These contradictions remain to this day, where neoliberals simultaneously argue for the weakening of state power on matters that impact individual pursuits of capital, and the strengthening of the state in protecting the civil and political rights of individuals.[46] In other words, neoliberals desire strong state intervention against an image of the state as interventionist.

Like Keynes, although for different reasons, Hayek is extremely critical of Benthamite utilitarianism. He juxtaposes Bentham against liberal thinkers, such as John Locke, David Hume, and Edmund Burke, and notes that the development of their liberal theories "suffered a new setback from the intrusion of constructivism in the form of Benthamite utilitarianism."[47] In particular, he criticises the "constructive rationalism" of Bentham's thought – which he also attributes to René Descartes, Thomas Hobbes, and Jean-Jacques Rousseau – which springs from "the erroneous conception that there can be first a society which then gives itself laws." Instead, Hayek suggests, "it is only as a result of individuals observing certain common rules that a group of men can live together in those orderly relations which we call a society."[48] Hayek's understanding of what constitutes a society forms part of his larger and often vitriolic critique, along with his mentor Mises, of socialism and social democracy.[49] In *The Road to Serfdom*, Hayek concludes that the collectivist ethics associated with socialism will always lead to totalitarianism: "Once you admit that the individual is merely a means to serve the ends of the higher entity called society or the nation, most of those features of totalitarianism which horrify us follow of necessity."[50] Thus while Hayek criticises Benthamite utilitarianism, he shares a similar view of society to Bentham.[51] He writes that "what are called 'social ends' are for it merely identical ends of many individuals – or ends to the achievement of which individuals are willing to contribute in return for the assistance they receive in the satisfaction of their own desires."[52] Hayek defends the social community as an aggregate of individual interests and the preservation of private property against the advances of socialism, which he believes has "persuaded liberal-minded people to submit once more to that regimentation of economic life which they had overthrown."[53] The liberal attitude, Hayek suggests, by way of contrast to socialism, is "based on the conviction that where effective competition can be created, it is a better way of guiding individual efforts than any other."[54] Consequently, "the successful use of competition as the principle of social organisation precludes certain types of coercive interference with economic life, but it admits of others which sometimes may very considerably assist its work and even requires certain kinds of government action."[55] We see here that neoliberals did not view this kind of government action as contradictory. Instead, they saw the role of government as facilitating the conditions for competition between individuals, and if certain measures got in the way of such competition, then governments were compelled to step in, not to provide individuals with support to live, but to get them back in the competitive game.

In his essay "Individualism: True and False," Hayek defines "true" individualism, which he finds in the work of Locke, Smith, and Burke, as "an attempt to understand the forces which determine the social life of man," which is "opposed to the belief that individualism postulates ... the existence of isolated or self-contained individuals, instead of starting from men whose whole nature and character is determined by their existence in society." While it seems that Hayek acknowledges the existence of society here, the social conditioning he imagines is vastly different to the kind Keynes puts forward. Rather, Hayek's view of society is informed by philosophical nominalism, which denies the existence of "social wholes like society." Rather, society is the culmination of "individual actions directed toward other people and guided by their expected behaviour." "False" individualism, which Hayek attributes to Benthamites and Cartesians, is characterised by the "rational" individual, which he claims, somewhat bizarrely, "tend[s] to develop into the opposite of individualism, namely, socialism or collectivism."[56] The point Hayek wants to make is that a proponent of false individualism views social processes as governable by human reason, which enables institutions and governments to set the conditions of the social into which individuals must adapt. An exponent of true individualism, however, "believes that, if left free, men will often achieve more than individual human reason could design or foresee."[57]

But there is an insurmountable contradiction at the heart of Hayek's account of true individualism, because the capacity of individuals to exercise their freedom – and form a society as a result – is always in conflict with the necessity that individuals compete against one another to ensure their freedom. As C. B. Macpherson puts it, "Hayek's attempt to humanise market individualism cannot hide the fact that his 'true' individualism, being tied to the free market economy, compels everyone to compete atomistically."[58] Furthermore, it is not clear how Hayek's version of individualism overcomes the very problems he perceives in the Benthamite tradition. As I illustrated earlier, Bentham is anything but opposed to the freedom of the individual. In fact, Bentham similarly calls for government intervention to guarantee the freedom of individuals, where the "art of legislature is limited to the prevention of everything which might prevent the development of their liberty and their intelligence."[59] Bentham might have placed a greater emphasis on the rational individual than some liberal thinkers, but he did not encourage the imposition of the social upon the individual, as Hayek claims.

Where Hayek sees rational individualism as a threat to the freedom of the individual, Keynes views the same rationality as a threat to the community. But neither Hayek nor Keynes move beyond utilitarianism entirely. Keynes adopts a somewhat utilitarian stance, through an adapted version of the greatest-happiness principle, to argue against the individualism of Benthamite utilitarianism. For Keynes, the happiness of the greatest number is paramount but, unlike Bentham, he thinks this should be protected through economic planning and not a result of the aggregation of individual utility-maximisers. Hayek, despite his desire to move beyond utilitarianism, ends up instituting a similar vision of the community to Bentham, which relies on the very atomistic individual he criticises in Bentham's work. The ensuing battle between the Keynesians and the Hayekian neoliberals in the mid-twentieth century was essentially fought over which aspect of the utilitarian tradition – majoritarian or individualistic – could be saved in order to overcome the totality of utilitarian reasoning.

The Futilitarian Condition

The neoliberals won the long game. The economic stagnation and political crises of 1970s crippled Keynesian logic. In its place, Hayek and the neoliberal cabal of the Chicago School of Economics chewed the ear of sympathetic politicians in the US, UK, and further afield. The violent overthrow of Salvador Allende's socialist government in Chile in 1973 was the beginning of neoliberalism as a political reality, and Hayek himself became honorary chairman of a neoliberal thinktank that oversaw the transformation of Chile to a neoliberal economy under Augusto Pinochet's dictatorship.[60] As the neoliberals attacked the Keynesian state, primarily at the economic level, the same state was undergoing a sustained social critique from the Left by those who saw this state as the distributor of social and cultural normativity.[61] For some critics of neoliberalism, this new social critique symbolises the ambiguous legacy of the May 1968 uprisings. Harvey has argued that "for almost everyone involved in the movement of '68, the intrusive state was the enemy and it had to be reformed. And on that, the neoliberals could easily agree."[62] Likewise, Alain Badiou concluded, on the fortieth anniversary of the May uprisings, that "the real outcome and the real hero of '68 is unfettered neo-liberal capitalism. The libertarian ideas of '68, the transformation of the way we live, the individualism and the taste for *jouissance* have become a reality thanks to post-modern capitalism and its garish world of all sorts of consumerism."[63] But as Kristin Ross illustrated in her indispensable book *May '68 and Its Afterlives*, the reading of the May uprisings as the birth of a new individualism is retrospective and reductive, ignoring the long genesis of the uprisings in protests against the Algerian war and various workers' strikes in the 1960s.[64]

Boltanski and Chiapello imply that the new individualism that emerged in 1970s was as much to do with the governmental and capitalist response to May 1968 as it was to do with any monolithic cultural logic of the uprisings. They note that in France, the governmental response to the uprisings entailed concessions on wages and social security as an attempt to "damp down class struggle." But these concessions subsequently drove up costs for those paying the wages, which, when combined with the economic crises of the early 1970s, pushed capitalists to look for innovative solutions to cut costs, especially since "the level of criticism they had to face did not seem to drop despite the concessions." As a result, firms developed new organisational frameworks for work, "which took the form of a mass of micro-developments and micro-displacements ... to render many of the provisions of labour law null and void in practice." And as Boltanski and Chiapello show, these developments tapped into only one aspect of the

1968 movement, the one concerned with the "oppression and sterilisation of each person's creative, unique powers produced by industrial, bourgeois society." Subsequently, "the transformation in working methods was ... effected in large part to respond to their aspirations, and they themselves contributed to it, especially after the Left's accession to government in the 1980s." The rise of a new individualism was not an inevitable consequence of the 1968 movement, Botlanski and Chiapello conclude, but instead was an effect of capitalists reducing the collective energies of the movement to the mere thirst for individual autonomy and building a new model of production around this thirst. By the beginning of the 1980s, Boltanski and Chiapello note, "autonomy was exchanged for security, opening the way for a new spirit of capitalism extolling the virtues of mobility and adaptability, whereas the previous spirit was unquestionably more concerned with security than with liberty."[65] The futilitarian condition emerged from the shadows precisely at this juncture, where capitalists colonised the demands of the anticapitalist Left, producing a new capitalist spirit that celebrated economic and social autonomy for the individual.

The concept of utility maximisation remains integral to neoliberalism – as I will discuss in detail in Chapter 6 in the context of the Covid-19 pandemic – because individuals are encouraged and even forced to *make themselves useful* in order to survive. But while neoliberalism is utilitarian in terms of its demand for utility maximisation – where "utility" is defined by employers, businesses, and corporations – it is most certainly not utilitarian in its effects. Undoubtedly, the idea that utility maximisation might lead to the wellbeing of the majority – even if it was a myth to begin with – has well and truly faded from the twenty-first century. The futilitarian condition transpires and proliferates when utilitarianism remains the justification for capitalism despite the fact that the general-happiness principle can no longer be experienced as an effect of utility maximisation.

Neoliberalism grants autonomy by making individual choice and flexibility the basis of the market economy. But this autonomy comes at the price of the social security that even utilitarians like Bentham and Mill saw as a fundamental aspect of ensuring the greatest-happiness principle. Neoliberalism simply generates the conditions for autonomy, irrespective of whether greater autonomy makes individuals happy or not. And, as the gross social inequalities, ubiquitous precarity, and mass depressions and anxieties of our age exemplify, neoliberalism primarily spreads *unhappiness* to the greatest number of people. On this matter, Franco "Bifo" Berardi makes a valuable point: "The masters of the world certainly do not want humanity to be able to be happy, because a happy humanity would not let itself be caught up in productivity, in the discipline of work or in hypermarkets."[66] Why would happiness be an end of capitalism if that very happiness might threaten the accumulation of capital?

This question reflects the intractable contradiction between autonomy and freedom that haunts the futilitarian condition. Under the fantasy of autonomy, the majority of us now contribute to the machine of capital without any freedom from its tentacles. Even our leisure time is colonised by surveillance capital.[67] As Marx maintained, "it is not the individuals who are set free by free competition; it is, rather, capital which is set free."[68] Freedom, Marx insisted, is an illusion that capitalism imprints onto human life, but it also uses individual pursuits of freedom to free capital from the restraints of social life. Neoliberals have aggressively pursued this duality by arguing that the only way humans can be truly free is by situating the market at the heart of all human endeavours, while liberalising the labour and social spheres, in the knowledge that humans (certainly, the majority of humans) and the market cannot simultaneously be free. Wendy Brown notes that "the neoliberal revolution takes place in the name of freedom – free markets, free countries, free men – but tears up freedom's grounding in sovereignty for states and subjects alike."[69] The trick here, as Byung-Chul Han helpfully points out, is that "capital generates needs of its own; mistakenly, we perceive these needs as if they belonged to us."[70] We believe that the freedom we desire can be achieved by our capacity to free capitalism from any constraints – and free ourselves from our relations to others – which often takes the form of our own exploitation and unfreedom.

The subject of the futilitarian condition is certainly autonomous, but only because this autonomy feeds the market. To be autonomous is to be chained to a much more volatile freedom, one that often blurs the distinction between liberty and precarity. Everywhere, we are told to be ourselves, celebrate our uniqueness, market ourselves as different to others, share our thoughts as if they will be heard. Simultaneously, we are expected to depend on our individual selves, be flexible and resilient, and view wider social and economic conditions as reflections of our individual characteristics. This is the price of autonomy in the neoliberal age. The great irony here is that this is not the world neoliberal thinkers had imagined in the mid-twentieth century. The ideas of Hayek, Milton Friedman, and the Chicago Boys were, in theory, aimed at protecting the economic freedom of the individual within the neoliberal market order. But the actual material processes of neoliberalisation have rendered even this insidious ideal futile. The forms of individual autonomy that have emerged in the early twenty-first century are not perfections of neoliberal theory, but mutations of this theory into an even more objectionable ideology as a consequence of neoliberal praxis. It is individualism without any freedom; individualism as commodity; individualism as surveillance; individualism as data; individualism as narcissism; *individualism or else.*

The benefits of using the term "futilitarianism" or "the futilitarian condition" to define this pervasive individualism, I suggest, are that it correlates more directly with the existential futility that permeates twenty-first-century life. When we are confronted with the very real calamities of our age – soaring inequalities, climate change, refugee crises, deadly pandemics – we are simultaneously confronted with our futility in dealing with these issues. Not that this futility is often acknowledged. Instead, many of us reflexively return to individual acts of (non-)resistance – swapping a plastic bag for a tote bag here, donating money to a humanitarian agency there. But futility haunts our every move, and we know it. To displace this haunting presence, we are quick to pat each other on the back for acts of philanthropy, celebrate and encourage each other's autonomy, and maintain the fantasy that we are ethical subjects taking care of our planet. To admit that our actions are futile is to concede that we have been hoodwinked by capitalism, that our desires for individual autonomy have been used against us to lock us even further into the throes of capitalist realism.[71]

This futility is not reflective of us as individuals, and perhaps it is the fear that it might be that stops us from fully acknowledging it. Rather, existential futility is the logical outcome of the historical relationship between utilitarianism and capitalism. Utilitarianism always carried the possibility of futilitarianism, since the aspects of a utilitarian ethics that benefit unbridled capital accumulation could always supersede the notion of social wellbeing, as occurred spectacularly when the neoliberals won the ideological battle of the twentieth century. As the neoliberal generation, we have been left with the devastating consequences of the metamorphosis of utilitarianism into futilitarianism. My goal in the rest of the book is not only to illustrate how futilitarianism manifests itself in contemporary society, but also to lay the foundation for a new politics to emerge that can confront the destructive logic of futilitarianism.

2
The Rise of *Homo futilitus*

Ideology, Slavoj Žižek likes to remind us, operates like a "thief in broad daylight."[1] It is that thing we do not perceive because we are so deeply immersed in it. And it is often in the seemingly innocuous events that the insidious effects of ideology reveal themselves. In 2013, for instance, Bill Manhire retired as director of the International Institute of Modern Letters (IIML) at Victoria University of Wellington, Aotearoa New Zealand. The IIML is a creative writing school set up in 2001 by Manhire, one of Aotearoa New Zealand's most prominent poets, with the support of a US philanthropist. The IIML has produced a conveyer belt of writers – including the 2013 Booker Prize winner, Eleanor Catton, and 2017 Windham Campbell Prize winner, Ashleigh Young – aided by its relationship with Victoria University Press. Manhire retired and was replaced by Damien Wilkins in 2013, who set about cementing the legacy of his predecessor in a way that suggested a thief had indeed reigned in broad daylight. In an interview not long after assuming the role as director, Wilkins was asked about the influence of Manhire on the IIML:

The thing I now say is, Bill Manhire is our brand, like Colonel Sanders. He's not actually cooking the chicken, he's a luminous cloud hovering and people don't care that he's not there. I think people recognise part of Bill's achievement was to make it just not about himself in every way.[2]

On the one hand, there is nothing particularly noteworthy about these comments. The IIML is shaped in Manhire's image and this image will live on beyond his tenure as director. On the other hand, the banality of Wilkins's comments is precisely the point. When someone is now reincarnated as a brand, we barely bat an eyelid. We have reached an age when it appears that the aim of human activity and creativity is to unlock a supposedly higher level of humanity, one in which the human attains the vaulted status previously reserved for products and services. And none of this seems to shock us. In fact, we celebrate this newfound autonomy, where we are encouraged at every turn to think of ourselves as brands – so much so that the term "on brand" has come to represent a human necessity, like breathing or eating.

For Wilkins, Manhire and the IIML operate according to the same principles as Colonel Sanders and KFC. And despite the comparison of Manhire to a figure who has his face splashed across every single KFC outlet in the world, Wilkins encourages us to see Manhire as self-deprecating and altruistic, an image which, of course, is good for the brand. My point here is not whether Manhire is an accomplished poet or whether the IIML is a good creative writing school. These things might well be true, but they are beside the point when Manhire and the IIML enter the world as brands. The success of an enterprise such as KFC is not that its fried chicken is superior to all other forms of fried chicken, but that it has aggressively cornered and monopolised the market, using successful forms of branding and franchising, and accumulating capital at every turn. If, as Wilkins suggests, we are to think of Manhire as Colonel Sanders, and the IIML as KFC, then we can similarly conclude that Manhire and the IIML share analogous operating principles to Colonel Sanders and KFC. Consequently, the art of creative writing becomes a means to an end at the IIML – like fried chicken to KFC – secondary to the practice of accumulating capital – economic, cultural, human, or otherwise. The point of this anecdote is that the triviality of such an event reveals the ubiquity of *self-branding* as an ideology across the globe, even in arenas that have historically been antagonistic to the advances of capitalism, such as the creative arts. Self-branding is as intuitive to us now as gaining an education or becoming adept at a trade skill.

The ideology of self-branding reveals itself in pretty much all spheres of capitalist society, from politics and entertainment to work and education. In her autobiography, for example, Michelle Obama offers a glimpse into the pressures of operating as a self-brand in the political realm, particularly as a woman. She bemoans that "it seemed that my clothes mattered more to people than anything I had to say." She goes on: "Optics governed more or less everything in the political world, and I factored this into every outfit."[3] While Obama discusses fashion specifically here, and the obvious gender disparities between men and women in politics, her admission that "optics govern[s] more or less everything in the political world" reveals the dominant cultural logic of politics today.

If we take the figure of Canadian Prime Minister Justin Trudeau – and he is by no means the only example – we see that his political rise is more a feat of marketing than it is a commitment to a coherent set of political principles. Trudeau and his PR team were widely credited with employing innovative and wide-reaching social media marketing ploys that set him on the road to his 2015 election victory. The headline of an article in the Huffington Post shortly after the election summed this up: "5 Ways Justin Trudeau's Social Media Game Trumped Other Leaders."[4] Even after assuming office, Trudeau has been relentlessly marketed as a humorous, funny, and down-to-earth guy, with a strong political emphasis on issues such as environmental protection, child poverty, and gender equality. His good looks and athleticism also help his brand. Stalking Trudeau's every move is his personal photographer, Adam Scotti, who takes shots of him jogging, surfing, hugging pandas, and even appearing to photobomb a school prom (as it turned out, this seemingly spontaneous moment was in fact a staged publicity stunt).

Canadian journalist Shannon Proudfoot writes that "branding a politician like Trudeau is not so different, really, from pitching a new car or facial moisturiser. You think about which category your product belongs to, who it's aimed at and what makes it different and better than the competition."[5] And like adverts for such products, the image that appears in marketing campaigns disguises the murky and exploitative realities behind their production – the slickness of Apple advertising, for example, masks the suicide nets at the factories in which its products are made; the cinematography of Nike commercials camouflages the sweatshops and child labour involved in making its trainers and clothing. In a similar vein, the image of Trudeau has concealed a largely neoliberal political agenda, in which he has continually cosied up to oil companies and big business and done very little to combat child poverty or climate change, or extend gender equality or indigenous rights.

There have been rumblings of discontent throughout Trudeau's term as prime minister. He has been accused of "token feminism," focusing primarily on equality in the boardroom – exemplified by his "roundtable" with female entrepreneurs and none other than Donald Trump.[6] Furthermore, his relentless pursuit of a multi-billion-dollar national pipeline on behalf of a major player in the oil industry, using taxpayers' money, has revealed both that his commitment to climate decarbonisation was expedient at best and that his promise to protect indigenous rights was disingenuous.[7] But the cracks between the image and the reality of Trudeau were fully exposed in 2019 by his aggressive pressuring of his former attorney general, Jody-Wilson Raybould, not to prosecute a Canadian engineering firm over allegations of bribery and fraud. Likewise, the discovery of his adornment of blackface on three separate occasions as a student has undermined his socially liberal image.[8] Trudeau has been uncovered by these scandals not only as a bully, but also as insensitive and entitled. As Leah McLaren playfully puts it, Trudeau's fall from grace, for liberals, has been like "watching a unicorn get flattened by a lorry."[9] The use of a mythical creature here is certainly apposite. The Trudeau brand is nothing more than a myth, a playful image of what a progressive politician might look like if conceived in a children's story. "The leader we believed to be special and unique," McLaren writes, "has behaved in ways that reveal him to be probably not all that" – a bit like the moment when a child realises that a unicorn is just a horse with a cone on its head.

The disintegration of Trudeau's image highlights some of the risks of inhabiting the world as a brand. If one wants one's product to be successful, then one must be committed to upholding the brand's image on all occasions. Vegan YouTube star Yovana Mendoza found this to her peril when she was recorded by a fellow vlogger eating fish.[10] But the real problem is that with the development of neoliberalism – and, within this, the notion of human capital – we have few options but to enter the world as brands. Consequently, we end up operating in a ruthless and highly competitive marketplace with fellow citizens, transforming not only how we think about selfhood, but also the ways in which we conceive of and relate to others. The world of self-branding and human capital consolidates the futilitarian condition, locking us into useless and repetitive behaviours that further our exploitation and immiseration.

Through human capital theory and the logic of self-branding, we have witnessed the birth of a new human – one who, in the pursuit of accumulation, tends towards futility rather than utility. I call this new human *Homo futilitus*.

The figure of *Homo futilitus* has lingered in the background of capitalism for centuries, often eclipsed by his rational and self-serving cousin, *Homo economicus*. The fact is that all human behaviour has carried an element of futility, one that capitalism has sought to minimise as much as possible in the pursuit of hyper-productivity and efficiency. But with the rise of financialisation in the neoliberal age, or, more broadly, the dominance of the rentier state, capitalism is less dependent on the fruits of human endeavours.[11] Instead, with the help of human capital theory, humans have been re-imagined as a new domain for capital exploitation, forced to conceptualise themselves as brands in a competitive marketplace. By drawing on the ideas of Michel Foucault, Wendy Brown, and Peter Fleming, I argue that the concept of human capital has facilitated a shift from *Homo economicus* to *Homo futilitus*. As I illustrate below, the figure of *Homo futilitus* manifests itself most concretely in the contemporary world of work, especially in Western societies, with the rise of useless labour, where many citizens are encouraged to dedicate almost all of their time towards tasks that have little, if any, social utility.

"Head Marketer for the Brand Called You"

To chart the rise of *Homo futilitus*, let me initially expand further on the logic of self-branding. In an influential 1997 article titled "The Brand Called You" for *Fast Company* magazine, motivational speaker and management consultant Tom Peters outlines the importance of self-branding in what he calls the "age of individualism":

Regardless of age, regardless of position, regardless of the business we happen to be in, all of us need to understand the importance of branding. We are CEOs of our own companies: *Me Inc*. To be in business today, our most important job is to be head marketer for the brand called You.

Peters encourages the reader to forget about their job title or affiliation with a company or institution: "Starting today you are a brand." With this new role as head marketer of yourself, you must "ask yourself the same question the brand managers at Nike, Coke, Pepsi, or the Body Shop ask themselves: What is it that my product or service does that makes it different?" To answer this question, Peters implores readers to identify "the qualities or characteristics that make [them] distinctive from [their] competitors" and suggests that, when they have done so, they have "to market the bejesus out of [their] brand – to customers, colleagues, and [their] virtual network of associates."[12] This "virtual network" has been granted a platform since Peters wrote his article through the development of social media and digital communication. In many ways, social media platforms are a manifestation of a growing social need in the neoliberal decades – the need to constantly distinguish ourselves from other self-interested individuals.

The outcome of this relentless self-marketing is "power," according to Peters. "It's not who's-got-the-biggest-office-by-six-square-inches power or who's-got-the-fanciest-title power." Rather, "it's influence power."[13] By "influence power," Peters means the power certain brands hold over consumers, a power that compels these consumers to keep buying the products sold under the auspices of this brand. The ubiquity of this kind of power today is evident in the rise of the online "influencer" industry, where some individuals build a popular social media brand – taking on the title of "influencer" – and, as a result, they are paid by the biggest brands to advertise and market their products on social media. There are even digital talent agencies set up to maximise the capital of these influencers, with one anthropologist predicting that between 2017 and 2020, the market value of Instagram influencers would rise from USD800 million to USD2.7 billion.[14]

Influence power entails the capacity to convince others to buy into your brand so that they might buy products associated with your brand. It is a form of piggy-back consumerism. But to be bestowed with the crown of "influencer," one has to create an image that is desirable. For Peters, influence power is more about "perception" than the actual quality of the brand. "If you want people to see you as a powerful brand," he proposes, "act like a credible leader. When you're thinking like brand You, you don't need org-chart authority to be a leader. The fact is you are a leader. You're leading You!" But most importantly, "being CEO of Me Inc. requires you to act selfishly – to grow yourself, to promote yourself, to get the market to reward yourself."[15] In Peters's world, Me Inc. can overcome the verticality of the traditional workplace – where, over time, an employee moves up through the ranks – by assuming the role of CEO of a corporation that looks like a self, but functions like a Coke bottle.

Peters's article – alongside many others on the same theme – has become a go-to source for budding entrepreneurs, recycled at business and PR forums and conferences over the last two decades. But the art of self-branding has not only engulfed the worlds of business and public relations; it has become the dominant mode of being-in-the-world for the majority of citizens in Western democracies. This development has been facilitated by an important ideological shift as an effect of neoliberalisation. The idea of being shaped by the social, cultural, economic, and political contexts in which we are immersed has been replaced by the belief that we can shape ourselves into whatever we want to be, irrespective of these contexts. As Byung-Chul Han puts it, "today we do not deem ourselves subjugated *subjects*, but rather *projects*: always refashioning and reinventing ourselves."[16] As "projects," we enter the world as seemingly active rather than passive participants, moulding the environments and situations in which we find ourselves to our advantage. In doing so, we believe that whatever unfolds is the result of the influencing power we exert over the world.

But the supposed empowerment of being head marketer of the brand called You obfuscates a debilitating human condition: complete and sole responsibility for one's circumstances – a condition that I discuss in more detail in the next chapter. For now, it will suffice to say that if the brand called You fails to attract consumers, as many brands do, the head marketer or CEO is responsible for this failure (which, it must be said, is often not the case in actual businesses). The celebrated autonomy granted by the transition from subject to project is the same autonomy that locks us into futile attempts to overcome the larger social, cultural, economic, and political conditions in which we find ourselves. Where we were once exploited by the owners of the means of production, we are now also exploited by ourselves. We end up in a *crisis of projectivity*. For Han, "people are master and slave in one. Even class struggle has transformed into an *inner struggle against oneself.*"[17] The real motive of the brand called You is not to enable mass personal empowerment, but to obscure the restoration of class power that lies at the heart of neoliberalism, as David Harvey has reminded us.[18] Each individual is pitted against themselves, carrying the effects of shared class struggle as markers of their personal failure. "The first lesson we must learn [from the effects of neoliberalism]," Harvey tells us, "is that if it looks like class struggle and acts like class struggle then we have to name it for what it is."[19] More often than not, we will name it as a failure of personal skill, ambition, or work ethic.

Paranoid Community

With the self as a brand, the other can only assume two roles: consumer or competitor. Almost all human interaction, as a result, becomes governed by capital. Han argues that "as entrepreneur of its own self, the neoliberal subject has no capacity for relationships with others that might be *free of purpose.*"[20] The brand called You requires relentless self-consciousness and self-restraint, where the self is required to continually think of how it appears to others, while also refraining from doing or saying something that might affect its image in the eyes of others. In such a scenario, how can we avoid a sense of paranoia, a fear that the other is always out to undermine us? The rapacious capitalist Jeff Bezos, the owner of Amazon, sums up this situation when he states: "your brand is what people say about you when you're not in the room."[21] What could be a more succinct expression of paranoia? There is a profound loneliness to the brand called You, another aspect of the art of self-branding that its preachers fail to mention. We are freed from the supposed weight of the other by continually accentuating and marketing our difference, only to discover that there is no form of freedom without the other.

The idea that individual freedom can come about only in relation with others was a point that Marx regularly returned to: "Only within the community has each individual the means of cultivating his gifts in all directions," he wrote, "hence personal freedom becomes possible only within the community." Capital creates an "illusory community," Marx argued, because it is dependent on "the combination of one class over against another," and therefore freedom only "existed for the individuals who developed under the conditions of the ruling class." "In the real community," he concluded, "the individuals obtain their freedom in and through their association."[22] A world of self-brands can only engender an illusory community, like the one Marx describes under capitalist class structures. Such a community is brought together by a sense of shared paranoia, where each inhabitant is suspicious and fearful of the other. Of course, some self-brands gain enough notoriety that they can gain a form of freedom from the wider community, like those individuals of the ruling class, safe in the knowledge that their brand will retain power over that wider community. But for most, the community of self-brands is characterised by *need* and *distrust* – the need for others to buy into the brand, and the distrust that others have and will continue to buy into the brand. There is no space for freedom in such a community, only paranoia.

PR gurus and entrepreneurs also often fail to tell their sycophantic underlings that the success of big brands rests on their ability to eliminate the competition and to foster the market conditions to make it almost impossible for potential competitors to emerge. The brand called You is not a "win-win logic," as Peters suggests, but a victory dependent on the defeat of as many others as possible. This should be evident to anyone who has ever watched *The X Factor*. That is, the success of one brand rests on the failure of the majority of others. For those whose brands have failed to find a regular consumer, the brand called You only leads to feelings of inadequacy, despair, and futility. And despite the fact we share these feelings with the majority of others, our desire to keep Me Inc. afloat means that we are usually entirely alone with these feelings. The autonomy that Peters and others celebrate as the precondition for a successful brand is also the albatross we carry around our necks. We are *branded* with the symbol of autonomy, forced to carry this mark as a representation of our individual failure.

Human Capital and the Self on Sale

The brand called You is a symptom of the entire economisation of life in the neoliberal age, where it has become almost impossible for us to think of the human as anything other than a conduit for capital. This fact has been concretised by the prevalence of the notion of "human capital," developed from the liberal thought of Adam Smith and John Stuart Mill and theorised more systematically by neoliberal economists in the twentieth century, especially Gary Becker. In theoretical terms, human capital, as the OECD definition tells us, represents "the knowledge, skills, competencies and attributes embodied in individuals that facilitate the creation of personal, social and economic well-being."[23] The development of human capital represents an historical break in the definition of what constitutes capital – with the emergence of what some theorists have called "neocapital" – breaking from classical definitions of capital as tangible and wrapped up in materials and labour practices.[24] Where capital had traditionally been held by the owners of the means of production, human capital, on a purely theoretical level, enables neoliberal economists – drawing on micro-economic modelling – to conceptualise the individual not merely as a holder of capital but *as capital*, as something that can acquire and lose value depending on how it invests itself.

Proponents of human capital celebrate this reconceptualisation as a heralding of a new age of human endeavour – backed up by a sluice of Nobel Prizes in Economics. But in practical terms, human capital simply marketises all human endeavours, viewing each act through its capacity to deflate or inflate an individual's potential to generate economic value either in the present or the future. Essentially, each individual must take on the risk inherent in all forms of investment. For example, if you want to be a lawyer, then you have to invest in education to achieve this goal. But if you can't afford university fees, then you can get a student loan in the hope that you will pay this off once you become a lawyer. Prior to neoliberalisation, a law student (and all other students) who could not afford fees or living costs would have received a stipend to go to university with the logic that the state should provide its citizens with such opportunities. The state knew that not all these students would become lawyers or whatever they wished to be, but it largely protected its citizens from the risk of not achieving this goal. But in the neoliberal decades, under the rationale of human capital, individuals must take on this risk by investing in the education themselves, with the failure to achieve their desired goal an indictment on their work ethic or investment choices, with a lifetime of debt as the punishment.

This passing of risk from the state to the individual inextricably ties the concept of wellbeing to the economy. Brown argues that "as we become human capital all the way down and all the way in, neoliberalism makes selling one's soul quotidian, rather than scandalous. And it reduces the remains of virtue to branding, for capital large and small."[25] By forcing us to sell our soul, human capital has enabled the economy to extend its tentacles into realms that have the potential to undermine the accumulation of capital, such as creativity, knowledge production, social interaction, and, ultimately, democratic deliberation. It has laid the conditions for the brand called You to emerge as the *prima facie* model of human behaviour in the twenty-first century. If distinctly human endeavours are reconceptualised as exchanges of capital – for example, thinking, communicating, sharing – then it is up to each individual to maximise this capital through whatever means possible. Self-marketing becomes an ontological necessity under such conditions.

Unsurprisingly, the notion of human capital has undergone rigorous critique, not that this critique has impeded the institutionalisation of human capital in all its forms.[26] Much of this critique has been channelled through the central figure of *Homo economicus*, initially conceived by classical and neoclassical economists as a self-interested and rational individual who maximises utility in order to develop individual wealth. This figure is shaped largely by a utilitarian ethics, as I noted in the opening chapter, whereby through maximising its individual utility, it can intersect with other self-interested and rational individuals to create the greatest happiness for the greatest number of people. But under conditions of neoliberalism – where the wellbeing of others has been once and for all eliminated from the accumulation of capital – *Homo economicus* becomes, to borrow Peter Fleming's words, "the organic seat bearer of 'human capital,'" interested only in the forms of investment that can help it accumulate economic wealth at the expense of other self-interested individuals.[27]

Foucault located this shift in the social function of *Homo economicus* in the transformation from classical liberalism to neoliberalism. In his "Birth of Biopolitics" lectures at the Collège de France, Foucault argued that the *Homo economicus* of classical liberalism was "one of the two partners in the process of exchange," which "requires an analysis in terms of utility of what he is himself."[28] In this sense, the classical model of *Homo economicus* was certainly self-interested, but crucially this interest emerged primarily in the realm of exchange and not production. That is, the classical economic human acted with its wellbeing in mind as a partner of exchange, where this wellbeing was calculated based on a series of needs that were shaped by its material and social life. But under neoliberalism, Foucault explained, *Homo economicus* is "not at all a partner of exchange," but instead, "an entrepreneur of himself ... being for himself his own capital, being for himself his own producer, being for himself the source of (his) earnings." As an "entrepreneur of the self," the neoliberal economic human is simultaneously consumer and producer of capital, whereby "consumption [becomes] an enterprise activity by which the individual, precisely on the basis of the capital he has at his disposal, will produce something that will be his own satisfaction."[29] And it this form of self-production that determines its economic potential as human capital, which is calculated through its own (dis)satisfaction.

Foucault chronicles the fledgling days of neoliberal *Homo economicus*, when the theories of Becker and the like were freshly hatched and only partially integrated into institutions and governmental policy. Four decades later, Foucault's theory seems more prophetic than ever, where "entrepreneurs of the self" reign supreme, with their apparent success characterising the futile aspiration of twenty-first-century humanity: one must not only produce but also produce one's self. Han notes that this self-production process is often performed under the umbrella of "authenticity," in which, he argues, one "develops a self-directed compulsion, a compulsion to continually question oneself, eavesdrop on oneself, stalk and besiege oneself."[30] He continues: "As a neoliberal production strategy, authenticity creates commodifiable differences. It thus increases the diversity of the commodities in which authenticity is materialised. Individuals express their authenticity primarily through consumption."[31] It is no surprise that the notion of "authenticity" is central to the online influencer industry. Influencers who advertises too many brands are at risk of being inauthentic, as they could not possibly like all of the products they share. As Sophie Elmhirst puts it, "in this new era of authenticity, influencers must display passion [for the products they advertise]."[32] Whether this passion is real or not is beside the point. The appearance of authenticity is all that matters. In the influencer world, authenticity becomes other to itself, used as a term to describe the marketability of commodified selves. "The I as its own entrepreneur *produces itself*," Han proposes, "*performs itself* and offers itself as a commodity. Authenticity is a selling point."[33] And, like all forms of capitalist production, we end up in a state of overconsumption, where resources have been pillaged to the point of extinction and we face a crisis of (re)production. But when the self is the very thing being produced, we are left with no resources. We become locked in the self, forced to continually commodify and consume ourselves in order to keep the production process alive, while we are simultaneously unable to connect to any kind of community that might relieve us from relentless self-production. The experience of being locked in ourselves, with no other option than to keep consuming ourselves and offering ourselves for consumption by others, is precisely the inexorable situation that produces existential futility. The entrepreneur of the self is the futilitarian condition *par excellence.*

From *Homo economicus* to *Homo futilitus*

Under the illusion of empowerment and freedom, human capital transforms the individual from an object of economic analysis to an active participant in the economy. But the whole point of this transformation is simply to privatise the risk inherent in the accumulation of capital in individuals rather than in businesses, corporations, or nation-states. In *Undoing the Demos*, Brown makes a similar point by arguing that "a subject construed and constructed as human capital both for itself and for a firm or state is at persistent risk of failure, redundancy and abandonment through no doing of its own, regardless of how savvy and responsible it is." The brute reality of human capital makes a mockery of Peters's concept of the brand called You as a form of equal opportunity, where everyone can be a winner. Rather, as Brown points out, "when we are figured as human capital in all that we do and in every venue, equality ceases to be our presumed natural relation to one another ... A democracy composed of human capital features winners and losers, not equal treatment or equal protection."[34] Human capital transforms *Homo economicus* from a "partner of exchange" – which at least required a dependence on others to exchange with – into a creature of competition, mercilessly seeking to eliminate others in order to enhance its capacity to accumulate as capital. The point here is that the classical figure of *Homo economicus* only operated in certain areas of human life, specifically the realm of exchange, leaving other realms relatively free of economic determinism, such as the realms of politics, law, and democratic participation. But at a time when we are *Homo economicus* in every domain of human life, "the construal of *homo economicus* as human capital leaves behind not only *homo politicus,* but humanism itself."[35] In other words, the traits that make us distinctly human have been co-opted by capitalism and reconfigured as nodal points in the accumulation of capital. This is truly the post-human nightmare in which we restlessly sleep.

Through decades of neoliberal economics, *Homo economicus* has been pushed to its rational endpoint, forced to carry the weight of the majority of human life, while those who benefit from the exertion of the economic human are freed from its chronic ailments. Its breaking point occurred during the 2008 financial crisis, when the catastrophic consequences of ordering humanity around such an abstraction materialised. Now, *Homo economicus* still dominates humanity, but its legitimacy as a model of human life has been demolished. It has become clear that "instead of being freer and wealthier, human capitalists are just as likely to be mired in debt, insecure and dominated by authoritarian management systems."[36] And yet the world imagined by neoliberalism offers us no other option than to carry on as atomistic human capital. In this respect, we are no longer *Homo economicus*, since this figure at least functioned on the premise – albeit an illusory one – that rational choice and ubiquitous competition could lead to the wellbeing of the majority and a prosperous future. Instead, in the aftermath of the financial crisis, we have inhabited the body of *Homo futilitus*, who operates in much the same way as *Homo economicus* but is perpetually shadowed by the futility of its plight. Most of us know that life should not be ordered this way, but in the desperation to survive, we currently have no way of behaving otherwise. *Homo futilitus* is the self-interested and rational economic human whose futility, rather than security, is the end of its means.

Neoliberalism's glorification of the entrepreneurial spirit entrenches the figure of *Homo futilitus* at the centre of everyday life.[37] William Callison and Zachary Manfredi note that "while neoliberalism demands that subjects conduct themselves as entrepreneurial individuals, producing value and profit through the optimisation of their human capital, it also creates political and social practices that systematically destroy the material conditions necessary to support this kind of individualism."[38] This dialectic between self-optimisation and social degradation, entrepreneurialism and austerity, follows a fundamental futilitarian logic – the more we behave as entrepreneurial individuals, the more the structures and relations that can provide any kind of collective security and welfare are dismantled. *Homo futilitus*, in this context, pursues what Fleming neatly terms "utility without purpose" – the pursuit of untrammelled utility maximisation without any concept of why such a pursuit might benefit society.[39] This blind pursuit of utility maximisation, despite its debilitating effects, institutes the futilitarian condition, and *Homo futilitus* is the archetypal individual of this condition: self-interested, entrepreneurial, obedient, unquestioning. In this respect, the hegemony of neoliberal capitalism relies as much on *Homo futilitus* as former versions of capitalism relied on the figure of *Homo economicus*.

Homo futilitus at Work

The existence of *Homo futilitus* is most obvious in the contemporary world of work, where the general experience of labour is increasingly mind-numbing and ritualistic on the one hand, and precarious and ubiquitous on the other. So many of us work jobs that are seemingly pointless and yet they take over our lives in ways that stop us from actually doing the things that make life worth living. Fleming describes this world as a "post-utility society" where "jobs and work have somehow drifted far away from the principles of utility. It is now a mistake to think of employment as strictly related to biological necessity – as if sending useless emails all day is akin to hunting and gathering."[40] Of course, futility has always been an aspect of human labour, to varying degrees. Fleming argues that "a degree of slack or spare capacity is inevitable in most human organisations given the lag between structure and need (or what economists call 'stickiness'), which hardly ever finds perfect symmetry. But only with the advent of neoliberal capitalism does this ritualised excess appear to be killing homo economicus off in such a determined fashion."[41] In other words, *Homo economicus* was always, in part, *Homo futilitus*, but the latter figure has emerged more prominently in the neoliberal decades, especially as capitalism has become less dependent on producing useful things.

In contemporary capitalist societies, more and more work is useless, both in terms of what workers actually produce and in their contribution to society more generally. In this sense, it is not that utility has disappeared from the world of work, but that utility has been increasingly detached from social needs. Neoliberals might argue that any labour is useful because the wage exchanged for their labour power enables individuals to buy the things that they need or want – although, we might counter that workers have less free time, or disposable cash, to buy or do the things they need or want. Furthermore, neoliberals could suggest that utility is judged on an individual basis; one person's futility is another's utility. And this might well be true. But for utility maximisation to work in the way that is often conceived by economists – that is, in a utilitarian context – then there must be some general consensus on what is collectively useful. If everyone pursues their own version of utility, then utility maximisation no longer necessarily produces a social need. Instead, utility maximisation simply becomes an end in itself.

Despite the fact that many jobs are no longer driven by utility, work is reverential in the neoliberal decades.[42] We could broadly argue, therefore, that there is an inversion of utility in the contemporary world of work; the more useless labour becomes, the more monetary value is attached to it. This inversion exemplifies the ideology behind what David Graeber bluntly calls "bullshit jobs," in which "huge swathes of people, in North America and Europe in particular, spend their entire working lives performing tasks they secretly believe do not really need to be performed." He targets specifically the managerial and administrative class, especially the creation of "whole new industries like financial services or telemarketing, or the unprecedented expansion of sectors like corporate law, academic and health administration, human resources, and public relations."[43] In an interview, Graeber elaborates on what he means by "bullshit jobs": "A lot of bullshit jobs are just manufactured middle-management positions with no real utility in the world, but they exist anyway in order to justify the careers of the people performing them. But if they went away tomorrow, it would make no difference at all." And this is the key point. If some jobs disappeared, we would notice a huge change in the functioning of the world – e.g., cleaners, teachers, care workers, builders, nurses, midwives; these are the jobs that provide a social utility. "If bullshit jobs go away," Graeber notes, "we're no worse off."[44] This has been abundantly clear during the Covid-19 pandemic, when suddenly the category of "essential workers" emerged, and it didn't include PR and HR consultants, corporate lawyers, and brand managers. There are jobs that are clearly "essential" to a healthy society – mostly, forms of care work in the sphere of social reproduction – but these are usually the jobs that are valued the least in terms of salary and security.[45] But we all (and even many of the people working them) know that the majority of these jobs in middle-management administration, public relations, or corporate law do not produce anything useful. Fleming observes that "organisations congratulate those who are able to master this melding of economic pointlessness and existential sacrifice."[46] In other words, not only do we keep up the fiction, but we are rewarded for doing so. The contemporary world of useless labour requires an employee that is willing to give over her or his entire life to the pursuit of futility; step up *Homo futilitus*.

In any capitalist system, it is unlikely that the majority of workers will enjoy their work, given that they are not the ones who benefit from their labour. As Charles Fourier, the French utopian socialist, wrote in the early nineteenth century: "'We must love work,' say our sages. Well! How can we? What is loveable about work in civilisation? For nine-tenths of all men work procures nothing but profitless boredom."[47] This is precisely why capitalism has required a spiritual realm, first outlined in detail by Max Weber, because without the idea that one's work is part of a bigger picture of human progress and spiritual fulfilment, many jobs make little sense.[48] But the neoliberal age is characterised not only by a dislike of work, or an alienation from the fruits of one's labour, but simply by a widescale pointlessness. It is a weird mix of futility and stress, not only boredom or resentment, that pervades the contemporary labour landscape. Graeber notes that "the moral and spiritual damage that comes from this situation is profound. It is a scar across our collective soul. Yet virtually no one talks about it."[49] Perhaps the collective shame of this reality stops us from talking about it. Perhaps we think this is as good as it gets. Or perhaps, subconsciously, futility feeds our death drive and relieves us from the pressure of having to actually live. This latter possibility is the scariest aspect of the phenomenon of useless labour. Maybe we like it this way. Maybe an overwhelming spirit of futility – a collective instinct towards pointlessness – is the very thing that will facilitate our transition from creatures capable of thinking, creating, and playing into mere pieces of data, vessels for capital to come and go.

Technology has of course transformed the world of work in the last century. Predictably, manual-labour jobs, particularly in agriculture and industry, have been largely automated, leading to mass agrarian emigration to cities alongside greater unemployment in industrial urban centres.[50] But where some theorists – such as Keynes and even tentatively Marx – predicted that the new age of technology would edge us towards a future with less, or even without, work, the opposite has become true. Technology has been used by capitalists not to free us from work, but to consecrate the ideology of work – to make us work harder but with less meaning (and for less money). Fleming contends that the primary purpose of technology has been to cheapen the expense of human labour; if a machine can do it for this much, then can we get a human to do it for cheaper? He writes: "Cheaper-than-machine labour conditions demonstrate how automation becomes a perverted standard – in terms of costs and maintenance – used to calibrate living labour against, compelling management to find an even better way to beat the machine."[51] Rather than freeing us from work, technology has lowered the standard and quality of the work conducted by humans. Fleming even goes so far as to say that "in the unlikely event that robots did develop AI, they would probably refuse to do the kind of work that millions of humans now must accept to make ends meet."[52]

There is clearly no economic justification for the prevalence of useless labour today. Why would a profit-driven society pay workers to perform tasks that produce nothing profitable? In volume one of *Capital*, Marx wrote that "if the thing is useless, so is the labour contained in it; the labour does not count as labour, and therefore creates no value."[53] And yet it seems as though useless labour not only counts as labour in the neoliberal decades, but that it is increasingly the dominant form of labour. The primary reason for this shift in the relationship between labour and utility rests in the emergence of financial capital or, perhaps more broadly, rentier capitalism. Our current capitalist mutation is dominated by financial markets, trading, and assets that no longer need workers to create things that can be sold for profit. Instead, profit is created by the mere circulation of money. But for financiers to go about their business unhindered, they require the majority of the population to be engaged in tasks that keep them eternally busy and less able or willing to question the practices of the financiers. The point of useless labour, I suggest, is to infect as much of the population with the spirit of *Homo futilitus*, not because this figure helps generate profit, but because this figure does not get in the way of profit-making. The best way to engineer this situation is not only to make work ubiquitous – with the help of communication technologies – but to also valorise the spiritual nourishment of work and to demonise those who do not or cannot work. Nick Srnicek and Alex Williams make the point that

Work has become central to our very self-conception – so much so that when presented with the idea of doing less work, many people ask, "But what would I do?" The fact that so many people find it impossible to imagine a meaningful life outside of work demonstrates the extent to which the work ethic has infected our minds.[54]

Our enjoyment of work is not even a question. *To be human is to work. To not work is to be other than human.* Jason Smith puts it well: "Work is a matter of discipline, the production of docility. When work becomes the site of libidinal and narcissistic investment, spinning a web of abjections and dependencies that exploits rather than represses desire – we become attached and bound to our own unhappiness."[55] And once we are compelled into a form of life that only reproduces our unhappiness, we are rendered completely useless in achieving anything resembling a happy life. We cling to work because we believe it might give us some meaning, even when that form of work is pointless. To think otherwise is to die.

The rise of useless labour in our age is a symptom of the widespread institutionalisation of human capital. When we are reconceived as capital, then the idea of utility is also transformed. We do not seek what is useful as and for human beings. Instead, utility is conceived in unconditionally economic terms, irrespective of whether an action might be useful or not for human life. The society of *Homo economicus* has not led to a self-governable community of competitive and rationally inclined citizens, as many (neo)classical economists believed, but instead evolved into widespread irrationality, inequality, and ungovernable misery, embodied in the figure of *Homo futilitus*. Instead of greater social freedom, we are trapped in the self, stuck in interminable narcissistic loops, forced to market ourselves against others who are stuck in similar loops. Instead of working towards social utility – a task that should be eased by technological innovation, giving us more free time – we work ceaselessly towards ends that are pointless in terms of human needs. Our only way out of this dilemma is seemingly to build a successful self-brand, to conquer the market, and free ourselves from the restraints of everyday human life. But even then, the pressure to keep up the image of the brand pulls us away from what actually satisfies us, towards a perverted sense of authenticity. Without us knowing, we have become as committed to futility as we used to be to utility. This transformation is the futilitarian condition in operation, like a thief in broad daylight.

3
Useless Responsibility

What's the point of responsibility? This seems like an odd question in an age when inequalities, human rights abuses, and climate change make it abundantly clear that we have an inescapable responsibility to others and the environment. And yet our age seems to be defined by an intractable paradox: taking on greater responsibility is ultimately useless in ensuring individual, collective, or environmental wellbeing. The reason for this paradox is not that responsibility is pointless, but that the kind of responsibility we are encouraged – and in many instances, forced – to take is one that places the entire burden of systemic problems on us as individuals. This reordering of responsibility was summed up in Ronald Reagan's first Inaugural Address in 1981: "if no one among us is capable of governing himself, then who among us has the capacity to govern someone else?" One need only take a glance at the ever-increasing shelves of self-help books to see that Reagan's question has been effectively answered in the last four decades. *Personal responsibility* is the order of the day.

The pervasive rhetoric of personal responsibility has transformed the role of government and society in the neoliberal era.[1] Where once the role of government was to safeguard the general happiness of the majority of citizens, albeit to varying degrees, its primary role now is to facilitate the conditions where each citizen can take on more and more individual responsibility, absolving the state from its responsibility towards its citizens. Can't get a job? Don't blame the casualisation and automation of labour, blame your inability to sell yourself or work hard enough. Feel depressed or anxious? Try cognitive behavioural therapy or mindfulness.[2] These will either change your thoughts or empty your head of any thoughts. Either way, the problem is yours and it has nothing to do with the rapid worsening of social or economic conditions.[3] Thinking about having children? Think again. You are single-handedly leading us towards a climate catastrophe, and it has nothing to do with the fossil fuel industry and the carbon dependence of Western society.[4] Forgot to recycle that plastic bottle? You're cancelled. Forget the centrality of cheap plastic to global trade.

This notion of personal responsibility rests on a problematic equality assumption: that all selves are equally capable of helping themselves. By starting from this assumption, the message of personal responsibility elides any socio-cultural histories of oppression, trauma, and exploitation. Hence we get statements like "poverty is a state of mind" by the former US secretary of housing and urban development and retired neurosurgeon Ben Carson, reminding us that we must reassess the status of brain surgeon alongside that of rocket scientist.[5] This equality assumption represents the real *end of history*, one where any sign of personal and cultural trauma evaporates to reveal the figure of the responsibilised individual lurking in the mist.

In this context, the state's retreat across Western democracies in the last three decades, in favour of privatisation, is more ideological than economic. Individual citizens have been inspired to view private welfare – particularly education and healthcare – as reflections of their ability to maximise their own utility. This simultaneously encourages a denigration of social welfare institutions as backward, inefficient, and repressive. Consequently, government divestment in public healthcare and education only serves to reinforce the image of a degrading social welfare system, which then enhances the supposed efficiencies and benefits of the privatised system. This divestment is a purposefully self-defeating cycle that is embodied in the everyday behaviours of citizens, who in being forced to take on more personal responsibility concretise the social conditions that require the need for more personal responsibility.

"Self-Help!"

To exemplify the ideology of personal responsibility in the neoliberal decades, let me turn briefly to Alan Duff's polemical and highly popular novel *Once Were Warriors*, which might not be too familiar to readers outside of Aotearoa New Zealand. The novel follows the travails of Beth Heke living in a low-socio-economic-status Māori community, which is shadowed by a wealthier Pākehā neighbourhood. Her husband Jake has been laid off from his job and the family are entirely dependent on welfare payments each month. And despite violent beatings at the hands of her husband, the rape and suicide of her daughter Grace, and a whole series of other devastating setbacks, Beth turns her life around through an odd mix of indigenous knowledge and neoliberal self-sufficiency.

By the time Duff published his novel in 1990, Aotearoa New Zealand had undergone the radical neoliberalisation of the economy by the Fourth Labour Government – known euphemistically as "Rogernomics," after the finance minister Roger Douglas.[6] Furthermore, a decade of the Waitangi Tribunal for claims into historical and relentless breaches of the Te Tiriti o

Waitangi – signed by several rangatira (Māori chiefs) and the British Crown in 1840 – had brought the idea of indigenous rights into the centre of Aotearoa New Zealand society. Neoliberalism and biculturalism emerged alongside one another and, in many ways, were iterative of one another. Literary scholar Jennifer Lawn notes in her reading of the novel that "*Once Were Warriors* exposes the tensions of th[e] split between Māori economic deprivation, on the one hand, and new forms of Māori economic autonomy on the other."[7] No doubt, *Once Were Warriors* is a powerful depiction of the everyday experience of poverty and systemic violence but, as Lawn points out, "the risk with Duff's work is that he will slide from his comprehensive awareness that poverty creates an associated mindset to the neoliberal position that poverty is merely a mindset."[8] And it is in this slippage that the moral message of Duff's novel reveals itself. He does not deny the brutality of poverty or even its relationship to colonial trauma, but, like the aforementioned Carson, he views poverty as a mentality that can be divorced from systemic forms of social, cultural, political, and economic violence.

In a telling passage from the novel, Beth is awakened to the healing effects of "self-help" from "reading somewhere, maybe it was the morning paper she'd taken to getting every day because it was a more serious publication, not so localised, trivial." The narrator goes on:

They gave her a pile of Teach yourself books: on a range of activities, from carpentry to making things from scraps of cloth material. She converted her sitting room to a rough sort of classroom. Spent the first month teaching to a class of one ...

Self-help!

She went to sleep at nights with the catchcry exclaiming itself in her increasingly happier mind. Her heart. Like this self-help idea was so beautifully all-embracing it was a wonder they, the Maori [sic] people in general, hadn't cottoned onto it before. Why, it helped the helpers, it helped the owners of the businesses they purchased from, it helped most of all the lost, unwanted, ill-directed kids. It was self-fulfilling.[9]

The reference to "the owners of the businesses" is particularly illuminating, because it exemplifies the implicit crossovers between the rhetoric of personal responsibility and the accumulation of capital. Those who exercise greater personal responsibility are better for business, both as workers and consumers, and will be less of a drain on government resources. And what better way to embed the ideology of personal responsibility in a society by linking it to self-fulfilment and empowerment.

Duff's novel exemplifies what Simon Barber observes as "a fundamental shift in the ideological orientation of Māori struggle [in the neoliberal decades] ... Where Māori struggle had previously positioned itself within working-class struggle more generally, a new basis in cultural nationalism called for Māori unity over and above class solidarities."[10] This shift initiated the dissolution of broader class divisions into two dominant cultures: Māori and Pākehā.[11] As Barber notes, "cultural nationalism ignores the location of the majority of Māori within the working class and so ignores their objective interest in abolishing capitalism ... It thus defines the struggle against oppression as one between Māori and Pākehā, and so forecloses the possibility of building a mass movement across these divisions."[12] *Once Were Warriors* reflects this reorientation by reframing the economic deprivation and social inequalities evident in the novel as reflections of a monolithic Māori culture rather than as a legacy of settler colonialism and the class relations engendered by capitalist forms of production, especially the division of labour and uneven geographical development. Throughout the novel, Māori culture is simply pitted against Pākehā culture, with the latter often glorified in Western versions of reading and education.

It is tempting to think that Duff uses *Once Were Warriors* to critique the very notion of self-help through the character of Beth – and, with it, the emergence of a neoliberalised cultural nationalism in Aotearoa New Zealand – but it is clear from interviews that personal responsibility is a message he values highly in his own life. In a rambling 1996 interview, we see many of the same traits in Duff as we witness in his character Beth. He states, for instance: "I had no formal training [as a writer], other than what I read myself and taught myself."[13] When asked the question whether he thinks institutionalised racism in Aotearoa New Zealand is the primary reason for Māori poverty and violence, he replies: "The answer is to respect yourself, to say, well, I'm not going to have a beer. I'm going to take my children somewhere. I'm going to stop hitting my wife. I'm going to stop blaming the world for my problems. I know it's harder for me to get a job, so I've got to try twice as hard. Don't cry about it. Someone's got to be the minority."[14] Later in the interview, Duff implies that this perceived defeatist attitude is collectively constructed and that it can be overturned by the company that you keep: "My friends are self-employed, they're business people, they're different. They're driven like me and they've got tons of energy and they want to get out and organise the world and fix it or achieve something."[15] Duff then injects this entrepreneurial spirit into the role of the writer, as he proudly tells the interviewer that he is writing a radio series so he can help pay for his daughter's school fees: "She's in a private school and not being one who runs to the government to say 'Well, I'm in the shit here, you know, give me some money,' I wrote a radio series and got the money to pay for her school fees."[16] It is perhaps churlish to note here that Duff filed for bankruptcy in 2011.[17] And to finish the interview, Duff puts forward his vision for Māori: "I've always said get economically strong, and the culture will get strong with it."[18] History only matters, he implies, when one is in a position of economic strength. Here, Duff takes the fundamentally neoliberal position that culture must always be subordinate to the market.[19]

The espousal of Duff's mantra of personal responsibility in *Once Were Warriors* is consolidated in the figure of Chief Te Tupaea, who embodies the convergence of mātauranga Māori with neoliberal economics. When he speaks, the community listens. But his message is fundamentally a neoliberal one of personal responsibility: "he was laying it on the line toem [sic]: telling em to jack their ideas up. Ta stop being lazy. ... Ta stop feeling sorry for emsleves. Ta stop blaming the Pakeha [sic] for their woes even if it *was* the Pakeha [sic] to blame." The Chief then goes on to compare colonisation to a storm. "Do I accuse the storm that destroys my crops?" he asks the community, "No! no, I don't accuse the storm. I *clean* up. THEN I PLANT AGAIN!"[20] Not only does this one-dimensional metaphor "naturalise a series of massive and deliberate colonial injustices into an elemental accident"; it perfectly characterises the motives behind the neoliberal ideal of personal responsibility.[21] The clean-up for the historical mess of colonisation (or capitalism) is disguised in the supposed empowerment of self-help, which is embodied in Beth's metamorphosis into the perfect neoliberal subject. In the metaphor, the Chief does not stop to think about building a different world, one that might be able to stand up better to the storm. Instead, he just plants again, certain that another storm will come along and destroy the crops in the future. Where Duff uses this metaphor to accentuate the virtues of personal responsibility – and to relegate the importance of history – he inadvertently provides an evocative image of how colonisation and capitalism initiate recurring cycles of violence.

Clinton and the Shame of Dependency

It is uncanny how Duff's proselytising novel mirrors the rhetoric of neoliberal politicians in the last four decades. While the language of personal responsibility emerged initially with the New Right of the 1980s and was present in the neoconservatism of the George W. Bush years, it emerged more systematically in the New Democrat and New Labour politics of Bill Clinton in the US and Tony Blair in the UK.[22] Nancy Fraser persuasively defines this development in left-wing politics, especially in the US, as "progressive neoliberalism," which constitutes the alliance of liberal social movements based on the extension of recognition with neoliberal views on economic distribution.[23] She notes that the neoliberal political economy was dreamed up by the Right, but "the right-wing 'fundamentalist' version of neoliberalism could not become hegemonic in a country whose common sense was still shaped by New Deal thinking, the 'rights revolution,' and a slew of social movements descended from the New Left." In short, the Right instituted neoliberalism; the Left made it cool. She continues:

It fell, accordingly, to the "New Democrats" to contribute the essential ingredient: a progressive politics of recognition. Drawing on progressive forces from civil society, they diffused a recognition ethos that was superficially egalitarian and emancipatory. At the core of this ethos were ideals of "diversity," women's "empowerment," LGBTQ+ rights, post-racialism, multiculturalism, and environmentalism. These ideals were interpreted in a specific, limited way that was fully compatible with the Goldman Sachsification of the US economy: Protecting the environment meant carbon trading. Promoting home ownership meant bundling subprime loans together and reselling them as mortgage-backed securities. Equality meant meritocracy.[24]

Progressive neoliberalism jettisoned the traditional corners of left-wing support in favour of a diverse entrepreneurial class who embraced the idea of personal responsibility with both hands. It was, in this sense, a progressive politics that could be endorsed enthusiastically by the financial sector. As Fraser puts it, "Bill Clinton won the day by talking the talk of diversity, multiculturalism, and women's rights even while preparing to walk the walk of Goldman Sachs."[25]

The rhetoric of personal responsibility was central to Clinton's progressive neoliberalism. In fact, his 1996 reform bill that effectively annihilated social welfare in the US was infamously titled: "The Personal Responsibility and Work Opportunity Reconciliation Act." The aim, Clinton argued, was "to achieve a national welfare reform bill that will make work and responsibility the law of the land."[26] Clinton's goal was not to merely encourage personal responsibility as part of his welfare reforms. He legally enforced it by placing time limits on welfare recipients and created a vast surveillance system in collaboration with law enforcement to monitor those who received assistance.[27] Furthermore, he created an inextricable chiasm between work and personal responsibility; in order to work, one must possess responsibility, and in order to take responsibility, one must work.

The pejorative juxtaposition of "dependency" with "responsibility" was key to Clinton's welfare politics.[28] He argued that the "current welfare system undermines the basic values of work, responsibility and family, trapping generation after generation in dependency." Like Duff in *Once Were Warriors*, Clinton viewed dependency as undermining the core values of work ethic and personal responsibility. The role of the state,

Clinton argued, "should be about moving people from welfare to work," which "gives structure, meaning and dignity to most of our lives."[29] To be dependent on welfare, he implied, was a mortifying condition, which effectively entailed living a meaningless and undignified life. On this point, Clinton certainly echoed the voices of the early neoliberal thinkers, who, as Jessica Whyte argues, "believed that only the self-reliant and responsible could lead dignified lives. Seeking welfare from the state, from this perspective, was inherently undignified. For the neoliberals, dignity required a competitive market order in which individuals were responsible for their own fate."[30] Furthermore, Clinton's welfare policies targeted and penalised African-American women especially, revealing the classist, racist, and gender connotations of neoliberal views on welfare.[31]

Clinton's bout of welfare-shaming epitomised neoliberal politics on the Left in the 1990s (and beyond), in which the notion of personal responsibility was viewed as the magic cure. Clinton's assault on welfare even received a glowing review from the influential Chicago School economist Gary Becker, who urged Clinton to "end welfare as we know it."[32] It is also important to note, as Melinda Cooper demonstrates in great detail, that personal responsibility for Clinton was not simply embodied in individuals but was also inextricably tied to the idea of the (heteronormative) family, which carried on a deep trend in the intellectual history of neoliberalism. Cooper illustrates that "an exclusive focus on free-market individualism obscures the recurrent elision between the personal and the familial in neoliberal discourse and thereby renders unintelligible its historical compatibility with various complexions of moral conservatism. Yes, neoliberals persistently exhort individuals to take responsibility for their own fate, and yet the imperative of *personal responsibility* slides ineluctably into that of *familial responsibility* when it comes to managing the inevitable problems of economic dependence (the care of children, the disabled, the elderly, or the unwaged)."[33] In this context, Cooper shows how Clinton's welfare reforms were informed by a new social conservatism that sought to "limit the potential social costs of sexual freedom among the post-Civil Rights poor by adapting and reinventing the family responsibility of the poor law."[34] In doing so, it reversed the trend of liberalisation in US family law and "unequivocally reaffirmed the importance of legitimate childbearing as a goal of social policy." This realised a dream of the neoliberals, who "hope[d] that many functions formerly 'usurped' by the welfare state [would] be returned to the private family, which they expect[ed] to automatically resume its 'traditional' role in the provision of care."[35] The valorisation of personal responsibility, therefore, was part of a larger moral project that tied individual opportunity to familial responsibility – with the male breadwinner discourse at its heart – in which the denigration of dependency on the state was also tied to moral panics about sexual liberation and unconventional families.

Blair and the Opportunity of Responsibility

Blair built on Clinton's re-imagining of social democracy through a similar glorification of personal responsibility and the denigration of any notion of dependency. In the 2002 Queen's Speech, Blair admonished previous social democrats who "divorced fairness from personal responsibility. They believed that the state had an unconditional obligation to provide welfare and security. The logic was that the individual owed nothing in return." He continued that the "language of rights was corroding civic duty and undermining the fight-back against crime and social decay," and commended

Thatcher and the New Right for "restor[ing] personal responsibility," because previously the "the obligation of society to advance the individual was denied." He argued that in the Thatcher years the Left "became a mirror image of the Right," as it stressed "social rights to the exclusion of individual responsibilities." In response, he proposed that "we [build] an enabling state founded on the liberation of individual potential."[36]

Not only did Blair present a bastardised history of left-wing politics in the UK here, but he also refashioned the Left in the image of the New Right – a political philosophy that many political commentators described as "Blatcherism."[37] Again, Blair follows Clinton's lead here, who, as Cooper shows, put into federal legislation welfare reforms that had been initiated by Ronald Reagan on a state level while he was governor of California in the 1970s.[38] This refashioning of the Left in the image of the New Right had been occurring already by the time Blair took power. In fact, Perry Anderson claims that Thatcher's "greatest achievement was the ideological adaptation of the Labour Party to her rule, a make-over confining its aims – this was still prior to Blair – to no more than a mild softening of the impact of a neoliberal regime."[39] Blair's victory was in many ways a triumph for the legacy of Thatcherism, a confirmation of its immutable impact on British politics across the political spectrum.

Part of Blair's political vision, which he shared with Clinton, was to re-imagine welfare not as a right, but as an *opportunity*. This linguistic shift enabled left-wing parties to link individual autonomy to notions of social justice and equal opportunities. We can see this in Blair's desire to continually tie opportunity to responsibility: "Respect ... makes real a new contract between citizen and state, a contract that says that with rights and opportunities come responsibilities and obligations"; "The New Deal ... seeks to provide new opportunities in return for new responsibilities"; "With these new opportunities comes responsibility."[40] Blair incentivised responsibility in a carrot-and-stick form of governance. And if you were not persuaded by incentives, then a strong criminal justice system loomed above your head to enforce responsibility. There is an obvious utilitarian logic operating here. Bentham, for example, claimed that "the business of government is to promote the happiness of society, by punishing and rewarding."[41] In combining welfare with the threat of punishment, both Clinton and Blair embraced the confluence of rewards and punishment that underpinned Benthamite utilitarianism.

The demonisation of the notion of dependency and the legal enforcement of personal responsibility by New Right and Third Way politicians is little more than an attempt to privatise risk. We see this most evidently in discussions around healthcare, where victim-blaming is a common tactic of the current political class. In 2018, UK Tory MP and Secretary for Health and Social Care Matt Hancock told us that "[illness] prevention is ... about ensuring that people take greater responsibility for managing their own health. It's about people choosing to look after themselves better, staying active and stopping smoking. Making better choices by limiting alcohol, sugar, salt and fat." Furthermore, and following a similar logic to Clinton and Blair, he claimed that "the biggest impact on your health from the economy is whether or not you have got a job."[42] And yet we could legitimately ask: if having a job leads to greater health, then why are governments going out of their way to make the world of work increasingly precarious? If the role of government is to ensure the wellbeing of its citizens, and if that wellbeing is tied to the security of employment, then surely the role of government should be to safeguard the labour sphere from exploitative practices by businesses and corporations. But the idea of prioritising the wellbeing of citizens over the freedom of capital would be to contravene the rule of individual autonomy that governs both the economic and social spheres under neoliberalism. Personal responsibility and work ethic – these are the only things that we can use to keep the cancerous cells and dark thoughts at bay.

Of course, the real reason for Hancock's remarks has nothing to do with the general health of the majority of citizens in the UK. Rather, his appeal to personal responsibility is a smokescreen to lay the foundations for the privatisation of the National Health Service (NHS), which effectively began with the introduction of the Health and Social Care Act in 2012. The narrative of personal responsibility is simply another story for austerity, but one that is masked as a tale of empowerment and liberty. Yet the effects of this tale are continually revealed as tragic and debilitating. In the UK, austerity has been cited as the primary reason for rapidly worsening child poverty, a sharp increase in suicides and suicide attempts, and even a decline in life expectancy, particularly in post-industrial areas.[43] Hancock is probably right. A bit less full-cream milk might help reverse these trends.

A number of NHS services have put in place "Personal Responsibility Frameworks" for their staff, which, according to one, "relies on all employees taking individual responsibility in order to improve the quality of services and personal experience of care for all patients/service users."[44] With the government envisaging all patients and staff taking personal responsibility for either their health or care, the government's responsibility to fund these services retreats to an infrastructural level, which crucially opens the potential for crossovers with private interests. The Covid-19 pandemic has exposed the devastating consequences of this manoeuvring in the last decade in the UK, as patients are unable to access the services they need, hospitals are overwhelmed, and staff are routinely put in dangerous situations with a lack of personal protective equipment (PPE). In fact, a report by the British Medical Association revealed that almost half of doctors in England were buying their own PPE – a sign of how far the ethos of personal responsibility has extended into the entire organisation.[45] Unsurprisingly, personal responsibility has been no match for Covid-19 in the UK, or elsewhere, for that matter. Boris Johnson has continually pedalled the personal responsibility line, drawing on the merits of "good solid British common sense."[46] In particular, the official "Stay Alert" slogan – an absurd directive in response to an invisible virus – explicitly passes the responsibility of limiting the spread of Covid-19 onto individual citizens. All the while, senior government advisors swan around the country, finding sunny riverbanks to test their eyesight, presumably so that they can remain alert.

My ultimate point here is that the denigration of the notion of dependency in favour of personal responsibility undermines an ontological necessity. We are, and always will be, dependent on others for our existential safety – no amount of personal responsibility can escape this fact.[47] Without any safeguards outside of our individual selves, we cannot trust that the external world will hold up its end of the bargain. There are endless events that can put us at risk – economic downturn, redundancy, pandemics – and the inability to guarantee our security outside of ourselves can only breed a culture of fear. We cannot know the inner workings of the market, the minds of our employers, or even our bodies. But we can hazard a guess, which can lead to crippling paranoia and hypochondria. This is the real opportunity of responsibility that New Right and Third Way politicians are so fond of encouraging: the opportunity to feel profoundly precarious in our responsibility.

The extension of opportunity is one of the central myths of neoliberalism. We are continually presented with the opportunity to take personal responsibility, but we are rarely granted with the responsibility to take opportunities. One only needs to experience the gruelling labour of contemporary unemployment to understand this paradox, where applying for employment takes on more rigorous characteristics and forms of surveillance than employment itself.[48] The labour of unemployment requires prodigious computer literacy, time management, and written and communication skills, not to mention dedication to the ethos of productivity. In short, unemployment demands high levels of personal responsibility. But no matter how much personal responsibility one takes, this does not necessarily increase the employment opportunities at one's disposal. In fact, a brigade of immensely responsible and skilful unemployed workers is ripe for exploitation by potential employers because they present the ideal mixture of desperation and productiveness.

The current labour structure of higher education is a prime example of the institutional exploitation of personal responsibility, where, in some countries, over 50% of academic labour is undertaken by casual and precarious staff.[49] These staff are highly educated, skilled, and capable, but opportunities for full-time employment are few and far between. No matter how much these staff members maximise their utility by obtaining more qualifications, publishing their research, and gaining teaching experience, the lack of opportunities for full-time employment disseminates the experience of futility throughout the university. University campuses are currently awash with the zombified precariat, who pump out back-to-back tutorials on a topic they have never studied, mark assignments like machines, and have long since forgotten why they were drawn towards thinking and learning in the first place.[50] The university is entirely dependent on this walking-dead workforce – it would crumble without it – but it provides them with few, if any, resources to perform their tasks. The university simply exploits the fact that many of these workers are dedicated to the disciplines that they teach, retain the idea of education as a social utility, and will take personal responsibility for their performance. And if they are not willing to spread this cheery message, then the threat of bad teaching evaluations will be used to ruin any future employment hopes, not in a dissimilar way to Clinton and Blair's reliance on a strong criminal justice system. This scenario does not encourage personal responsibility. Rather, it spreads the message: *personal responsibility or else.*

The more opportunities a government, institution, or corporation provides for citizens or workers to take personal responsibility, the less responsibility they take for the welfare of those citizens or workers. This dynamic reveals the cognitive dissonance of Clinton and Blair's progressive neoliberalism. The current relationship between government and citizens is not a tit-for-tat transaction, as they propose, where the government provides resources to citizens that take on greater personal responsibility. Rather, the aim is to create a self-regulating society where the behaviour of citizens absolves the government of responsibility towards these citizens. Again, a futilitarian logic operates here. Taking personal responsibility for our individual wellbeing alleviates any need for the provision of social welfare in the accumulation of capital. Not only do citizens end up taking responsibility for things that are beyond their capabilities, but any responsibility they do take is ultimately useless in providing a sense of existential security. That is, by taking responsibility for our own individual utility, a social system emerges where that utility is exploited to further disseminate the experience of futility. It is *useless* to have responsibility in such a society, because, as Brown puts it, "the subject is at once in charge of itself, responsible for itself, and yet a potentially dispensable element of the whole."[51] This self-perpetuating cycle is what Isabell Lorey describes as "precaritisation as an instrument of governing," in which "individuals are supposed to actively modulate themselves and arrange their lives on the basis of a repeatedly lowered minimum of safeguarding, thus making themselves governable."[52] Precarity becomes the new equality, and personal responsibility our daily medication.

Obama and "A New Era of Responsibility"

The 2008 financial crisis presented serious challenges to the ideology of personal responsibility, one that Obama and his administration in the US confronted by doubling down on responsibility rhetoric. His first Inaugural Address in 2009 was, in retrospect, an ominous moment for the future of leftist politics in the wake of the crisis. "The question before us [is not] whether the market is a force for good or ill," he stated; "its power to generate wealth and expand freedom is unmatched."[53] At exactly the time when the illogicality of the market was laid bare for all to see, Obama eschewed any critique of the capitalist system. Of course, none of this came as a surprise. As David Graeber reminded us:

> Whenever there is a choice between one option that makes capitalism seem the only possible economic system, and another that would actually make capitalism a more viable economic system, neoliberalism means always choosing the former. The combined result is a relentless campaign against the human imagination ... [W]e are left in the bizarre situation of watching the capitalist system crumble before our very eyes, at just the moment everyone had finally concluded no other system would be possible.[54]

In Obama, the leftist "campaign against the human imagination" – specifically the imagination that there might be an alternative to capitalism – that was instigated initially by

Clinton and Blair's politics in the US and UK, respectively, was made concrete precisely at the moment when the sanctity of neoliberal economics had been exposed as fraudulent. Nancy Fraser accurately sums up Obama's legacy in this regard: "All told, the overwhelming thrust of his presidency was to maintain the progressive-neoliberal status quo, despite its declining popularity."[55] The financial crisis removed any illusion that neoliberalism might bring about greater collective prosperity. And, faced with this reality, Obama chose neoliberalism.

Obama's response to the crisis, particularly his decision to bail out the banks and financial institutions that caused the collapse, represents the intractable contradiction for progressive neoliberals. Even when they can see that neoliberal policies lead to greater social and economic inequality, unemployment, and environmental degradation, even if they know that something needs to be done, their devotion to the doctrine paralyses any form of political action. Yes, they say, we need greater environmental protections, but more regulation might put off foreign investors. Yes, we need greater social and economic security, but we cannot stymie the entrepreneurial spirit and the freedom of the market. Yes, we need a more deliberative democracy, but we cannot get elected without corporate money. Yes, your life is miserable, but GDP is growing.

In his 2009 Inaugural Address, Obama employed the language of personal responsibility to legitimise the bailout of banks authorised in the 2008 Emergency Economic Stabilisation Act:

What is required of us now is *a new era of responsibility* – a recognition, on the part of every American, that we have duties to ourselves, our nation, and the world; duties that we do not grudgingly accept, but rather seize gladly, firm in the knowledge that there is nothing so satisfying to the spirit, so defining to our character than giving our all to a difficult task.

But while Obama implied that this "new era of responsibility" extended to all American citizens, his bailout of the banks and strengthening of financial institutions suggested that this new era absolved certain citizens of responsibility. Here, he tapped into an important loophole in the doctrine of personal responsibility. Both Clinton and Blair, following Reagan and Thatcher, preached the gospel of universal personal responsibility, while encouraging a small section of citizens, predominantly those in the financial sector, to be freed from the shackles of responsibility. And when the irresponsibility of this select few came to fruition in the first term of Obama's presidency, Obama drew on the very same doctrine to legitimise the passing of responsibility for the post-global financial crisis clean-up to those citizens who had already been carrying the weight of responsibility: "we must pick ourselves up, dust ourselves off, and begin again the work of remaking America," he implored.[56]

There is a great irony in the fact that after decades of proselytisation about personal responsibility by its mainstream politicians, the US elected a president who refused to accept any for his actions. Of course, Donald Trump still demanded it from the majority of US citizens – although not, it must be added, from his billionaire cronies – but he was the embodiment of the very loophole in the gospel of personal responsibility created by Reagan, Clinton, and Obama. He was the cartoonish personification of untrammelled capitalist irresponsibility.

The Futilitarian Spirit of Capitalism

Where Clinton and Blair could construct a fanciful image of an economically and socially prosperous future as justification for the grim reality of personal responsibility, Obama made this speech amid the economic ruins of the global market. Unlike Clinton and Blair, Obama could not even vaguely promise that progressive neoliberalism would provide economic stability, social justice, and equal opportunities. To remake America, Obama invoked the pioneering spirit of sufferance and sacrifice: "Time and again these men and women struggled and sacrificed and worked till their hands were raw so that we might live a better life" – the use of "might" here is no coincidence. Obama did not pretend that hard work would bring about greater prosperity for all or moral evolution for humanity – it *might*. He did not give any material compensation for citizens taking responsibility, but simply called on them to "give [their] all to a difficult task." And to finish, he warned citizens, "this is the price and the promise of citizenship."[57]

Obama was aware that to reconstruct the US and global economy along the same lines on which it had operated prior to the 2008 crisis, he had to rely on something other than the material realities of the current economic system – realities that revealed themselves as painful and debilitating. In this respect, Obama constructed what we might call *the futilitarian spirit of capitalism*. Capitalism, as Max Weber famously pointed out, has always relied on this spiritual realm, which Weber attributed to an initial symbiosis between the rise of capitalism and Protestant ascetic ideals. And while there are significant problems with Weber's thesis on the Protestant work ethic, as Ellen Meiksins Wood exposed, the idea of a spirit of capitalism remains important.[58] Weber noted that "in order that a manner of life so well adapted to the peculiarities of capitalism could be selected at all, i.e. should come to dominate others, it had to originate somewhere, and not in isolated individuals alone, but as a way of life common to whole groups of men."[59] The spirit of capitalism is precisely what binds together disparate strands of human lives within a wider ideological system, a system that requires the compliance of the majority of citizens.

Like previous spirits of capitalism, from Weber's Protestant work ethic to the managerial and libertarian "new" spirit of capitalism, the futilitarian spirit relies on a series of "shared representations – capable of guiding action – and justifications, which present it as an acceptable and even desirable order of things: the only possible order, or the best of all possible orders."[60] The futilitarian spirit shares many of these representations and justifications with previous iterations, such as the ideals of utility maximisation and the benefits of hard work synonymous with Weber's version and the blind pursuit of economic growth and endless accumulation, autonomy, freedom of choice, and competitiveness in more recent forms. But what separates the futilitarian spirit from its former iterations is the perceived pay-off. Where previous spirits compensated hard work with the promise of religious salvation, greater individual freedom, the democratisation of the workplace, or equal opportunities and rights, the futilitarian spirit demands utility maximisation with little, if any, reward. There is no afterlife, there are no promises of pastures new, no job security, no expectation of future prosperity, not even a guarantee of a planet on which to live; there is only the promise of hard work, suffering, and perpetual debt. This is what Obama called "the spirit of service – a willingness to find meaning in something greater than [our]selves." Where this greater meaning used to be theologically or morally constructed, it now rests solely in the act of serving the market, which is the deity that governs our behaviours and demands sacrifice to something beyond our material lives. Obama's eight-year term characterised the re-visioning of the state under the futilitarian spirit, in which "economic growth has become both the end and legitimation of government" and "commitments to equality, liberty, inclusion, and constitutionalism are now subordinate to the project of economic growth, competitive positioning, and capital enhancement."⁶¹ It is no surprise that one of Obama's first speaking appointments after leaving office was on Wall Street, to the very people he had bailed out.⁶²

Self-Destruction

The language of personal responsibility is the flywheel of the futilitarian spirit of capitalism; it is a background mantra that sustains the public sphere and conditions its inhabitants. But this mantra conceals its real motive: to legitimise divestment in education, training, and social security for citizens. The "sharing" or "gig" economy, for example, is a consequence of this divestment, and it similarly rests on a set of mantras, which are often celebrated as the zenith of freedom – *be your own boss, work whenever you want, do whatever job you like*. But the flexibility of the labour market allows employers and corporations to ask a couple of key questions that significantly impact an individual's responsibility in such an economic system. If workers own their own productive potential, then should they not be responsible for investing in its development? Why, neoliberal capitalists argue, should employers pay for developing an employee's skills when that worker might leave and apply those skills in another position at another company? These questions also apply at the state level in the belief that taxpayers' money should not fund the training or education of individuals who solely benefit from it, which is often a logic used to legitimise the hiking-up of university fees.

In granting workers "freedom" to choose how and where they apply their skills, employers and governments can shield themselves from the very relationship that threatens their power. This re-imagining of workers as individual corporations, Fleming notes, negates the Marxist call for workers to own the means of production. "If each person is already *their own* means of production," he writes, "then the intractable conflict at the heart of the capitalist labour process must logically dissolve."[63] Rather than being the antithesis to the capitalist employer, the worker is merely a mini-version of the employer or corporation that they work for. They operate on the same principles, but the relationship is deeply hegemonic. The employee is entirely dependent on the employer or corporation for her or his capacity to self-invest – because they set the terms of employment – whereas the employer is freed from any responsibility towards providing the employee with the training, skills, or security to further this investment. In fact, governments regularly facilitate this hegemonic relationship by relaxing employment laws and restricting unionisation, all in the name of unleashing individual creativity and ingenuity (and further enriching the corporations on which governments so depend). Rather than supposedly liberating the worker from the disciplinary restraints of the industrial workplace or the hierarchical structure of the office, the futilitarian spirit of capitalism encourages utter sacrifice and surrender to the capitalist cause, without any safety nets.

Neoliberal ideologues tell us that personal responsibility gives meaning to our otherwise miserable lives. But most of us experience personal responsibility as merely an act of survival in a deeply unstable world. Is this the price of freedom? If so, then we must divorce the confluence of human and capitalist freedom. Greater freedom to be responsible for our individual selves might free capitalism from responsibility to us, but it does not free us from our responsibility to the accumulation of capital. This is a one-way and abusive relationship, in which we are encouraged to see this violence as a reflection of our own inadequacies. This is ultimately Duff's point in *Once Were Warriors*, as it is in the progressive neoliberal politics of Clinton, Blair, and Obama. The violence of capitalism, they imply, is not inherent to the system itself but in the response of the general populace to this system. By forcing citizens to absorb the punches of this violence through the mythical empowerment of personal responsibility, capitalists can escalate violence without the fear of a fight back. Self-help becomes merely another term for self-destruction.

4
Semio-Futility and Symbolic Indigestion

The colonisation of everyday life by communication technologies means that we are bombarded by words, every day, everywhere. Silence has been effectively conquered and annexed by digital communication. Conversation has been replaced by endless information exchange. The act of listening has become almost impossible. We are constantly left frustrated by the incapacity of language to affect others in meaningful ways. The predominant production process in the early twenty-first century depends on communication and yet never has language been so useless as a source of meaning.[1] This futility has arisen primarily because language has been released from bodies – both individual and collective – and acts of enunciation, and now circulates in a communicative sphere where the relationship between the hyper-production of words and their declining semiotic value is vastly disproportionate. Words no longer need to mean anything to have value. Their value is as information. Like money, they only need to circulate to acquire value. If once, as Ludwig Wittgenstein observed, "the meaning of a word is its use in the language," then we can now say that meaning is no longer dependent on use.[2]

The hyper-acceleration of word production instils a market logic at the heart of language. Words compete against one another for attention and value, and utility is repurposed in the process. This is the # era, where the digitised use of a particular word, term, or phrase can be linked to other instances of the same linguistic formulation through algorithms that are not based on direct communication between human bodies.[3] We speak to one another incorporeally through the #, and when we do, we say the same thing as each other. Our communication not only resembles the market exchange of commodities, but we willingly enter into this exchange by freely offering up our thoughts and ideas to anyone with internet access. We are beyond commodity fetishism. We *are* commodities and we have the language to prove it.

It has long been clear that in the late twentieth and early twenty-first century signs and symbols are essential cogs in the machine of capital. This is the basic thrust of "semio-capitalism," a theory that traces a lineage through the ideas of Jean Baudrillard, Félix Guattari, and Franco "Bifo" Berardi. While my analysis here undoubtedly overlaps with the notion of semio-capitalism, I am less concerned with how capitalism creates value from immaterial production – what some call "immaterial labour" or "cognitive capitalism" – or how semio-capitalism acts as a "machine of subjectivation" that merges human and non-human behaviour.[4] These ideas are certainly present in what follows, but I diverge from them to explore a more direct, perhaps even phenomenological, relationship between the use of language and the act of making-meaning in the early twenty-first century. When I say that *meaning has been separated from use*, what I mean is that the act of making meaning – which is grounded in human bodies – is increasingly dissociated from the use value of language, which is determined by its market utility as information. I call this phenomenon *semio-futility*, and in what follows I explain how it currently dominates the sphere of human communication.

"For Those It Affects, It's a Crisis"

Allow me to begin with an example from Aotearoa New Zealand, which, at the time of writing, is in the midst of a serious housing shortage. This shortage exemplifies the illogical rush to double down on neoliberal economics in the aftermath of a globalised financial collapse, so while wages stagnate and household debt explodes, house prices continue to rise year in, year out in Aotearoa New Zealand. The average house value has increased by 51.5% since 2007, with the Auckland region, the country's most populous area, increasing 91.6% in the same period. Needless to say, the average household income in this period did not increase at the same rate (44%).[5] Many reports illustrate that people in full-time employment, sometimes working numerous jobs, are unable to buy a house, particularly in Auckland, and are increasingly finding it difficult to cough up rent. Unsurprisingly, homelessness and child poverty have become pressing social issues. Stories of people forced to sleep in their cars, entire families included, is a recurring trope in the news media over the last few years, and a news article in August 2018 noted that this demographic now includes a worrying amount of the post-retirement population.[6] For a country of approximately 5 million people – a third of whom are located in Auckland – and considerable land mass, the image of elderly car dwellers and children in poverty is deeply incongruent with the discourse of cultural unity and egalitarianism of which Aotearoa New Zealand politicians are so fond of flaunting on the world stage.[7]

A day after he assumed the role of leader of the centre-right National Party in February 2018, Simon Bridges was interviewed on Aotearoa New Zealand national radio about the housing shortage. He conceded that his party's government could have done more for housing during its three terms in office, but he was then pushed by the interviewer to answer the question: "Do we have a housing crisis in Aotearoa New Zealand?" After a long sigh, Bridges responded: "You can call it what you like. Is it a crisis? Yeah, for some it is, for those who don't have houses." He then repeated, "For those it affects, it's a crisis."[8] What are we to make of this statement? For one, Bridges tied himself in knots trying not to criticise his party's former leaders, John Key and Bill English. This was hardly a new development in governmental politics, irrespective of political leanings. Bridges, at this point, was leader of a party that won the largest share of the votes (44.5%) in the 2017 general election under the leadership of English, but he ended up in opposition to a Labour-led coalition with the Green Party and New Zealand First. To criticise his party's former government would have been to disregard the fact that their policies received the backing of a large proportion of the electorate in the 2017 election. Furthermore, a lot of citizens were, and still are, doing very well, financially speaking; Aotearoa New Zealand was ranked first on the World Bank's 2020 "Ease of Doing Business Index" and third on the 2019 "Index of Economic Freedom." A crisis? What crisis?

However, there is a lot more happening in Bridges's statement than a simple defence of his political allies and his party's electorate. When he told the interviewer, "you can call it what you like," he implied that the relationship between the word and the event it described is irrelevant. Of course, such a formulation was not a new thing; political discourse has always relied on deflection. But Bridges implicitly tapped into the growing anaesthetisation of meaningful public discourse in the twenty-first century. We can think of Michael Gove's dismissive "I think people in this country have had enough of experts," Donald Trump's "fake news" catch-cry, or the general trend of post-truth politics on the populist Right. Journalists, scientists, political commentators, and rationalists reply with facts to counter these dismissive or false statements, but because these facts are presented through language, which has become increasingly useless as a source of meaning, then they have little resistance against the tide of bullshit.[9] The Right has enthusiastically embraced the phenomenon of semio-futility and used meaninglessness to build a populist politics of apathy, deception, and conspiracy. The Left has been thoroughly outflanked on the terrain of language. In this context, Bridges did not merely deflect; rather, he recognised that the very act of definition was meaningless. *You* can call it what *you* like. *I* can call it what *I* like. I do not need to respect your definition, and vice versa.

A Crisis is a Crisis is Not a Crisis

The term "crisis" is a good example of how semio-futility functions. In a bloated media market, where news outlets not only compete against one another for breaking information but with almost everyone who owns a smartphone, 24-hour news outlets resort to hyperbole to distinguish themselves from the competition. Everything is described as a crisis. But rather than rising above the noise, hyperbole becomes the norm and reverberates around the communicative environment, and the semiotic variation between the adjectives that surround "crisis" is flattened out. And when hyperbole becomes the linguistic norm, then there is no way to transcend the noise, and we become trapped in a loop of semio-futility. Berardi calls this process "semio-inflation," where "you need more signs, words, and information to buy less meaning."[10] Just as money loses its purchasing power in periods of inflation and becomes almost meaningless, the hyper-accelerated production of particular words in the infosphere renders the meaning of these words useless. Semio-futility is the result of long periods of semio-inflation, where events eventually become almost indistinguishable from one another; we have no way of separating out their significance through language. The financial crisis is the same as the refugee crisis is the same as the plastic bag crisis is the same as the midlife crisis. Or, perhaps more precisely, while these adjectives point towards a difference in the quality of an event, the noun "crisis" has been emptied of affect, which makes the difference between the adjectives increasingly aesthetic.

When words are hollowed out of affect, we become locked into a Baudrillardian dilemma, where the emergence and circulation of a word brings about its disappearance.[11] The more we call something a crisis, the more the meaning of this word evaporates. Berardi, who takes much of his inspiration from Baudrillard, is helpful in navigating this terrain. For him, the accelerated contemporary infosphere leads to linguistic "automatism," in which "we find [the word] frozen and abstract" in its social use.[12] The media's instinctive rush to label any event a "crisis" is a form of automatism, which stymies the social importance of such a term. Crises matter because they materially affect lives. But for the media, crises matter because they might improve viewing figures, sell papers, or increase clicks on a website. The meaning of the term "crisis" is separated from its actual materialisation in the social field and its use takes on a new meaning in the sphere of what Jodi Dean calls "communicative capitalism," in which the proliferation of networked communication technologies engenders new forms of self-exploitation as "our basic communicative activities are enclosed in circuits [of exploitation] as raw materials for capital accumulation."[13]

In her book *Anti-Crisis*, the anthropologist Janet Roitman notes that "evoking crisis entails reference to a norm because it requires a comparative state for judgement: crisis compared to what?"[14] Its use today, however, implies an endless condition, where crisis has itself become the norm. Thus, as Roitman asks, "can one speak of a state of enduring crisis? Is this not an oxymoron?" When the term "crisis" becomes the normative condition for contemporary life, then it ceases to carry any use as a way of demarcating moments of time. Roitman points out that "crisis signifies a purportedly observable chasm between 'the real,' on the one hand, and what is variously portrayed ... as fictitious, erroneous, or an illogical departure from the real, on the other."[15] But this chasm can no longer appear when crisis is enduring and, as a result, it becomes very difficult to distinguish between the real and non-real, or fact and fiction. This is precisely why a certain brand of populist politician can deny the existence of the climate crisis, the inequality crisis, the refugee crisis, the Covid-19 crisis, or the like. The capacity of crisis to create a juncture, to demarcate between a previous and present state of affairs, has been rendered useless by the over-use of the term. This allows a politics of the non-real to emerge.

Marx showed us that the internal contradictions of capitalism meant that it was always destined to repetitive crises, so that "the real barrier of capitalist production is capital itself."[16] But neoliberalism has seemingly removed this barrier by making crisis central to the functioning of capitalism.[17] Pierre Dardot and Christian Laval argue that under neoliberalism, crisis has become a "method of government," where "every natural disaster, every economic crisis, every military conflict and every terrorist attack is systematically exploited by neoliberal governments to radicalise and accelerate the transformation of economies, social systems and state apparatuses."[18] It is clear, therefore, that today crises do not matter exactly in the way that Marx imagined. This is not to say they do not have destructive and irreversible effects, or that they are not felt as sharply as ever, but that they do not matter to the evolution of capitalism; they do not *materialise* as a barrier. This failure to materialise is partly an effect of semio-futility. When the use of the term "crisis" is an everyday phenomenon, the default starting point for politics, then the term cannot be used to counter the present state of affairs. Consequently, politicians like Bridges can use the term dismissively when discussing a social issue that materially affects the lives of many people, because they know that term has little meaning. When Bridges says to the interviewer, "you can call it what you like," what he really means is, "you can call it what you like, *it doesn't matter*."

Until it really does matter. The Covid-19 pandemic is a crisis of epic proportions, and suddenly politicians who have been busy hollowing out the term desperately require its profundity. Covid-19 is not just a crisis for "those it affects." Instead, it affects everyone, even those who do not have the virus. But when crisis becomes the norm, then it is very hard to believe that there is a crisis that extends beyond this norm. It is no surprise, then, that across the globe we see many citizens either ignoring official guidelines, campaigning against lockdowns, or spreading conspiracy theories about the severity of the virus. The pandemic is just another crisis to add to the list.

We have seen a similar phenomenon with the term "climate emergency," which obviously aims to capture the apocalyptic severity of the climate crisis, but, instead, merely serves to show how inured we have become to emergencies. In 2019, the European Parliament declared a climate emergency, as did over 11,000 scientists, and several local state administrations and councils around the world. One in ten of the world's population live in a location that has been declared as a "climate emergency." And while this fact clearly is an emergency, the naming of it as such has not really changed anything. It certainly doesn't seem like the majority of citizens are acting as if their house is on fire. Like "crisis," the term "emergency" is another victim of semio-futility, which undermines the capacity of language to adequately represent the severity of a situation.

The semio-futility of the word "crisis" highlights that the materiality of language is at stake under neoliberalism. This is a point that Christian Marazzi foregrounds in his analysis of the language economy. He draws on biological and linguistic theory to argue that "the language faculty, the fact of talking, *is one and the same with our bodies*. Our language faculty developed *physically/psychologically* (in *nature*) inside the phenomena of *life*, right from our very first proto-semiotic interactions."[19] Human bodies and language do not develop concomitantly, but rather operate in a chiastic relationship. The human is language, language is human; the human body both makes language and is made by language. We can say, therefore, that the human body is the material site of semiotic production; it is where meaning is created in the intertwining of body and language. When the circulation of words overloads their embodied use value, the body usually acts as a trip-switch in the current. The production of words is always regulated by the ability of the body to use these words, in the same way that in industrial capitalism material production was determined by the use value of the things being produced.

But what happens when communication is separated from the human body, as is increasingly the case in digital communication? For one, the production of meaning is separated from the bodily use of language. That is, meaning is no longer grounded in the human body because communication is not solely dependent on this body. Berardi describes this phenomenon as "parthenogenesis" where "signs produce signs without any longer passing through the flesh" in the same way that "monetary value produces more monetary value without being first realised through the material production of goods."[20] Meaning once relied on the chiastic relationship between human body and language, which necessarily decelerated the production of language because it always had to be useful for that body. But in the parthenogenetic process, meaning is liberated from its utility to the human body, takes on a different use value, and can be almost infinitely accelerated. "The word is no longer a factor in the conjunction of affective bodies," Berardi observes, "but a connector of signifying functions transcodified by the economy. Once deprived of its conjunctive ability, the word becomes a recombinant function, a discreet (versus continuous) and formalised (versus instinctual) operator."[21] When the word is "deprived of its conjunctive ability," it is decontextualised and is not solely dependent on a symbolic order that takes the human body as its reference point. Meaning, like money in a financial market, can be freed from the constraints of use value.

Hyper-Complexity and the Swarm

Semio-futility creates a non-linear and emergent communicative environment, where perpetual semiotic unpredictability overlaps with a complex self-organising network of systems and algorithms. John Urry describes this process as "hyper-complexity," which he likens to "walking through a maze whose walls rearrange themselves as one walks. New footsteps have to be taken in order to adjust to the walls of the maze that adapt to one's movement through the maze."[22] Hyper-complexity, in this sense, is an experience of reacting to a world that is continually changing as we move; every step is a shadow of itself. The paradox of hyper-complexity is that it severely reduces the semiotic complexity of communication. When we step towards somewhere and it changes its shape before we land, then we are required to find more simplistic forms of navigation that limit our potential to fall or misstep. In terms of language, if our decelerated attempts to make meaning are always overrun by the accelerated production of words, then we must reduce the complexity of the act of meaning-making so that we can communicate.

When we speak through our communication technologies, we might speak to digitised versions of one another and share more than information between ourselves, but, more importantly, our words are turned into information for a non-human infrastructure that governs the conditions of our interaction. Data is the new gold. And whereas mining gold required a big manual labour force, we now freely offer up valuable raw materials by messaging, liking, and tweeting. Furthermore, the proliferation of communication technologies and networked media has not led to greater democratic participation, access, and inclusion, as many techno-optimists claim. Rather, it has produced the phenomenon of what Dean calls "talk without response," where "everyone is presumed to be a producer as well as a consumer of content."[23] And because our interaction is mediated through technologies, and not bodies, then how can we tell if anyone is listening, even if we get a response? This fear can lead us to talk more, which only produces more information and more value that is not related to the corporeal act of meaning-making. In other words, our attempts to *use* language to *make* meaning always come up against the reality that the act of making meaning is no longer tied to the bodily use of language.

Hyper-complexity obliterates the capacity of individuals to understand and process the abundance of continually emerging information. In response, acts of interpretation become homogenised and simplified. Some critical theorists call this homogenised human collective the "swarm," which Berardi describes as "a plurality of beings whose behaviour follows (or seems to follow) rules embedded in their neural systems."[24] Semio-futility is the glue of the swarm. When meaning is separated from the bodily use of language, then human behaviour must conform to restore order. Our conformity is not based around a set of shared meanings that have been collectively integrated, but the communal (and largely unconscious) experience of the inability to use language to make meaning. "In conditions of social hypercomplexity," writes Berardi, "human beings tend to act as a swarm. When the infosphere is too dense and too fast for a conscious elaboration of information, people tend to conform to shared behaviour."[25] The complexity of communication supersedes the capacity of human beings to interpret what circulates in that communication and, consequently, the possibility of making new meaning is replaced by semiotic conformity, mainly as an act of survival.

Symbolic Disorder and "Gaplessness"

Importantly, semio-futility is not characterised by a dearth of materials to make meaning. In fact, Marazzi argues that "the opposite is true: we live in a genuine 'fair of meanings' where each of us can 'freely' appropriate the images, symbols, and myths that s/he prefers. What we lack is a 'symbolic order' capable of structuring and unifying the scattered fragments of our lives."[26] We certainly have the materials and the capacity to make meaning – we have a surplus – but the "symbolic order" that gives meaning its shape has been atomised by neoliberalism and digital technologies. We live in an era of *symbolic disorder*, where the separation of the human body from the production of symbols only serves to remind us that we cannot keep up with the chaos. Moreover, neoliberalism depends on this disorder so that we are rendered incapable of creating symbolic orders that might challenge its hegemony.

Marazzi makes the point that the lack of a symbolic order has created the room for a conservative and reactionary politics to flourish: "At the very time when the 'absence of meaning' brings within our reach an era in which human beings finally seem able to speak to one another, by virtue of free access to communication, we are witnessing the return of the idea of 'race' and of every myth of origin and belonging."[27] Marazzi wrote these words in Italian in 1994 (and revised them in 1999), but they could have been written today. A new right-wing populism feeds on the general populace's hunger for meaning, and primitive symbols emerge as avenues to feed this hunger. The symbol of borders, for instance, implies some form of geographical order and defence against perceived infection. Orthodox gender roles provide a social order, albeit one that inherently favours one gender over another. The nation-state provides existential order, a sense of belonging. Predictably, borders are fortified, gender roles reinforced, and the nation-state reinvigorated. These primitive symbols absorb the feelings of *Homo futilitus* – precarity, loneliness, disposability. They promise to alleviate the symptoms of semio-futility by restoring a previous (mythical) order.

Symbolic disorder is a consequence of the lateralisation of the communicative environment by digital technologies, where the endlessness production of language flattens out the distinction between the saying and said, self and other. Byung-Chul Han argues that "hypercommunication ... destroys both the *you* and *closeness*. *Relationships* are replaced by *connections*. Gaplessness supplants closeness."[28] The #, with its obliteration of the gaps between words, exemplifies the lateralisation of communication by digital language production.[29] Words are not distinct from one another in the #; they are both one word and many. The # demands that we create the gaps ourselves in order to understand what is said. There is no time for *gaps* in digital hyper-communication. Gaps are derelict spaces, wasted energy that could be used in the production process. Gapless communication, as Han calls it, can be deciphered more quickly by algorithms than human beings.

The body creates the gap. One body does the *saying*; the other body turns it into the *said*. The gap is necessary for the creation of meaning. Without this gap, the saying and the said become indistinguishable. In gapless communication – or "information exchange," as it might be called – there is nowhere for meaning to materialise. The bodies of the sayer and the said are nowhere to be seen. As Han points out, even handwritten letters retain "*signs of the body,*" whereas "all digital writing is the same."[30] My text is the same as your text, my voice sounds like your voice. How can one speak or listen without gaps? Where do the speaker and listener begin and end?

The desire of the conservative Right to reinforce borders, reinstate fixed gender roles, and reconstruct national identities is in part a response to the gaplessness of contemporary society. The border wall, especially, is a retort to the borderless world of global capital, where some people move across borders as if they are not there. Of course, the people that inhabit a borderless world are not the migrants and refugees that are violently repelled by militarised borders, but the nomadic capitalists who move and invest their money as if geography does not exist. These borderless citizens are the ones we should be worried about.[31] The border is at once the barrier to a universal capital and the very thing that facilitates the accumulation of capital.

On a more fundamental level, the border is an attempt to distinguish between *here* and *there*, and to protect here from infiltration by there. But here and there cannot exist without a gap, without a hinge that separates here from there. The border wall is an attempt to create a gap. But the construction of a border wall also aims at an irrevocable gaplessness – that is, at creating something that plugs gaps. It is not a porous gap, such as the gap between sayer and said or self and other, but a hermetic gap. In fact, as Reece Jones points out in his work on borders and migration, "the border creates the economic and jurisdictional discontinuities that have come to be seen as its hallmarks, providing an impetus for the movement of people, goods, drugs, weapons, and money across it."[32] Reinforcing the border only embeds the very violent and illegal practices that a hard border is supposed to prevent. The border wall, predictably, appeals to a symbolic order that is at odds with actual order. It is a gap pretending to be gapless.

The border wall does not facilitate a relationship between here and there. Its primary role is to violently distinguish here from there, to eliminate all otherness. When scholars like Han criticise the gaplessness of contemporary society, we cannot simply reply by saying that we must reinstate gaps, because not all gaps are created equal. Some gaps, like border walls, are not aimed at creating a distance so that the self can communicate with the other, but in *distancing* the self from the other. Such gaps attempt to instate an irrevocable distance, one that can become a gap to end all gaplessness. Their aim is not to overcome gaplessness in a constructive sense, but to create a world in which the gap is so vast that here no longer bares any relation to there. The border wall is a destructive gap.

The Vulnerability of Listening

To counter a destructive gap, we require a gap that opens a space for a relation between the self and the other. But the difficulty here is that digital communication depends on a misplaced conflation of gaplessness with relationality. Han writes that "today, by means of digital media, we seek to bring the Other as close as possible. This does not give us more of the Other; rather, it causes them to disappear."[33] Gapless communication, we are told by digital enthusiasts, represents the radical democratisation of communication, where everyone has the right to speak and be heard. But while everyone is talking, no one is listening. This is not relationality, but deafness. "Listening means something entirely different from exchanging information," Han argues; "listening does not involve any exchange whatsoever. Without neighbourliness, without listening, no community can form. *Community is listenership*." For Han, in distinctly Levinasian language, listening requires a "desire for the Other" in which "the listener undertakes the unreserved exposure of the self to the Other."[34] But in gapless communication, where the body is hidden, there is so space for this desire to flourish. We are not related but isolated from one another. A truly relational gap is dependent on listening.

Listening requires vulnerability; it demands an openness to the voice of the other. But gapless communication encourages invulnerability, where the self is better able to shield itself from the other. Simone Drichel notes that when vulnerability "signal[s] the openness to wounds and wounding," then the "the experience of vulnerability ... leads to efforts to transform openness into closure by creating and protecting proper – impermeable – boundaries."[35] The border wall is the most obvious example of a response to vulnerability conceived as exposure, but the refusal or incapacity to listen is just as violent. Not listening is a form of self-defence; it is an ethically violent act that attempts to overcome our exposure to the other.

Drawing on Levinasian philosophy, Drichel argues that vulnerability "is the precondition for ethics: exposed to and defenceless before the other, the ethical subject is pure affectivity; unable to shut itself off against the other, it cannot evade the responsibility it is assigned by (and for) the other."[36] We are destined to vulnerability precisely because of this exposure to the other. We are condemned to listening to the other. And yet the world of digital, disembodied, and gapless communication seems entirely aimed at eradicating this fundamental ethical responsibility. In fact, as endless accounts of online trolling exemplify, digital communication offers a platform for the self to try and dismantle ethical responsibility. The ethical command of the other, what Levinas famously described as "the face of the other," is hidden behind layers of screens, algorithms, and digital images. The "pure affectivity" is mediated. The ethical subject is deadened. Not listening proliferates under such conditions.

Symbolic Indigestion

The other side of not listening is not being heard. For some, the lack of a listening other might prompt anger with others, which in some cases can provoke another into listening. But if this anger is not listened to, which is usually the case in gapless communication, then eventually it can only be directed inwards towards the self. The subject creates a gap within itself, because that gap cannot be created outside of itself. Anger turned inwards is translated into *anxiety*. Soon, all communication (or lack thereof) is permeated with inchoate anxieties: anxiety that no one is listening; anxiety that one cannot be heard; anxiety that one cannot speak; anxiety that one cannot stop speaking; anxiety that one might be overheard; anxiety that speaking is meaningless; anxiety that one might be misinterpreted; anxiety that meaning is meaningless. In fact, as Han observes, "the diabolical logic of neoliberalism is this: *anxiety increases productivity*."[37] An anxious subject works harder, partly out of fear of losing their job, and partly as a distraction from anxiety.

Anxiety is lodged in the body and it manifests itself in a series of psycho-physical symptoms: fatigue, restlessness, sweating, dizziness, racing thoughts, lack of concentration, insomnia, palpations, lack of appetite, nausea, and indigestion. We can trace many of the same symptoms to the effects of the communicative sphere today. Berardi writes that "the explosion of the semiotic sphere, the utter intensification of semiotic stimulation, has provoked simultaneously an enhancement of the horizon of possibility and a panic effect in the social neuro-system."[38] But while we might think that anxiety is a fundamental pathology of our times, alongside a whole host of other psychological disorders, I tend to agree more with Dean's assertion that "the real pathology is the individual form itself," and that psychological disorders are a response to the pressure to maintain this form. "Depression, anxiety, autism, and hyperactivity signal the breakdown of a form that has always itself been a problem," she writes, "a mobilisation of processes of individuation and interiorisation in a reflexive inward turn that breaks connections and weakens collective strength. The individual form is not under threat. It is the threat."[39] Anxiety is first and foremost a defence. On an autonomic level, anxiety is a defence in times of physical danger. On a psychoanalytical level, anxiety is a defence in times of existential crisis. On a social level, anxiety is a defence in times of precarity. On a linguistic level, anxiety is a defence in times of semio-futility.

Anxiety reveals itself in several ways in digital communication, such as the fatigue of trying to be heard, fluctuating attention spans, racing and dizzying jumps in conversation topics, linguistic insomnia (or the incapacity to take a break from the production of language), and the inability to digest endless flows of information. This last point is of upmost importance. *Digestion* is key to the semiotic process. It enables us to break down language and transform it into meaning. But in gapless communication, where everyone is producing and consuming language at the same time, indigestion becomes the dominant form of semiotics, because the symbolic digestive process cannot keep up with the hyper-accelerated production of symbols.

In the biological body, digestion is a catabolic process that breaks down large food molecules into smaller molecules that can be absorbed into the blood and distributed throughout the body. For the semiotic body, digestion is a cognitive process of absorbing language and translating it into understanding. These definitions are clearly complimentary. For us to convert what we eat into nutrients, the digestive system must break down bigger food forms into smaller ones. Likewise, the understanding of what we read or hear requires larger chunks of language to be digested, broken down, and distributed into the capillaries where meaning-making can take place.

Like eating, listening is a form of ingestion. It is the act of taking something from outside the body – the voice of the other – and putting it inside the body. It enables the saying to be digested into the said. Time is important here. Digestion, of any kind, needs time. But time is at a premium in neoliberal everyday life. In fact, many jobs, particularly of the precarious variety, barely include any time for eating, and, if they do, they are often unpaid. In such a world, it is only logical that we have witnessed the proliferation of fast food, eating at our desks and on the run, or even the replacement of real food with powdered meal replacements, as occurs among the tech entrepreneurs of Silicon Valley.[40] It is not a surprise, in addition, that we have seen the rise of a range of digestive problems in the late twentieth and early twenty-first century, such as irritable bowel syndrome, celiac disease, and diabetes.[41] These issues are also an effect of globalised food production, where not only is the evolution of the biological body unable to adjust to ingredients from different geographical regions, but the quality of ingredients in foodstuffs differs vastly depending on price, accessibility, and the preservation process.

But neither is it surprising that when biological digestive problems proliferate, we simultaneously encounter the phenomenon of semio-futility: the inability to fully digest language and turn it into meaning. Biological and symbolic indigestion are two sides of the same coin, because there is little room for digestion in the machine of neoliberalism; it is unproductive and hinders the circulation of capital. We can simultaneously eat and work, in the same way that we can listen and speak at the same time. But while we are physically capable of performing these contradictions, they have long-term effects on our health. The "gut-brain axis" is a new medical phenomenon, with the discovery that the gastrointestinal tract is connected to the central nervous system.[42] What happens in our gut directly affects our brain, and vice versa. The key question here is not how we can improve our gut flora or what medication we can take to alter neuro-chemical processes that connect to our digestive system to improve our moods. Rather, the question is: why has the "gut-brain axis" become significant now? Anxiety is the answer. It has exploded across social existence. It plays havoc with the (symbolic) digestive system.

A daily and prolonged dose of listening should be the prescription for this condition. Listening to the other. Listening to our bodies. They can open us towards new ways of feeling. They can reveal to us the virtue of vulnerability. But so many of us are locked into anxiety because it is inextricably linked to production. We might even desire this anxiety because it is familiar, and we have no idea what to do with silence. Han proposes that "what is needed today is a *temporal revolution* that ushers in a completely different time; we must rediscover the *time of the Other*. Today's temporal crisis is not acceleration, but rather the totalisation of the *time of the self*."[43] Listening is a means of silencing the self. It is a way of reclaiming time. It can unblock the symbolic digestive system. Most importantly, listening can help us combat the phenomenon of semio-futility because in listening, the act of making-meaning is not solely the responsibility of the isolated subject – as almost everything is under neoliberalism – but is created in affective correspondence with the other. The other breathes meaning into our language again. The other makes language useful again.

Digital technologies are obviously not going anywhere. They will continue to expand and dominate everyday life. But they are not deterministic. They do not have to function in the way that they do now. To change how they function requires a re-conceptualisation of how digital technology has transformed our understandings of our social conditions. McKenzie Wark's concepts of the "vectoralist" and "hacker" classes can be helpful in this respect. The former "owns and controls ... the infrastructure on which information is routed, whether through time or space."[44] The hacker class produces new information for this infrastructure, often understood as intellectual property. Conceiving of the world through these new social formations radically transforms traditional notions of class. "We have a hard time thinking what the writer and the scientist and the artist and the engineer have in common," writes Wark; "well, the vectoral class does not have that problem. What all of us make is intellectual property, which from its point of view is as equivalent and as tradable as pink goo [meat]."[45] The vectoralist class has released language almost infinitely across space and time through the invention of new technologies of communication. But is has also captured language by using these technologies to create a new commodity in the form of information. On the one hand, the production of language has been hugely accelerated. On the other hand, the function of language as a relational act between human beings has been radically diminished.

The hacker class embodies the figure of *Homo futilitus*, destined to endlessly maximise its utility through the production of new information but, in doing so, further entrench the social conditions that mean it cannot experience the benefits of this production process. Semio-futility is the language of this hacker class, and symbolic indigestion is its semiotic code. Changing these phenomena cannot simply occur at the level of language. Yes, we can think of anarchic and revolutionary ways to use language, to make it occur in surprising and seemingly unsuitable environments, to separate it from the predictable rhythms of production. But without the building of a politics that can harness these new inventions of language, they will eventually be transformed into information and commodified by the vectoralist class. Wark writes that "words have to connect to everyday life in all its vulgar glory and idiocy, and right at the point where the emerging forces of production are shaping that everyday life, driven perhaps by quite distinctive forms of class struggle and experience."[46] Semio-futility and symbolic indigestion are abstractions that foreground experiences of everyday life and class struggle. In showing how we currently communicate, they also intimate towards a way of living otherwise, a world in which language can be used to make meaning again.

5
The Politics of Futility

On one of his many post-presidential speaking tours, Barrack Obama told a 2017 summit on food innovation in Milan: "People have a tendency to blame politicians when things don't work, but as I always tell people, you get the politicians you deserve."[1] A neat soundbite, delivered with characteristic languidness. But what exactly did he mean? Most obviously, he bemoaned the low voter turnout and leftist apathy that facilitated, he believed, the election of Donald Trump. "If you don't vote and you don't pay attention," he told the audience, "you'll get policies that don't reflect your interest." We might counter that his eight-year term was characterised by a set of policies that did not reflect the interests of the majority who voted for him – from the bailout of corrupt financial institutions to the escalation of drone warfare and American imperialism.[2] We could also suggest that his extension of a largely neoliberal agenda throughout his term could only lead to political apathy. Even the extension of healthcare provisions to millions of uninsured US citizens under the euphemism of Obamacare – the major political victory of the Obama era – reinforced the marketisation of healthcare and further enabled insurance and pharmaceutical companies to capitalise on the ill-health of millions of Americans.[3] The fact that the parts of the Affordable Care Act were written in collaboration with these very companies was a warning sign.[4]

If Obama represented hope, as his initial election campaign promised, then his decision to reinforce the very economic and social system that engenders hopelessness undoubtedly helped stoke the right-wing anger and left-wing apathy that permeated the 2016 US presidential election.[5] Also, if voter turnout was the real problem with the 2016 election, then the huge turnout for the 2020 election showed that Trumpism is built around a sizeable anger against, and deep desire to move beyond, the neoliberal status quo in the US. While Biden won the presidency, the Democrats will have to reckon with this reality sooner rather than later.

But, more significantly, Obama promulgates here a kind of mythical democracy, where there exists a direct connection between the people and their representatives, and where legislation straightforwardly reflects the will of the majority of the people. This imagined democracy of universal inclusion, participation, and unity is the holy grail of contemporary liberal politics. *We all have a say. Every voice matters.* The danger in promoting this simplistic democratic vision is that it bears no resemblance to the actual reality of contemporary democracy. Governmental politics is increasingly influenced by a whole host of unelected officials – from PR gurus and lobbyists to choice architects and nudge theorists – and legal and bureaucratic systems routinely silence voices through modes of exclusion and punishment. Moreover, Obama's mythical democratic image obfuscates the fact that contemporary democracy is routinely used to cement neoliberal hegemony – especially a US democracy that has legalised corporate bribing of political parties – endlessly reinforcing the interests of the wealthy and reducing the role of the demos to the capacity to vote every few years. How could we possibly get the politicians we deserve in such circumstances? The more pertinent question is: what have we done to deserve this?

Emily Apter provides an indirect answer to this question in her book *Unexceptional Politics*. She observes that the contemporary "political environment ... is severely pockmarked by obstructionism, obstinacy, the marketing of affairs and financial scandals, rude-boy tactics (incivility, tactlessness) and the submersion of political struggle in the vagaries of managerialism."[6] Apter locates a disconnection between the relentless expression of the political in everyday life and the institutional practice of politics. Here, she makes a distinction between "'small p' politics" – what might be described as micropolitical expressions that anticipate large-scale political action – and "big P" politics, which deals with analyses of power, governmentality, capitalism, and the like. Apter argues: "the abandonment of 'small p' politics to pundits and members of the chattering classes risks putting 'big P' politics out of action. By framing the Political in terms of that which is extraneous to or other to problems of statecraft, constitutionalism, and institutionalism, many thinkers have left undertheorised the formless force field of 'smallest p' politics that keeps the system of capitalo-parliamentarism in place and prevents emancipatory politics from taking place."[7] In the spirit of Apter's focus on "small p" politics, I focus here on micropolitical events – although not as "micro" as those in Apter's study – to emphasise how "emancipatory politics" are negated, even by political acts that aim at fundamental changes to the world order. Apter calls this "unexceptional politics," which challenges political theory's tendency towards the "states of exception," which, ultimately, "blocks the representation of what is unintelligible or resistant to political theorisation."[8] Crucially, this unexceptional politics can often take the form of a politics that thinks of itself as exceptional – that is, as doing something antithetical to the status quo. Taking Apter's theory in a slightly different direction, I locate in an unexceptional politics that sees itself as exceptional what I call the *politics of futility*, where politics routinely takes on a futilitarian form that only consolidates neoliberalism. In some cases, political expression mirrors capitalist behaviour; in others, capitalism is relegated to the background and the responsibility of individuals is foregrounded. But what ties the various examples of the politics of futility together is a negation of emancipatory politics and a retreat into the safety of political forms that do not threaten the hegemonic order.

Political Disillusionment and Pretence

Before I look at some specific examples of the politics of futility, I want to reflect on the relationship between political desire and the practice of politics. The Covid-19 pandemic has not only exposed the catastrophic impact of a decade of austerity, as I discuss in the following chapter, but it has highlighted the complete incompetence of many politicians and problems with political systems and institutions. The pandemic has accentuated the simultaneous decline of political deliberation and increase of political desire for the wider populace. These developments might seem paradoxical, but increasingly we are inhabiting a political environment in which serious political debate is negated – exemplified by figures like Donald Trump – but there exists a desire for some change in the current state of affairs – which leads to the election of leaders like Trump. William Davies highlights this paradox when discussing the proliferation of political referendums and binary choices in the last decade. Situating this development within the rise of social media platforms, and specifically the centrality of the "like" function, Davies illustrates that "clicking a button marked 'like' or 'dislike' is about as much critical activity as we are permitted," creating what he calls "a society of perpetual referendums." When this situation overlaps with an increase in political engagement – especially on fundamental questions of national sovereignty, colonial histories, or how to respond to a pandemic – the binary choice simplifies political deliberation to good versus bad and like versus dislike, generating bitter divisions on each side of the fence. Deliberation takes a backseat and an instantaneous rating system is prioritised. But as Davies points out, "a polity that privileges decision first and understanding second will have some terrible mess to sort out along the way," which, he notes, is evident in the post-Brexit debacle.[9] This situation is exploited by populist politicians, especially of the conservative variety, who can mobilise an electorate by presenting them with simple and extreme binary choices that mirror their online behaviours. For example, Stalinist Soviet Union or contemporary North Korea is seemingly the only alternative to capitalism, an elaborate hoax is the flipside to climate change, and burning down 5G towers is a substitute for a coherent response to a pandemic.

Davies observes that "it is easy to lose sight of how peculiar and infantilising this state of affairs is. A one-year-old has nothing to say about the food they are offered, but simply opens their mouth or shakes their head. No descriptions, criticisms, or observations are necessary, just pure decision."[10] No one on Twitter, for instance, wants to hear from the person who asks how the UK is going to navigate its way out of EU agricultural regulations. In any case, there is no room to actually present this argument in 280 characters. It is much easier to write "Boris Johnson is a knob" or to rant against "woke warriors" who have the temerity to raise the issue of colonisation or child poverty. The relationship, then, between the desire for politics – actual deliberation and participation – and the environment in which politics is expressed is increasingly fractious. And what develops in the space between political desire and this environment is disillusionment, not with the idea of politics itself, but with the options for political participation.

When Obama indicts people for not voting, he mistakenly believes that this absence is down to a lack of political desire. But we could as easily argue that the lack of voting is an expression of political desire. That is, the desire to have a politics that does not boil down to a choice between Donald Trump and Hillary Clinton. Perhaps Obama has it the wrong way around; politicians get the voters they deserve. My point here is that political disillusionment is often mistaken as a lack of political desire, when in fact it can often be more a consequence of the logic of futilitarianism. If your desire to participate in political discussion can only be met by joining ranks with increasingly diverse poles of political expression, represented by objectionable politicians, then it is the sense of futility that this situation precipitates that brings about disillusionment.

Where the current political environment might entail an abandonment of political participation, it can also breed subcultural forms of political pretence, where groups of people engage in small-scale activities that they perceive to be political, but instead either reinforce the status quo or turn away from the stickier aspects of the political altogether. I turn to some examples of political pretence below, because this is where the relationship between the politics of futility and neoliberalism is most evident, creating forms of political expression that proliferate the rationalities of individualism, competition, and personal responsibility. These forms of political pretence are often tied to consumption practices, which deepens the idea that politics can only be expressed through capitalist behaviour. Thus, neoliberal hegemony is defended against the political on two fronts. First, disillusionment ensures that large swaths of the populace see no means to change the current state of affairs, even if they desire to do so. Second, those who translate this desire into forms of consumption or lifestyle ethics reduce politics to a level that is unable to challenge the universality of neoliberalism. Stuck in this dilemma, many glorify the heroic individual as the archetypal political subject, who sees her or his own reflection in systemic injustice.

Buycotting and the Consumer-Activist

This heroic individual is exemplified in the increasingly popular practice of *buycotting*. Unlike consumer boycotting, which entails avoiding purchasing products from a particular company, buycotting is the process through which people express their dissatisfaction with a particular company by "rewarding" what are perceived to be more ethical companies through buying their products. As one commentator puts it, "political consumerism is on the rise and presents an opportunity to bring serious social justice issues to the marketplace."[11] Setting aside the fact that buycotting requires a certain amount of disposable income and that companies can exploit the desire for political consumerism by marketing themselves as ethical, the point of buycotting is it allows us to spend money and still *feel* political. Furthermore, if consuming certain products makes us good political and ethical subjects, then why not consume more and more of these products?

The buycott emerged in the 1990s as a positive alternative to negative forms of political consumerism, which usually entailed boycotts of particular companies or products. In a 1996 article, behavioural psychologist Monroe Friedman observed that evidence of the success of boycotts was very limited, and that buycotts represent a promising alternative. Friedman compares a series of buycotting events, from the Florida Gay Rights Buycott of the early 1990s to the *Twin Peaks* Buycott, where in the wake of its cancellation by ABC, loyal fans of David Lynch's cult classic TV series started buying products that were advertised on the show, hoping that these advertisers would persuade ABC to renew it. But it is not so much the examples of buycotting that are revealing about Friedman's analysis, but rather a point he makes about the expectations of the consumer engaged in the practice. "While it may be reasonable in theory to employ buycott campaigns to reward business firms for their contributions to the community," he contends, "most consumers would balk at participating in such campaigns if the products or services to be purchased are deficient from a consumer economic perspective."[12] The key difference between boycotting and buycotting, therefore, is the relationship between politics and consumerism. In the former, the political is used against consumerism, whereas in the latter, consumerism becomes the condition for the political, even to the point that the political is abandoned if the products consumed are not fulfilling enough.

It is hard to overestimate the consequences of this subtle shift in forms of activism in the late twentieth century. For one, it exemplifies the inability to think of politics as anything other than a marketplace. Many of us believe that in order to enact social change, we must first of all locate the market manifestation of a social issue, and then, through changing market behaviours, reap the rewards in the social sphere. Doing so leads us into further acts of consumption, as the corporations that govern this marketplace adjust to our consumer behaviours. What really happens is that capitalism presents us with the problems it has created, and we respond to these problems by further cementing capitalism. As Jason Hickel and Arsalan Khan write, "rebellious and virtuous consumption are products of a neoliberal logic that posits market solutions for political and economic problems, celebrates 'the consumer' as the supreme agent of change, and obscures the coercive dimensions of capitalism that generate the very problems that these forms of consumer activism aim to remedy."[13] In this sense, the phenomenon of buycotting reveals a futilitarian logic, where political interventions in consumer practices perpetuate the very conditions that precipitate the need for such interventions in the first place.

Buycotting has become a mainstream form of consumer activism in the early twenty-first century. There is an even an app called "Buycott" that matches users with products that reflect their political and ethical concerns. Buycotting is undoubtedly a form of sociality, but it is reflective of the transformation of the social in the neoliberal decades, where social capital becomes a synonym for social solidarity. In an essay from the mid-1980s titled "The Forms of Capital," Pierre Bourdieu argues that "it is impossible to account for the structure and functioning of the social world unless one reintroduces capital in all its forms and not solely in the one form recognised by economic theory."[14] Alongside economic capital, Bourdieu introduces cultural and social capitals. Where cultural capital entails a symbolic order that binds or differentiates individuals – from one's taste in music to qualifications and education – social capital is built through relationships "of mutual acquaintance and recognition ... which provides each of its members with the backing of the collectively-owned capital."[15] These relationships are protected by what Bourdieu calls "institutionalised forms of delegation," which enable a spokesperson to "shield the group as a whole from discredit by expelling or excommunicating the embarrassing individuals."[16] The point of these forms of "delegation" is the "conservation and accumulation of the capital which is the basis of the group" and to "regulate the conditions of access to the right to declare oneself a member of the group." The role of delegation is to facilitate the "reproduction of capital" within that social group and to prevent the infiltration of that group by others who do not hold the same amount or kind of capital.

Bourdieu's ultimate aim was to try and explain the social reproduction of capital, illustrating how power is maintained and protected through social relationships between the privileged. The concept of social capital has come a long way since. Other theorists challenged Bourdieu's theory, teasing out the potential for social capital to complement theories of human capital and to contribute to ideas about civic society.[17] Most notably, in his popular book *Bowling Alone*, Robert Putnam reframed social capital in democratic terms, around notions of community and "civic virtue." For him, social capital referred to "norms of reciprocity and trustworthiness" that arise from "connections among individuals." His point was that virtuousness could only be expressed collectively when individuals were bound together by "reciprocal social relations," which he felt were rapidly disappearing from American society in the late twentieth century.[18] Rather than ensuring the inter-generational hoarding of wealth, Putnam viewed social capital as essential to ensuring communal bonds and, consequently, to protecting democracy. Such an analysis could have led to a critique of neoliberalism, accentuating how the neoliberal assault on the concept of the social had dissolved communal bonds or how the inability to access healthcare or affordable housing reduced trustworthiness. Instead, in a study of 41 urban and rural communities across the US, Putnam turned towards diversity and immigration as reasons for this decline.[19] While he acknowledged that diversity and immigration are likely to be good things in the long run, his conclusion played into the hands of US conservatives. It gave them the sociological evidence to directly tie notions of social capital or civic virtue to race and cultural homogeneity.

In our century, social capital has become a buzzword at organisations like the International Monetary Fund (IMF) and World Bank, and politicians routinely throw it around when discussing policy. In all these cases, social capital looks much more like Putnam's definition than Bourdieu's. Social capital is a helpful way for governments to compartmentalise all social relationships and institutions into one concept, often obfuscating the ways in which specific policies are designed to dismantle such relationships and institutions. Furthermore, as both Bourdieu observes and Putnam implies, the development of social capital depends as much upon who is excluded from a group as it does on those included. Consequently, social capital can be used to justify systems of exclusion, from tight border regimes to gated communities. But, perhaps more significantly, certainly in terms of shoring up neoliberal hegemony, social capital is often employed to protect the rights of capital. For instance, in his IMF Working Paper on "Social Capital and Civil Society" at the turn of the century, the liberal philosopher *par excellence* Francis Fukuyama writes: "states indirectly foster the creation of social capital by efficiently providing necessary public goods, particularly property rights and public safety." He continues:

States can have a serious negative impact on social capital when they start to undertake activities that are better left to the private sector or to civil society ... If the state gets into the business of organising everything, people will become dependent on it and lose their spontaneous ability to work with one another.[20]

So, in other words, social capital works best when private property is protected and the state either steps aside for the private sector or gets its nose out of our business. Sound familiar? It is not hard to see why this term has become ubiquitous under neoliberalism.

The most important question, in terms of my argument, is why it is necessary to conceive of the social as *capital* at all. Many economists have asked this question, contending that the social does not meet the criteria to be defined as capital.[21] But more interesting is how the term "social capital" exemplifies Mark Fisher's definition of "capitalist realism," what happens when "capitalism seamlessly occupies the horizon of the thinkable."[22] To think that social relationships produce something tangible that can be accumulated like capital fundamentally alters how we conceive of society itself, much in the way that human capital transforms the very idea of the human. And, if social capital and economic capital are interdependent, as the theorists above would have it, then any attempts to change the distribution of social capital can be conceived as interventions in the accumulation of economic capital. To enact social change, therefore, becomes as much about how one engages in the production and accumulation of economic capital as it does about how one relates to other individuals. This lays the foundations for a form of political participation that prioritises marketplace interventions over concrete social relations, because to intervene in the market is to alter the flow of economic capital, even in a minor way, which subsequently modifies social capital. This is precisely why something like buycotting becomes a desirable alternative to boycotting. The latter might stem the flow of a form of economic capital, but only by retreating from actively engaging in the market. Social capital might develop, but economic capital is reduced. Buycotting, by comparison, not only develops social capital through the relationality of those engaged in buying certain products, but it also directly leads to the accumulation of more economic capital as it attempts to redirect this accumulation in more desirable ways. By developing both forms of capital, the world supposedly becomes a better place.

"Vote With Your Dollar"

Buycotting is the kind of social movement that develops when the social is filtered through the lens of capital. Hence we get statements like: "by continuing to engage in acts of buycott, consumers can support admirable or reject objectionable marketplace practices while bringing social change every time they take out their wallets."[23] This statement reminds us of Davies's "society of perpetual referendums," where people display their admiration or disgust by "voting with their dollars," which is a sentiment that has gained significant traction in recent decades. For instance, the ethos of Green America, a large non-profit membership organisation with over 140,000 members, is to "harness economic power – the strength of consumers, investors, businesses, and the marketplace – to create a socially just and environmentally sustainable society."[24] To help consumers achieve this goal they have developed a "Vote with your Dollar Toolkit," which provides information on environmentally friendly clothes and food shopping, as well as socially responsible investment opportunities. "Voting with your dollar works," they tell us, "[because] if many of us shift our spending at once – to preference non-GMO foods, for example – it can force large corporations to scramble and drop harmful ingredients from their products. And in the case of small businesses, it helps them stay afloat in a competitive, deal-driven market."[25] The use of a modal verb here leaves a lot of wiggle room – "it *can* force large corporations to drop harmful ingredients" is very different to "it *will*."

The idea of voting with your dollar presumes a simple relationship between individual consumer behaviour and what Apter calls "big P" Politics. That is, it is premised on the idea that a series of individual behavioural changes can directly initiate political ruptures, skipping the frustrating aspects of actual political organising and participation. Instead, Green America tells us that "every time you buy organic, you tell the world you want more farmers to grow healthy, safe food"; "every time you buy fair trade, you fight poverty."[26] But just because a shop sells organic food does not mean that its employees are treated well, as Nichole Aschoff illustrates in her analysis of the militant anti-union practices of the organic supermarket Whole Foods in the US.[27] Likewise, the ethics of fair trade has been a continual debate, with Ndongo Samba Sylla showing how the Fairtrade organisation favours large producers over smaller ones and the costs of certification disadvantage those in countries with low-income economies. As Sylla notes, "FT does not partake in a logic of international redistribution in favour of the poorest countries. In reality, this movement seems to follow a plutocratic logic, in other words, one that serves the government of the rich."[28] When we find market solutions to problems caused by the market economy, these solutions merely create new market problems that will require new market solutions.

This vision of the world in which money and credit cards carry magical political properties allows us to believe that every time we buy something, we are either making the world a better place or contributing to its downfall – another referendum. Consequently, organisations like Green America can pitch themselves as a supposedly radical alternative to the stagnation of governmental politics. Witness this example from the Vote with your Dollar Toolkit:

Green America's mission of creating a green economy that works for all – one that preferences [sic] social justice, environmental preservation, and healthy communities, has been under direct threat from Washington lately, but no matter whether it's election day or one of the hundreds of days between casting ballots, decisions we make every day cast votes for our values.[29]

Here, Green America proposes that we can change the world by simply bypassing the minutiae of governmental politics. On this point, Green America shares with the neoliberals a suspicion of governmental politics, confirming the neoliberal thinker Ludwig von Mises's conclusion in the mid-twentieth century that "the average man is both better informed and less corruptible in the decisions he makes as a consumer than as a voter at political elections."[30] And not only that – voting with our dollar means we do not have to do any of the messy and mundane aspects of actual politics, whether this is developing relationships, institutions, organisations, or party structures. Instead, we can simply get out our credit card and suddenly the world becomes a better place.

This post-political fantasy draws a straight line between capitalism and the individual, failing to grapple with the ways in which the state and governmental politics facilitate and sanction the very problems organisations like Green America attempt to confront. Green America is by no means the only organisation to promote this post-political vision, especially when it comes to environmental concerns. Aschoff notes that "current global frameworks of environmental power place consumers on an equal plane with states, corporations, and civil-society actors."[31] The political implications of such a shift are huge. Jodi Dean, for instance, argues that "the individualisation of politics into commodifiable 'lifestyles' and opinions subsumes politics into consumption. That consumer choices may have a politics – fair trade, green, vegan, woman-owned – morphs into the sense that politics is nothing but consumer choices, that is, individuated responses to individuated needs."[32] When politics becomes "nothing but consumer choices" – a variation of the like-or-dislike binary – it becomes impossible to think of politics as anything other than a variant of capitalist experience. This acceptance, Dean notes, "enchains us to collective failure, turning us ever inward as it holds back the advance of a politics capable of abolishing the current system and producing another one."[33] In other words, capitalism is buttressed against any kind of social relationship that threatens its hegemony.

The Politics of Babies (or Fossil Fuels)

Voting with your dollar and the practice of buycotting present two ways that the politics of futility operates in the early twenty-first century – principally that we can buy our way out of systemic social and ecological problems. Another avenue is to recast these systemic problems through the prism of personal responsibility. This avenue is evident in another variant of the climate change movement: anti-natalist environmentalism. A cursory glance across some major media outlets confirms the ubiquity of this idea, where we have headlines such as: "How to Save the Planet? Stop Having Children" (*The Guardian*); "Science Proves Kids are Bad for the Earth. Morality Suggests We Stop Having Them" (NBC News); "The Couples Rethinking Kids Because of Climate Change" (BBC); "Should We Stop Having Babies in the Age of Climate Change?" (NPR); "If You Care about Climate Change, Stop Having Children" (Newshub NZ); "How Should a Climate Change Reporter Think about Having Children?" (*Vanity Fair*); "How Climate Change is Shaping Family Planning" (*The New York Times*); "Climate Change Fears Put Young People Off Having Children, YouGov Poll Shows" (*The Times*); "Why Having Kids is the Worst Thing You Can Do for the Planet" (*Fast Company*). And so on, and so forth. The most obvious thing about these headlines is that all of them focus on individual moments of decision-making. But a key difference is that some suggest that individuals have to seriously question the ethics of bringing another human into a world that is heading towards a climate apocalypse, whereas others imply that the decision to not have children is somehow going to save the world from that apocalypse. The former understands that the individual is constitutive of its social and ecological milieu, to the point where bringing a new individual into the current milieu might seem unethical. The latter sees society in the individual, and all social and ecological issues are reduced to the level of individual decision-making. Like the idea of voting with your dollar, this is another form of magical thinking, where individuals are encouraged to believe that their daily life choices either save or annihilate the world.

Much of the anti-natalist environmental movement characterises the politics of futility. It treats the carbon footprint as a natural phenomenon and immutable fact about the world, rather than something that is both the result of historical processes of production, colonisation, extraction, and exploitation, and a manifestation of neoliberalism's translation of systemic problems into questions of personal responsibility.[34] The trickier details of Western imperialism, the power of the fossil fuel industry and its hold over governmental politics across the globe, and the impotence of global climate accords retreat into the background. In doing so, this form of anti-natalism negates any possibility of overcoming the very system that makes climate change a reality. Instead, it largely encourages us to find individual ways to mitigate and survive the oncoming apocalypse. This is not only defeatist but extremely dangerous, because it concretises the social and economic conditions that make climate recovery impossible. Fisher is particularly helpful on this point when he argues: "instead of saying that *everyone* – i.e. every *one* – is responsible for climate change, we all have to do our bit, it would be better to say that no-one is, and that's the very problem."[35] But to admit that no "*one*" is responsible for climate change would be to undercut the ethos of triumphant individualism that fortifies neoliberal subjectivity. It is much easier to believe that individual choices can effect systemic change than to admit one's life has little impact on how the world functions. If the choice is between saving the individual subject or the climate, neoliberal rationality ensures that the former will always win out.

In an essay titled "Don't Blame the Babies," Liza Featherstone points out that when the anti-natalists highlight the carbon footprint of each individual human, they do not ask: "why does each human have such a huge carbon footprint? It is not inherent to your (possibly quite charming) baby." She continues:

> A Zambian has nowhere near the environmental impact of an American; even though her nation has a much higher birth rate, her society isn't nearly as carbon-intensive. The problem, then, isn't kids. It's the carbon dependence of our society, which is set up to ensure that we drive, fly, heat, cool, shop, and eat in all the most polluting ways possible.[36]

Furthermore, fertility rates have been steadily declining across the globe over the last 70 years – mainly because of economic pressures and inadequate childcare provisions, and not environmental consciousness – and yet, global temperatures and sea levels have been heading in the other direction in the same period.[37] Either we're not reducing the fertility rate quickly enough or there is something else going on. That "something else" is much more difficult to confront because it constitutes an entire social and economic system that requires more and more environmental plundering just in order to repropagate.

To believe in the myth that individual behaviour can change society is to cement the logic of futilitarianism, where in supposedly being useful – by, in this case, refraining from having children in order to save the planet – we actually facilitate the worsening of collective social and ecological wellbeing because we let capitalism off the hook. As Featherstone puts it: "ExxonMobil doesn't care whether you have another kid. The actual 'best thing you can do' for the planet is anything that will reduce the political power of the fossil fuel industry, while 'the worst thing you can do' is try to convince people otherwise."[38]

This is all a long way around to say that any environmental politics that is not fundamentally anticapitalist is ultimately destined to futility. It is this problem that undermines the rebellious energy of Extinction Rebellion (XR). When one protestor turned up to a rally carrying a sign reading "Socialism or Extinction," the official XR Twitter account in the UK responded by saying: "Just to be clear we are not a socialist movement. We do not trust any single ideology, we trust the people, chosen by sortition (like jury service) to find the best future for us all through a #CitizensAssembly. A banner saying 'socialism or extinction' does not represent us."[39] Of course, direct action is a legitimate form of rebellion, and it has been shown to work in grassroots movements, but a climate movement that retreats from "big P" Politics, to the point where it is moved to distance itself from socialism, is one that is inevitably doomed to failure. Many people responded to this tweet with the words of the Brazilian trade union leader and environmentalist Chico Mendes, who reportedly said: "ecology without class struggle is just gardening."[40] XR has undoubtedly harnessed a disruptive collective energy but without continually tying climate change to capitalism, colonialism, and global systems of exclusion and exploitation, it will routinely retreat back into the safety of the politics of futility.

Politics beyond Futility

In his book *The Death of Homo Economicus*, Peter Fleming asks a very pertinent question in the context of the politics of futility: "Is resistance to capitalism still possible after such a devastating process of individualisation has taken place?"[41] If buycotting and anti-natalist environmentalism are anything to go by, then the answer would be a resounding no. Even contemporary anti-capitalist movements have faltered precisely because of this process of individualisation. Dean gives a good example in her experience of an Occupy Wall Street rally at Washington Square Park in New York in 2011. She notes that as police tightened the cordon around the park, the energy of the crowd built. "Speaker after speaker," she writes, "amplified by the People's Mic (where the crowd repeats the words of a speaker so that those who are farther away know what is being said), urged us to take the park. *We are many. We can do it. We must do it.*" And then a young man stood up to speak through the human microphone: "We can take this park! ... We can take this part tonight! ... We can also take this park another night ... Not everyone may be ready tonight ... Each person has to make their own autonomous decision ... You have to decide for yourself ... Everyone is an autonomous individual." As Dean notes, "the mood was broken ... We were no longer a 'we' ... Collective strength devolved into the problem of individuals aggregating by choices and interests that may or may not converge. Reducing autonomy to individual decision, we destroyed the freedom of action we had as a crowd." Exactly at the moment the crowd threatened to inhabit the political subjectivity of a "we," it disappeared through fear of stepping on the toes of individual autonomy. For Dean, "Occupy Wall Street foundered against a contradiction at its core. The individualism of its democratic, anarchist and horizontalist ideological currents undermined the collective power the movement was building."[42] Despite the Occupy movement naming its enemy – the 1% – neoliberal rationality won out indirectly in the end.

The human rights movement is another that routinely suffers from neoliberal intervention. David Harvey made this point in the early part of this century:

Undoubtedly, the neo-liberal insistence upon the individual as the foundational and essentialist element in political-economic life does open the door to extensive individual rights activism. But by focusing on those rights rather than on the creation or re-creation of substantive and open democratic governance structures, the opposition cultivates methods that cannot escape the neo-liberal trap. The neo-liberal attachment to the individual is allowed to trump any social democratic concern for equality, democracy and social solidarities.[43]

But it is not only the attachment to the individual form where human rights and neoliberalism overlap. In her remarkable book *The Morals of the Market*, Jessica Whyte elaborates how neoliberals manipulated the discourse of human rights to advance the neoliberal project, especially around preserving private property and individual liberty. She quotes Milton Friedman, who believed that "property rights are not in conflict with human rights. On the contrary, they are themselves the most basic of human rights and an essential foundation for other human rights."[44] Whyte documents the parallel histories of neoliberalism and human rights, accentuating that "the neoliberals of the Mont Pèlerin Society reinvented human rights as the moral language of the human market" and "they developed their own account of human rights as protections for the market order." The neoliberal reinvention of rights, Whyte illustrates, influenced new forms of non-governmental advocacy, especially global charities and humanitarian organisations, which shared with the neoliberal thinkers a deep fear of decolonisation and antagonism towards politics. Whyte writes: "[international human rights and humanitarian NGOs] defended the same (anti-)political virtues the neoliberals attributed to the market: restraining political power, taming violence and facilitating a margin of individual freedom."[45]

Where it seems almost sacrilegious to even question the idea of human rights in an age where rights issues dominate the political landscape, we should be concerned with the conflation of human rights and the rights of capital. Moreover, despite the rise of human rights, it seems like rights abuses are only increasing, so we need to think seriously about how the notion of human rights neatly corresponds with a neoliberal value system that stymies the construction of political and social solidarities, all in the name of freedom. By placing the liberty of the individual at the centre of politics, human rights activists risk accepting the premise of hyper-individuality that consecrates the neoliberal project. A human right for the neoliberals, generally speaking, is basically the right to fend for one's self in a competitive world order.

There are, however, reasons to be hopeful. In the Introduction to this book, I mentioned an important generational divide between what we might crudely call the baby-boomers and the millennials in the Global North. The boomers, for the most part, are relatively secure, especially if they bought their houses at the right time and have seen huge appreciation in the value of their properties. The millennials, however, have grown up into a deeply insecure world, where work is increasingly sparse and precarious, house prices are extortionate, higher education requires the absorption of serious debt, and the natural environment is irrevocably damaged. On top of this, Covid-19 has shown that deadly viruses can bring the world to a standstill at any moment and, even then, the rich seem to get richer. Some millennials are fine, of course, especially if they have access to the assets accrued by their boomer parents and families. But many are not, and the most precarious are the ones who are starting to make their voices heard across the globe.[46] In this context, Grace Blakeley asks a simple but powerful question: "Why ... should young people support capitalism when they never expect to own any capital?"[47] This presents a deep dilemma for neoliberal hegemony. The centralisation of wealth in an ever-decreasing few might have worked for a few decades, especially in the wake of the collapse of the Soviet Union and the momentary end of history, where capitalism seemed to answer every question posed against it. But a new generation has emerged who do not necessarily see capitalism as the golden ticket. In fact, they find themselves excluded from and exploited by capitalism every single day, whether it is by their boss, landlord, university, or government. Indeed, why would young people support this system?

Ultimately, this book is written for this generation of doomed youth. It is an attempt to give a name to those feelings and thoughts we encounter on a daily basis. *Futility*; it is not ours, no matter what we are told. Capitalism, especially in its neoliberal guise, creates the conditions for futility to spread, but through its operating logic, it manages to pass the upkeep of this futility on to us as individuals. Political expressions like buycotting, voting with your dollar, or anti-natalist environmentalism are the kinds of politics that emerge when we accept responsibility for this futility. It is not that these movements aren't trying to make the world a better place, but that by accepting responsibility for the state of the world, they also accept the fundamental premises of neoliberal rationality, that the world is made in the image of the individual. It is worth quoting Dean at length on this point.

[E]ven when we are fully conscious of the deep inequity of the system in which we find ourselves, we confirm and conform to the dominant ideology: turn inward, enclave, emphasise the singular and momentary. Sometimes we don't feel like we can do anything about it (maybe we have too much work to do already). Or we find ourselves participating in individuated, localised, or communicatively mediated activities without momentum, duration, or a capacity for political memory. Or we presume that we have to focus on ourselves, start with ourselves and thereby redirect political struggle back into ourselves. In a brutal, competitive, and atomised society, psychic wellbeing is so difficult that success on this front can feel like a significant accomplishment. Trying to do it themselves, people are immiserated and proletarianised and confront this immiseration and proletarianisation alone.[48]

Under such circumstances, where people are "proletarianised alone," it is unsurprising that the political forms that have come to dominate the twenty-first century also situate the individual at the heart of systemic problems. The politics of futility is a symptom of futilitarianism; individuals attempt to make themselves as useful politically as possible – often with genuinely good and ethical intentions – but in doing so, they end up reinforcing the logic of neoliberalism, which worsens the collective conditions for the majority of people. No matter what Obama and the like tell us, we deserve better than this.

6
Futilitarianism in the Age of Covid-19

On 22 March 2020, in the early stages of the Covid-19 pandemic, Donald Trump tweeted (originally in block capitals): "We cannot let the cure be worse than the problem itself. At the end of the 15 day period, we will make a decision as to which way we want to go!"[1] Trump appears to have come to this conclusion after watching *The Next Revolution with Steve Hilton* on Fox News. On his show earlier that day, Hilton – the former director of strategy and close friend to British Prime Minister David Cameron, before straining his relationship with the former prime minister by enthusiastically supporting Brexit – said: "You know that famous phrase, 'the cure is worse than the disease?' That is exactly the territory we are hurtling towards."[2] Hilton then went on to quote an article from *The Guardian* that referred to a study that had calculated austerity measures were to blame for at least 130,000 deaths in the last decade.[3] Bearing in mind that Hilton had worked for the government that was largely responsible for these measures, it was a bizarre source to turn to. But perhaps that contradiction was lost on many US-based viewers. This is also not to mention that modelling, at this point, had predicted that the potential deaths from Covid-19 were exponentially higher than the figures attributed to austerity. Hilton finished: "The years of austerity for America to pay the costs of this shutdown will be worse."[4] Here, Hilton flaunted his lucrative lack of imagination.

Of course there will be austerity in the wake of the pandemic, he implied. What else could there be?

In the post-pandemic world, the economy will be in ruins, a liquidity crisis is brewing, and unemployment will be at record highs across the Global North.[5] The 2008 financial crisis will look like a minor blip in comparison. Neoliberalism will be dead (again). And Hilton does not even stop for a moment to think that there might be any other post-pandemic policy measures than austerity. This is certainly understandable, given the response to the 2008 global financial crisis. Post-2008, as governments and central banks attempted to save the financial system through a mixture of quantitative easing and bailouts, a political rhetoric emerged that convinced vast swaths of the general populace that social spending and benefit cheats were really to blame for the crisis. In doing so, governments could market austerity as the only fair response.

William Davies notes that austerity regimes represent a shift in the logic of neoliberalism, which prior to the 2008 crash had simply "elevat[ed] economic judgements of 'efficiency' and 'competitiveness' above moral judgements of social justice." But the post-2008 austerity measures exemplify a "shift to unreason by the governing powers ... [with] more vindictive policymaking, which often operate outside of the norms of policy evaluation, evidence gathering or public appeal." Austerity is a prime example of this shift, Davies observes, because "history offers scant examples of pro-cyclical fiscal-contraction programmes that have succeeded in avoiding macroeconomic stagnation ... Yet no amount of empirical evidence of austerity's failings seems adequate to derail those who pronounce its necessity."[6] Sound economics, therefore, is not the point of austerity. Instead, it is an authoritarian flexing of muscles on behalf of neoliberalism, which was most evident in the EU's brutal bullying and brinkmanship in response to

Greece's democratically elected anti-austerity government in 2015. This is precisely why Pierre Dardot and Christian Laval argue that the post-2008 neoliberalism "openly adopted the paradigm of war *against the population*."[7] A new war, more illogical and punitive, is what Hilton and many others imagine will emerge in the aftermath of the pandemic.

But who are these governments going to blame this time? Some have turned on China, and the World Health Organisation, but such entities are hardly valid reasons for imposing austerity on national citizens. Moreover, the pandemic has revealed the total decay of health and social institutions under a decade of austerity, so blaming social spending will be much more difficult this time (not that this will stop many governments trying). Even the right-wing think tanks that aggressively pushed the austerity agenda in the last decade in the UK, such as the Adam Smith Institute, the Institute of Economic Affairs and Policy Exchange, and the Centre for Policy Studies, have conceded that the age of austerity is over.[8] There are very few plotlines that could come together to rebuild the austerity narrative. This time, governments would have to force austerity on their citizens without any accompanying narrative other than *we know of nothing else.*

Neoliberalism is supplemented in Hilton's logic by the more subtle yet equally persuasive rationality of utilitarianism. Throughout this book, I have argued that the principle of utility flipped into futility as a result of the confluence of neoliberal economics with new political, social, and economic forms of individualism in the late twentieth century. It would be wrong, however, to conclude that utilitarianism therefore disappeared in the neoliberal decades. In fact, as Jonathan Wolff notes, "while philosophers have turned away from maximising consequentialism, public policy decision making has embraced it."[9] Jeremy Bentham would have been very pleased with his lasting impact on public policymaking. After all, his aim was social and legal reform, not philosophical legitimacy. In his book *The Happiness Industry*, Davies charts the influence of utilitarianism on twenty-first-century obsessions with happiness and wellbeing, especially in public policy. Davies argues that utilitarianism was Bentham's attempt to eliminate the metaphysical from political and legal policy in the late eighteenth century. In this respect, Bentham was "the inventor of what has since become known as 'evidence-based policymaking,' the idea that government interventions can be cleansed of any moral and ideological principles, and be guided purely by facts and figures."[10] Since the turn of the century, policymakers have thoroughly embraced "evidence-based policymaking," backed up by a new breed of psychologists and social scientists, who are armed with contemporary behavioural science and psychology, neuroscience, and data analytics, and claim to have irrefutable empirical evidence of pleasure and pain in neural pathways and affective responses.

In the neoliberal decades, utilitarian logic has become predominantly economic in character, in the sense that almost all policymaking responds to one simple question: what is the least amount of funding (cost) required to keep a service or system functioning (benefit)? These calculations usually take the form of the cost-benefit analysis, which draws on data and modelling to ascertain whether a policy is worth the financial cost. Wolff observes that cost-benefit analysis is currently used across a vast range of policy areas: "From the building of a new airport to the permissibility of performing a particular animal experiment." The advantage of cost-benefit analysis, we are told by its devotees, is that it removes prejudice or subjective reasoning from decision-making, much like Bentham thought utilitarianism could do to moral philosophy. But Wolff implies that the real attraction to cost-benefit analysis is that it financialises all activities, even subjecting each human life to financial valuation. The problem, he identifies, is that cost-benefit analysis "in its purest form is a particularly crude form of consequentialism: consequentialism of money."[11] It is easy to see why philosophers might disregard cost-benefit analysis as a flawed morality – since it prioritises money over any ethical reasoning – but policymakers view it as a magical formula for determining the distribution of public funds. A consequentialism of money is exactly what any treasury desires as it attempts to map the future.

For his reading of the pandemic, Hilton undertakes a simple cost-benefit analysis. He acknowledges that there might be a way of limiting the amount of infections and deaths as a result of Covid-19, but these all involve shutting down the vast majority of economic life. The benefit would be a much smaller loss of human life, but the economic cost would be catastrophic. But if we do not shut down the economy, he suggests, then the loss of human life might be catastrophic, but the economy might survive. In hushed and solemn tones, Hilton dresses up this cutthroat utilitarian logic as a deep concern for the welfare of the everyday citizen. He states: "Our ruling class and their TV mouthpieces whipping up fear over this virus, they can afford an indefinite shutdown. Working Americans can't."[12] Never mind that many workers are fearful of returning to work in the midst of a pandemic, or that it is actually the contemporary ruling classes – large corporations and business owners – who have been pushing to restart the economy. None of these facts really concern Hilton, or Fox News for that matter. The ultimate point of Hilton's diatribe is to remind viewers that the economy and the financial system are much more important than the lives of everyday citizens, even if he disguises this belief as a concern for those same citizens. For those who have benefitted from this utilitarian stance throughout the neoliberal decades, any kind of state intervention and social policies enacted to combat the pandemic are illogical. The financial valuation of human life is far too high, they conclude.

Counting the Costs

This cost-benefit imbalance has plagued many initial governmental responses to the virus. In the UK, Boris Johnson spoke in early March 2020 of "taking it on the chin" and letting the disease "move through the population, without taking as many draconian measures." He spoke of "bizarre autarkic rhetoric" coming from the rest of the world, which might "trigger a panic and desire for market segregation."[13] His advisors spoke of "herd immunity" and "flattening the curve," of mitigating rather than suppressing the virus. Herd immunity is utilitarianism 101, approaching the Covid-19 virus from a purely consequentialist perspective. The herd immunity strategy allows the virus to spread with the hope that when it has infected approximately 80% of the population, the antibodies developed to fight the virus by the infected part of the population protect the 20% who are uninfected. The illness will therefore kill a certain proportion of those infected in the initial stages but, in the long run, the virus will be held in check. According to the herd immunity logic, the long-term benefits outweigh the short-term costs, and a certain number of deaths is deemed acceptable.

Johnson's amaurotic former chief advisor, Dominic Cummings, reportedly pushed the herd immunity strategy forcefully in the initial stages of the pandemic, with his approach summarised by Tory ministers, according to one newspaper report, as: "Herd immunity, protect the economy, and if some pensioners die, too bad."[14] By mid-March, however, Johnson, Cummings, and other members of the Cabinet were infected with the virus, and Cummings performed an abrupt U-turn on the herd immunity theory after modelling predicted that the mitigation approach could lead to at least 250,000 deaths in the UK. An initial utilitarian approach had proved disastrous, and any kind of benefit had been eliminated from the cost-benefit ratio. There have been unprecedented deaths in the UK as a result of this initial approach, and the economy will still be in ruins in the long run. This is a cost-cost scenario.

The pervasiveness of utilitarian logic was not confined to the UK and United States in the early stages of the pandemic. In Aotearoa New Zealand, Prime Minister Jacinda Ardern has been rightly credited with a proactive and urgent response. But her decision to put Aotearoa New Zealand into lockdown at a very early stage did not go down too well in parts of the business community. A prominent businessman and former leader of the Opportunities Party, Gareth Morgan, chastised Dr Souxsie Wiles, a public-health academic, who argued that the lockdown needed to stay in place after many were calling for its abandonment after only two weeks. Morgan berated Wiles on Twitter (with barely disguised misogyny): "Do you have any appreciation of how important the economy is? ... The official value of a life in NZ is $10k (ask Pharmac) ... cost so far = $5bn! Wake up!"[15] PHARMAC is the governmental agency that funds medicine and medical equipment in Aotearoa New Zealand. According to Morgan, this agency has managed to render redundant millennia of philosophical reflection on the value and meaning of life. Turns out, life is worth NZD10,000. If only Plato had known this, it might have saved us all a lot of hassle.

Morgan's calculation of the value of life raises many questions, however. For one, his economic valuation is not only ethically indefensible but also empirically problematic. Morgan had a friend who was denied medical treatment that cost NZD10,000. The friend subsequently died. Morgan uses this example as evidence for the universal cost of a life, which he then puts into his version of the utilitarian calculator. As of 28 November 2020, Aotearoa New Zealand has 25 deaths from Covid-19, equalling NZD250,000, according to Morgan's equation. If the economic cost was NZD5 billion in mid-April when Morgan tweeted Wiles, then we can assume it is much higher now, even though large parts of the Aotearoa New Zealand economy have opened up again (although, the lack of tourism provides a gaping hole). Such a disparity between economic cost and social benefit is unthinkable under utilitarian policy-making. The cost-benefit ratio is far too unbalanced.

Perhaps the most overt public display of utilitarian logic amid the pandemic came from the vice chancellor of the University of Melbourne, Duncan Maskell. In an interview for a Victorian newspaper, Maskell postulated: "the question everyone is skirting around here is what is the appetite in any country for disease and mortality associated with this virus." Ultimately, Maskell concluded, "it all comes down to a basic but very hard moral philosophy" – a succinct definition of utilitarianism if ever I saw one. Maskell argued that one might very well conclude that there is no appetite for death in any country, but one must come to that conclusion understanding the consequences. "If that decision stops people dying now from the virus," he questioned, "what are the economic consequences of that for people and how will that play out in terms of future mortality? It would be crazy if, hypothetically, we stop 100 people [dying] from the virus but over the next two years, 200 people died from [the effects of] poverty and mental health." We see here a familiar thread running from Trump, Hilton, Johnson, Cummings, Morgan, through to Maskell. Although they all put it in different terms, whether a faux worry for the American working class or a pseudo-medical calculation of human life, their main concern is with the idea of equality and equivalence in a neoliberal society. Some lives are more valuable than others, they imply, and the economy is the sphere where such valuation is concretised. Maskell is the only one who literally asks the question they are all thinking (although, Cummings was reported saying something similar): "What is the value of a 90-year-old's life versus the value of continuing livelihood and happiness of a 25-year-old?" Of course, "value" here is a very limited definition, with the implication that a happy and healthy 25-year-old can contribute to economic growth and productivity in a way that an elderly person cannot. The baldness of Maskell's "basic but very hard moral philosophy" is apparent when he grimly states: "What people need to keep front and centre is the only certainty in life is death. The only event in our life with a probability of one is you are going to die."[16] This is probably a reminder that most readers do not need in the middle of a pandemic.

But while some media commentators, politicians, and academic administrators call for utilitarianism to guide the response to Covid-19, the pandemic seriously undermines the utilitarian calculators and exposes the disastrous effects of decades of utilitarian policymaking. Cost-benefit analysis is all well and good in the abstract, especially if the human costs emerge over a long period of time. Austerity, for example, has undoubtedly contributed to many deaths in the UK and beyond, as even Hilton acknowledges, but its effect is indirect. Austerity does not infect the body, clog the lungs, or stop the heart. It puts people in positions where they are more likely to experience such things, but it does not appear on any records as the cause of death. The effects of austerity can therefore be hidden by governments, even translated into a lack of sufficient personal care, work ethic, or responsibility on behalf of the deceased. But when thousands of citizens die daily from the same virus, cost-benefit analysis can no longer hide behind the surface of everyday life. Suddenly, policymakers must directly calculate deaths versus the economy. And no matter how ruthless and utilitarian a government might be, this is a very difficult sell to the general populace. There is no cost-benefit model that has the capacity to protect human life and the economy at the same time. Hence, we find arguments like those discussed above, where some propose that the economy should be prioritised over human life. When Maskell wonders whether stopping 100 people dying now might lead to 200 deaths from poverty, he does not for any second consider that perhaps poverty need not be an inevitability, much in the same way that Hilton views austerity as an unavoidable consequence of the pandemic.

Over the last four decades, healthcare, welfare, education, social care, and the like have all been subjected to utilitarian scything. Hospitals, in many countries, have been cut back to bare levels of staffing and equipment, with short-term profits and high patient turnover prioritised over patient welfare and staff resources. Care work has been increasingly casualised, with many workers employed on zero-hour contracts that cut costs on wages but endanger the people whom these workers care for. Universities likewise maximise financial benefits by cutting costs on permanent academic staff, relying instead on a vast army of precarious and casual lecturers and tutors. But when the world stops turning, as it has in the early stage of this decade, and when we really need healthcare, welfare, education, and social care, none of these institutions or services are capable of effectively providing the aid that they are supposed to because they have all been focusing on doing something else: namely, maximising benefits (financial profits) and minimising costs. It is in the degradation of these services and institutions, starkly exposed by the Covid-19 pandemic, that we see the social consequences of futilitarianism. The practice of utility maximisation since the turn of the century, primarily through the widespread adoption of cost-benefit analysis by governments, has led not to the safeguarding of the vast majority of the population but to the endangerment of this majority because the services and institutions that are supposed to protect the wellbeing of the majority have been serving the interests of the monied minority.

The CARES Act and Corporate Socialism

In *Nine Lives of Neoliberalism*, published in early 2020, Quinn Slobodian and Dieter Plehwe ponder: "Only time will tell when neoliberalism will use up its next – or even final – life."[17] Neither could have imagined how quickly and spectacularly that time would come about in the early 2020s. In many ways, the pandemic, like so many crises before, seems to spell the end of neoliberalism, especially as the global economy retracts and governments around the world intervene in national economies. But while many of the pandemic aid measures might look like they are prioritising citizens over the economy, there have been several developments that suggest the neoliberal status quo is being shored up. To explore these developments, I turn to two examples of governmental responses to the pandemic – the Coronavirus Aid, Relief, and Economic Security (CARES) Act in the US and the Australian higher-education reforms rolled out in the Job-Ready Graduates Package. Both of these governmental responses, I propose, offer a glimpse into the post-pandemic world, where the tactics and rationalities of futilitarianism I have outlined in this book will be extended and cemented.

The immediate context of the CARES Act is essential to understanding its long-term consequences.[18] On

March 23, 2020, the US Federal Reserve announced that it was introducing new measures, many of which mirrored the 2008 financial crisis response, to combat the economic consequences of the pandemic. As the press release stated, "our nation's first priority is to care for those afflicted and to limit the further spread of the virus."[19] The CARES Act was signed into law by Donald Trump on 27 March, with the aim "to provide emergency assistance and health care response for individuals, families, and businesses affected by the 2020 coronavirus pandemic."[20] The CARES Act appeared to supplement the actions of the Federal Reserve to provide urgent and much needed welfare and economic security to millions of American citizens. On the surface, these were both interventions in the economy that protected the wellbeing of the majority of citizens over the financial system.

Unusually, and suspiciously, the CARES Act had almost unanimous bipartisan support. In fact, Robert Brenner outlines in his analysis of the legislation that the Democrats ceded the initiative of the drafting of the CARES Act to the Republicans, with the Democratic-led House of Representatives, where such Acts are supposed to originate, allowing the legislation to go to the Republican-led Senate in the first instance. Brenner argues that the Democrats ensured the ratification of the Act "as it was a top priority for their most important allies, 'the donors' – viz. their corporate backers – and was supported by the great majority of the Party's elected figures in Congress."[21] But this raises the question: why would an emergency piece of legislation that aims "to provide emergency assistance and health care response for individuals, families, and businesses" be supported by large corporations? The short answer is that the CARES Act is a relief package in the way that Amazon's Alexa is a close friend. It seems to be going out of its way to help you, but it really is just using you to further line the pockets of the capitalist elite.

Brenner argues that the Act was "the required first step to enable the Federal Reserve to take over the bailout's actual administration." When granted authority by the treasury, the Federal Reserve can buy debt from large and small businesses, which it announced its intention to do on 23 March. In emergency circumstances, the Federal Reserve can leverage funds from the Treasury, which it did in this case, turning USD454 billion into approximately USD4 trillion. And with the Federal Reserve taking the lead on how to distribute the funding, the CARES Act takes on a very different outlook from a relief package. Brenner observes that

> $4.586 trillion, roughly 75 per cent of the total $6.286 trillion derived directly or indirectly from CARES Act money, would go for the "care" of the country's biggest and best-off companies. By contrast, as unemployment soared, just $603 billion in total was allocated for direct cash payments to individuals and families ($300 billion), extra unemployment insurance ($260 billion), and student loans ($43 billion).[22]

Crucially, the loans issued by the Federal Reserve placed no stipulations on how the funding should be spent, allowing "top managers and stockholders ... to line their own pockets via share buybacks, dividends and executive salary increases while reducing employment and investment."[23] And thus an emergency relief package that was supposed to help the most vulnerable citizens in the midst of a pandemic became a "billionaire coronavirus bonanza."[24]

When the CARES Act was announced, the newspapers and periodicals that reflexively defend capitalism trotted the old party line. A headline in *The Wall Street Journal* pleaded with readers to "save capitalism from the CARES Act," with the columnists suggesting that it is "the largest step towards a centrally planned economy the US has ever taken."[25] A contributor to *Forbes* magazine called the CARES Act "coronavirus socialism," and claimed "Mao Zedang would be pleased."[26] In many ways, the CARES Act is a kind of socialism, but it is one that ensures only the distribution of wealth at that top end of the economic pyramid. Writing in *The Independent*, the former Wall Street trader Sameer Butt describes the CARES Act as a "reverse Robin Hood legislation," where big corporations steal emergency funding from those who desperately need it. Butt notes, "Americans have a preternatural aversion to socialism. Except we have the most liberal socialism imaginable. It's just not for the average citizen. It is for multi-billion-dollar, faceless corporations."[27] This kind of corporate socialism is evidenced by a report released in early November 2020 by the progressive think tank the Institute for Policy Studies, showing that since mid-March, US billionaires increased their wealth by almost USD1 trillion.[28] Every day there seems to be a headline alerting us to the rapid increase in wealth of Amazon CEO Jeff Bezos, who has now become the first ever person to be worth USD200 billion.[29] This exponential growth in wealth for the very richest has even led to the laughable claim that billionaires are now worried that their wealth might lead to political anger. Josef Stadler, a senior official from the Swiss bank UBS, tells us that the billionaires he looks after are fearful they "may be singled out by society" because of their wealth concentration.[30] If only there was a way that some of this wealth could be redistributed – say, by progressive taxation or pay rises for their employees – so that we could relieve these billionaires of their anxiety.

The Threat of the Humanities

If the CARES Act is a sign of the economic future, then another development points towards the cultural landscape of the post-pandemic world. On 19 June 2020, Australian Minister for Education Dan Tehan announced the "Job-Ready Graduates Package," which instigated a series of reforms to the higher-education sector in Australia. The aim of these reforms, we are told by the Ministry, is to "deliver more job-ready graduates in the disciplines and regions where they are needed most and help drive the nation's economic recovery from the Covid-19 pandemic."[31] Under these reforms, the cost of a humanities degree (except for language courses) increases by 113% – from AUD20,400 to AUD43,500 for a three-year degree – while students in agriculture and mathematics will see a 62% reduction, and those enrolled in STEM subjects and IT will receive a 20% fee decrease.[32] In a speech outlining the package, Tehan followed the standard neoliberal mantra on universities, by tying education to employment. The role of universities, he argued, "is to teach Australians the skills needed to succeed in the jobs of the future." He rolled out another line from the neoliberal handbook: "Our package offers universities a strong partnership with government and business to ensure they play a key role in Australia's recovery from Covid-19." He even provided some sage advice for humanities students by reminding them that the fees are based on each individual course: "So if you want to study history, also think about studying teaching. If you want to study philosophy, also think about studying a language. If you want to study law, also think about studying IT." In other words, if you are dead-set on studying something useless, then do yourself a favour and at least combine it with something useful (at contributing to GDP). And to really ram home the logic of these reforms, as if we were in any doubt, Tehan stated: "A cheaper degree in an area where there's a job is a win-win for students."[33]

For humanities students, lecturers, and researchers within a university system, none of this rhetoric will come as a huge surprise, although perhaps the bluntness of the package is jarring. The idea that university is a pathway to employment has been drilled into generations since the millennials. The introduction of tuition fees, forcing students into cycles of debt, was the price they had to pay for this opportunity. But as the labour sphere becomes increasingly unpredictable and precarious, and wages continue to flatline, the magical passport into full employment granted by a university degree rarely materialises in the way imagined by figures like Tehan. Daniel Bresner, reflecting on the impact of the pandemic on higher education in the US, writes that "exploding tuition costs obliged students to take out enormous loans that compelled them to view higher education primarily as a precursor to employment – employment that, as the economy worsened, was rarely guaranteed. This house of cards, built on exploitation, anti-intellectualism, and massive debt, was doomed to collapse."[34] With its collapse will come its rebuild. And if the Australian measures are anything to go by, the policies of the previous four decades will only be resurrected and extended.

Boris Johnson has already hinted that the UK will follow a similar programme, as he warmly commended the Australian reforms by criticising the UK measures under David Cameron's government:

If you remember, what basically went wrong with the higher education degree courses [in the UK] was everybody charged the maximum whack, because no further education institution felt that they could accept the loss of prestige associated with offering a course that was cheaper. In reality, it would have been much more sensible if courses had been differently priced. We are certainly looking at all that.[35]

Donald Trump's administration has also repeatedly attempted to eradicate the National Endowment for the Arts in the US, deeming the arts a pointless endeavour.[36] Beneath the blustering rhetoric of these politicians, it is easy to see that the assault on the humanities is not for economic reasons – although that might be a byproduct – but overwhelmingly political. The humanities are not useless, as many governments might imply; they are *dangerous*. And if we are going to properly defend the humanities, it is extremely important to grasp this fact.

The assault on the humanities has heightened since the 2008 financial crisis. The standard governmental narrative is that the humanities do not provide a coherent vocational pathway and, as a result, governments cannot calculate exactly how a humanities graduate would contribute to economic growth. This narrative also engenders two broad counterarguments: one that pleads the humanities' usefulness and one that defends its uselessness. Some argue that the humanities develop soft or transferable skills which a graduate can apply across a range of different jobs, especially in the industries filled with STEM graduates, while others suggest that art, history, literature, and the like should be studied for their own sake as cultural phenomena. Both these counterarguments are doomed to failure. The former turns the humanities into what Rosi Braidotti provocatively terms "a glorified finishing school" that readies graduates for technical jobs in the private sector.[37] The latter counterargument empties the humanities of their political and subversive potential, relegating them to a hobby or purely cultural practice, which has little impact on economic life.

There are of course many defences of the humanities in-between these broad counterarguments, but instead of taking a defensive position on the humanities, it is better, I contend, to reframe such education reforms as the "Job-Ready Graduates Package" not as a threat *to* the humanities, but a threat *of* the humanities. Neoliberal governments do not attack the humanities because they see no value in humanistic education. Rather, they see the cultivation of value systems that are persuasive and alternative to the one that underpins their power, and thus this alternative must be shut down, especially in times of crisis when the dominant worldview is up for debate. Hiking humanities fees can ensure that arts and culture are redirected to the realms of the elite, who can admire the beauty of art and experience the joy of intellectualism without feeling threatened by their subversive and revolutionary potential. Meanwhile, the rest of us can stick to functional and vocational endeavours, without being exposed to the critical and creative techniques that might question the economic and social relations that underpin these endeavours. If we attempt to adapt humanities education to the needs of these vocational practices or simply defend the uselessness of such education, we enter the fight on the terms given to us by those who attack the humanities. Rather than making the humanities more relevant or cementing their irrelevance, their threat to the status quo needs to be politicised and radicalised within and against the university.

The threat of the humanities is evident in the culture wars of the present, especially as nationalist tendencies emerge worldwide. Davies argues that, in the context of the UK, "the new conservative ideology coalesces around one theme in particular: hostility towards the modern humanities, and their elevated status in British public life." He observes that the humanities were at the centre of public life in the UK in the twentieth century, especially with the postwar investment in the arts and humanities. But in the neoliberal decades, the humanities graduate has come to embody an elitist and metropolitan liberal, one that "sit[s] in the crosshairs of both Thatcherite neoliberals and nationalists." For neoliberals, "a humanities degree is a simple waste of money," and "a high-risk investment, which [the student] should be personally liable for." For nationalists, fuelled by fears of historical revisionism, "humanities are an enemy within, a segment of the liberal elite that lacks national loyalty."[38]

This nationalist concern towards the humanities has come to the surface in the wake of the Black Lives Matter movement and its radical confrontation of colonial histories and racial capitalism.[39] The crucial thing on the side of the humanities is that while governments can attack education institutions, the principles and techniques of the humanities are not restricted to the walls of the academy. No one can split an atom in their bedroom, but they can read a book on the history of British imperialism. The Black Lives Matter movement, alongside other global rights movements, is a kind of activist humanities, performing a grassroots immanent critique grounded in the principles of humanistic education. It is no surprise that, for many, these protestors have also become the "enemy within" precisely because they can put history and critique into practice. The now infamous photo of a woman standing beside a statue of the Scouts founder, Robert Baden-Powell, holding a sign that reads "British history matters" exemplifies nationalist fears towards the humanities. None of the Black Lives Matter protesters would disagree that history matters – in fact, this is precisely their point – but the kind of history they practice is one that a new conservative nationalism is deeply afraid of. As a result, we get a strange phenomenon where the concept of history – or, more precisely, a nationalist version of history – is defended against the actual practice of history. Humanistic education is paradoxically constructed by the new nationalism as antithetical to the understanding of history.

A Futilitarian Future?

While it seems logical to conclude that the vast shutdown of many aspects of the global economy puts neoliberalism's life on the brink again, there are many reasons to also suggest that neoliberalism is mutating into a new form, one that will find new and innovative ways to concentrate wealth in the hands of a few and impose brutal austerity on the lives of the many. The CARES Act and Australian education reforms point towards this aggressive mutation of neoliberalism in the post-pandemic world, but they are by no means the only examples. Telehealth, for instance, has been a neoliberal pet project for years, with significant political support, especially in the US.[40] The marketing line is that telehealth can expand access to healthcare, especially in rural areas. The reality is that telehealth further privatises healthcare, enabling tech-health companies to find new ways to make money out of patients, while also reducing physical infrastructure costs. It also provides a pretext for governments to cut funding to rural hospitals and clinics. Telehealth has exploded during the pandemic, for obvious reasons, with Donald Trump signing an executive order to extend telehealth and even suggesting that its exponential rise is "one of the only good things we've gotten out of this horrible situation."[41] The rise of online education follows a similar trajectory to telehealth, with schools and universities seeing the possibility of developing vast digital campuses, creating the chance to sell off lucrative physical assets like buildings and land.

In many ways, the pandemic confirms and exemplifies the central claims of this book, especially when you see the chaotic and incompetent response to the pandemic by many governments around the world. The pandemic has exposed the vacuity of the rhetoric of personal responsibility and self-help, as hospitals and public institutions are ill-prepared exactly at the very time they are desperately needed. The rise of conspiracy theories and anti-lockdown protests is surely a sign of semio-futility, as leaders across the world are unable (or don't even try) to use words like "crisis," "pandemic," "emergency" to convey the seriousness of this global event. *Homo futilitus* is everywhere, and no amount of self-branding will be able to counter the current and most likely prolonged unemployment crisis. And with more people looking for jobs, the potential for employers to find new ways to precaritise work will only increase. The environmental plundering required to renew economic growth could well be the final nail in the coffin of the planet in terms of human life. Few can surely deny now the futility of the world-system that we live in. The worry is that neoliberalism has trapped us in this futility to the point where we have been rendered useless in doing anything about it.

The pandemic, however, undoubtedly reveals some chinks in the armour of neoliberalism. For one, it has initiated a crisis of utilitarianism. This is not merely a philosophical or abstract crisis. As I noted in Chapter 1, utilitarianism has been at the heart of governmental power and capitalist expansion since the early nineteenth century. Bentham's aim was to reform social and legal policy and to rid philosophy of the metaphysical and replace it with rational and predictable calculations of human emotion, precisely the kind of calculations undertaken by governments in the early twenty-first century. The philosophical limitations of such a project have been outweighed by its potential to justify the exertion of capitalist power over citizens under the ethical dictate that the consequences of such exertions of power are deemed to be for the benefit of the majority of people in the long run. But as new generations find themselves worse-off than their predecessors, not even the most ardent capitalists could argue that neoliberalism succeeds at securing a future in which the wellbeing of the vast majority is protected. Not only that, but the exploitation required to achieve utility maximisation in the neoliberal decades has taken on a new geographical formation, with the Global South maximising utility for the Global North. Instead of leading to a prosperous future for the vast majority, utility maximisation under capitalist conditions only disperses class relations, on a global scale, trapping much of humanity in inter-generational forms of poverty, exploitation, and immiseration while ensuring the consolidation of wealth in the hands of an ever-decreasing few. This potential has always been latent in the intermingling of capitalism and utilitarianism; neoliberalism has unleashed it.

All of this is to say that a crisis of utilitarianism is simultaneously a crisis of capitalism and power. This is precisely why certain politicians, advisors, and media mouthpieces, like Steve Hilton or Gareth Morgan, are ranting against the preventative approach to the pandemic. They know that neoliberal hegemony depends on utilitarian policymaking, because when governments stop thinking purely in terms of the calculation of financial costs and benefits, as most have been forced to do during the pandemic, then suddenly the logic of neoliberalism makes very little sense. And if a crisis of utilitarianism is simultaneously a crisis of capitalism and power, then it also presents an opportunity to confront capitalist power. Understanding and uniting around the experience of futility can be the first step in building the necessary collective movements that can go about abolishing capitalist power.

Conclusion: The Becoming-Common of the Futilitariat

> The course our future takes will depend on whether we prove able, beyond the world of production, to *make use of the useless*.
>
> Byung-Chul Han

Futility captures so much of what *feels* wrong about the world we currently inhabit. By giving this feeling a name, this book has attempted to show that our various experiences of futility are not reflections of our individual characters, as the peddlers of personal responsibility rhetoric tell us, but are created by the operating principles of neoliberal capitalism and the monstrous logic of neoliberal rationality. While my futility might differ to yours, its origin is the same, which gives us a common enemy. Precarity is another name often given to these experiences, and while this term has been extremely productive theoretically and practically in organising a myriad of individual experiences, I contend that futility can push us further. To do so, I want to briefly imagine here how futility could become the basis of a new theory of the common.

In her book *States of Insecurity*, Isabell Lorey makes an important distinction between precariousness and precarity, building on the work of Judith Butler. "Precariousness," she observes, "designates something that is existentially shared, an endangerment of bodies that is ineluctable and hence not to be secured, not only because they are mortal, but specifically because they are social." Precariousness is a relational phenomenon that emerges from our primary ontological entanglement with others (human and non-human). Precarity, on the other hand, "is to be understood as a category of order, which designates the effects of different political, social and legal compensations of a general precariousness. Precarity denotes the striation and distribution of precariousness in relations of inequality, the hierarchisation of being-with that accompanies the process of *othering*."[1] In other words, precarity is precariousness striated by regimes of class, gender, race, sexuality, age, and so on, and it can be located in political and legal structures that protect the precariousness of some and augment the precariousness of others. In this sense, we all share the experience of precariousness because life is inherently precarious, but precarity classifies a particular status of being-in-the-world in which some are more precarious than others.

The primordial nature of precariousness has the potential to bind us together or to pit ourselves against one another. Lorey writes: "precariousness that is shared by all can also be understood as a separating factor: on the one hand, it is what we all have in common, but on the other it is what distinguishes and separates us from others." Precarity is a means of ordering and giving name to the separating factor of that which we all have in common. For Lorey this is the key aspect of the relationship between precariousness and precarity. "Shared precariousness as a relational difference does not exist beyond the social and the political," she writes; "[t]herefore it does not exist independently from a second dimension of the precarious, namely that of hierarchising precarity."[2] This process of hierarchisation undercuts the inherent relationality of precariousness. Instead, it creates a world in which the precarious are ranked against one another. And while precarity creates the potential for the development of political subjectivities that protect against precariousness, it is also guards against a truly collective form of politics that is based on the shared precariousness of us all and not simply the precarity of one being or group over another.

This relationship between precariousness and precarity has been transformed under neoliberalism. Lorey observes that older forms of state power demanded "obedience in exchange for protection." There is a clear relationship of utility in such power relations. By providing citizens with provisions and safety nets, the state gets an obedient populace it can use to create goods, generate economic growth, and even defend the state against foreign invasion. The state recognises that its citizens share precariousness and, in return for its citizens' obedience, the state guards against their precariousness through its apparatuses. But in the neoliberal decades, the relationship between the state and citizens is re-imagined not as a relation of mutual utility, but as a form of management or governance. The citizens might be useful – in fact their utility is exploited to its extreme – but their usefulness is not exchanged for protection, but for greater insecurity. Lorey writes:

In the course of the dismantling and remodelling of the welfare state and the rights associated with it, a form of government is established that is based on the greatest possible insecurity, promoted by proclaiming the alleged absence of alternatives. The way that precaritisation has become an instrument of government also means that its extent must not pass a certain threshold such that it seriously endangers the existing order: in particular, it must not lead to insurrection. Managing the threshold is what makes up the art of governance today.[3]

Neoliberal hegemony relies, therefore, on extending precarity as far and as wide as possible across social life, but in a way that it can protect itself against the shared experience of precariousness. To do so, it creates a governing rationality – outlined throughout this book – that atomises populations, lionises competition, and glorifies individuality. Rather than turning to others to guard against precarity – that is, by recognising in others a shared precariousness – the neoliberal subject is forced inwards to find coping mechanisms against extreme forms of insecurity. Even in "managing the threshold" between precarity and insurrection, neoliberalism outsources this labour to us.

The concept of precarity has undoubtedly helped define the experiences of a growing proportion of global citizens, and in doing so it has enabled disparate groups of precarious workers and individuals to collectivise against the operating principles of neoliberal capitalism, from the feminist collective *Precarias a la deriva* to the various unions supporting precarious workers in the gig economy.[4] Moreover, the term "precariat" has categorised a new social class that seems to capture the metamorphosis of the human being into pure human capital in the neoliberal age.[5] This new social class is the productive force of the neoliberal project, brought into existence by the proliferation of insecure and exploitative labour conditions, especially zero-hour contracts, sometimes with the addition of unstable immigration or citizenship status, social isolation, various mental health issues, and ecological degradation. The precariat can only sell a small proportion of their labour power to an employer because their jobs are cut up into micro-utilities that arbitrarily distinguish between productive and non-productive time. This social class extends beyond traditional class divisions, encompassing jobs such as fast-food workers, taxi drivers, and adjunct university lecturers.

Despite occasional threats to its hegemony, neoliberalism has just about managed the threshold between precarity and insurrection thus far. One reason for this is precisely its ability to separate experiences of precarity from the shared experiences of precariousness, so that campaigns against precarity focus on specific domains of precariousness. Another reason, I contend, is quite simple; the term "precarity" is too narrow to describe the myriad of experiences of neoliberal life. Precarity cannot, for instance, characterise the experience of someone in a full-time bullshit job, who to all intents and purposes is socially and financially secure, yet still feels an emptiness in what they do. Precarity cannot account for the useless behaviours that many citizens repeat on a daily basis, from buycotting to voting with their dollar. Precarity is not a strong enough word to describe the ways in which people are unable to make their voices heard in the vast ocean of digital communication. Precarity might capture the disastrous effects of climate change but it does not explain our individualised attempts to avert these effects. And in the midst of a pandemic, precarity does cover the entirety of the fundamental restructuring of all social life. These are experiences of *futility*, and they take us closer to the shared precariousness of all life because they are experiences that permeate more lives than precarity. But this can only happen if futility is conceived in a way that prioritises the shared precariousness of all life instead of differentiating between categories and manifestations of futility.

Becoming-Common

It is worth repeating here that, like precarity, not all experiences of futility are equivalent and there are of course people who feel more useless than others. But this is precisely why futility matters, because individual experiences of futility expose us to a fundamental "social relationality," to borrow Lorey's term, that intersects all life forms.[6] Lorey contends that,

> In light of the existential precariousness of every (living) being, understanding social relationality as primary does not mean starting from something that is equally common to all. Recognising social relationality can only be the beginning of an entry into processes of *becoming-common*, involving discussions of possible common interests in the differentness of the precarious, in order to invent with others new forms of organising and new orders that break with the existing forms of governing in a refusal of obedience.[7]

As a reader, you may or may not feel like you are in a precarious situation, but there might be parts of this book that have struck a chord with your lived experience of the present. If you feel trapped in a job that pays well but feels pointless, then you have something in common with the migrant worker who flits between jobs and worries about their immigration status. If you suspect that your zero-waste and organic lifestyle is minuscule in the face of climate change, then you have something in common with the climate refugee. If you feel like all your consumer activism has not made one blind bit of difference, then you have something in common with the precarious workers protesting against their exploitative employers. These are not relationships of equivalence, but they do attest to a social relationality. If we make equivalence the basis of political collectivity, then not only does this restrict entry into forms of collectivity, but futility also becomes a means to demarcate difference, and existing forms of governing – that is, neoliberal forms of competition and individualisation – remain dominant. But if we prioritise the social relationality of futility, then we can start a process of *becoming-common*, as Lorey calls it, one in which futility acts as the experience that bonds rather than separates us.

My hope is that this book has laid some of the historical and theoretical foundations for this becoming-common, first by outlining the transformation of utilitarianism into futilitarianism, and second by illustrating how futilitarianism manifests itself in contemporary everyday life. For all its major faults, utilitarianism, at its basic premise, was at least aimed towards a conception of the common. However, as Bentham's work testifies, utilitarianism was committed to a capitalist worldview, which meant that it could never conceive of utility maximisation outside of a framework that attached concepts of utility to labour exploitation, consumerism, and the accumulation of wealth. In doing so, utilitarianism provided the philosophical legitimation for the common – or the happiness of the majority – to be inextricably linked with capitalist social and economic forms, under the idea that utility maximisation (or labour exploitation) and economic growth (even in the hands of a few) were unalloyed goods for the wellbeing and progress of humanity. The nefarious skill of the neoliberals was to conceive of a social and economic system that maintained utility maximisation and economic growth as socially accepted goals, but completely detached these goals from ideas of the common. And thus, futilitarianism was born, where the pursuit of utility maximisation actively deconstructed the common, and individuals competed against one another for a slice of the good. Futilitarianism is aggressively antithetical to the common; it provides no space for the becoming-common. Instead, it presents us with a non-future – the inescapable knowledge that if we continue as we are, we are all doomed – and tells us that we must continue doing what we are doing as we have no other choice. This is the existential entrapment of the futilitarian condition.

The common is our only shot at a liveable future. But the becoming-common cannot aim towards the common in the way that it has been by conceived by utilitarians, enlightenment philosophers, (neo)classical economists, or liberal theorists. The common cannot be reconstructed *a priori*. The common, instead, must develop from the material conditions of our times. Austerity, financialisation, refugee crises, pandemics, climate emergencies, militarism, rentierism, these are the conditions that we share in common, whether we like it or not. Part of the problem here, as Pierre Dardot and Christian Laval observe, is the very tying of the common to the idea of *good*, which has been the basis of Western moral philosophy. They insist that "one should avoid, at all costs, speaking of 'common goods' or even '*the* common good.' *The common is not a good* ... because the common is not an object of the will, whether as a possession or as that which is constituted by the will." As soon as the common becomes associated with conceptions of "good," then a process of judgement must necessarily take place on what constitutes good, both in a material and metaphysical sense. And such a process can never be separated from power, from the distinction between those who are called to judge and those who are judged. The legacy of utilitarianism shows us this fact, whether it is in the shape of imperialism or cost-benefit analysis. The good has always been tagged onto the common externally, from those who own the means of production, sit in the seats of parliaments, and, as is increasingly the case under neoliberalism, hold financial power. But what is truly good to the common develops organically from within the activities that continually create and constitute the common; it cannot be attached independently. "The common can only be rethought," Dardot and Laval argue, "by breaking with the metaphysical confrontation between the free subject and the inert material object offered up to this subject's grasp." Passive observation and detached judgement can never produce a good that is worthy of being associated with the common, no matter how much Kantians and neo-Kantians try to persuade us. Instead, "only *practical activity* can make the common, just as it is only practical activity that can produce a new collective subject."[8] The neoliberal mutation of capitalism has persuaded the vast majority of us that the good can only come about by aggressively denying the common, to pitch workers against each other, citizens against migrants, or old against young. A becoming-common cannot allow the good to be dictated by the market or data analysts. It must insist on an immanent good, a good that is only roughly aimed towards but is concretely produced through the activity and needs of the common.

The Futilitariat

How, then, can a concept like futility become the basis of a practical activity, especially in a political sense? The simple answer is as a language that articulates the shared experiences of the individuals that make up the common. By "language," I do not mean an official or spoken language, but an affective correspondence between lived bodies that generates a mutual recognition that does not require enunciation. I must stress here that I am not advocating a form of self-organising and autonomous common, one in which the common works together without any tangible unification.[9] As I noted in Chapter 5, with Jodi Dean as my interlocutor, it was precisely this autonomous form of social organisation that eventually undercut the Occupy movement. At some point, a unitary political subject must emerge, a "we" must be formed in a concrete sense, and the common must translate from an in-itself to a for-itself, to invoke the Marxist theory of class consciousness. If we take futility as the shared language of the common, then at some point *the futilitariat* must be born. Precarity is therefore a helpful precursor (and warning) to futility as the instigator of practical political activity. The precariat emerged from a shared language of precarity, but as Guy Standing pointed out (prior to Trump and Brexit), "[the precariat] are floating, rudderless and potentially angry, capable of veering to the extreme right or extreme left politically and backing populist demagoguery that plays on their fears or phobias."[10] The precariat is socially organised and politically disorganised. The futilitariat has the same potential contradiction at its core. This is why political organisation must be central to the becoming-common of the futilitariat.

The urgency of this becoming-common has been accelerated by the Covid-19 pandemic. The pandemic has underlined our shared relationality of precariousness in a way like no other event in living memory. This exposure to a shared precariousness is of course differentiated by precarity itself, so that certain social groups are more likely to experience the extreme precariousness of the deadly virus. But, nonetheless, the pandemic has revealed that we do share a world in common, that what happens in one part of the world affects another part of the world, that human beings are not islands but ontologically and biologically interdependent, an interdependence that neoliberalism has disavowed at every juncture. The pandemic has also shown that so many societies are completely ill-equipped to deal with such an event, not only because of decades of austerity, privatisation, rentierism, and financialisation, but also due to a governing rationality that forces individuals to see others as competitors and threats. Throughout its hegemony, neoliberalism has rapidly increased the potential for destruction of the common world while simultaneously reducing the kinds of social and political formations and practices that can prevent such destruction. Futility is the logical outcome of this dynamic, and it will only become more pervasive in the post-pandemic world, unless a new process of becoming-common emerges.

The practical activity of acting in common has been evident in the grassroots response to the pandemic (as, sadly, has its opposite), whether it be in rent strikes, mutual aid networks, or debt collectives. Likewise, the Black Lives Matter protests against police brutality across the US and beyond are a sign that authoritarian and punitive neoliberalism cannot hold the weight of collective expression. The spontaneous protests in Chile have succeeded in overturning the Pinochet-era constitution, which was not only associated with violence, but, thanks to the work of the Chicago Boys, steeped in neoliberal economic orthodoxy. There are numerous examples from around the world that prove there is a growing belief in the benefits of and need for acting in common. There is no greater threat to neoliberal hegemony.

Futility can be the shared language that transforms this practical activity from the becoming-common into the common. The futilitariat can be the name given to the political organisation of the common. And futilitarianism must be the logic that the common rejects. If this can happen, we can give capitalism back the non-future it had originally given to us.

Notes

Introduction

1 Karl Marx, *Capital: A Critique of Political Economy*, vol. 1, trans. Ben Fowkes (London: Penguin, 1976), 131.
2 Jeremy Bentham, "The Philosophy of Economic Science," in *Jeremy Bentham's Economic Writings*, vol. 1, ed. Werner Stark (London: Routledge, 2004), 117.
3 The French economist Gilles Saint-Paul theorises the term "post-utilitarianism" in his book *The Tyranny of Utility: Behavioural Social Science and the Rise of Paternalism* (Princeton, NJ: Princeton University Press, 2011). However, Saint-Paul uses the term to describe state intervention in the economy, which he claims is a result of the infiltration of economics by utilitarianism, especially in the form of contemporary social sciences and behavioural psychology. While he is right to be concerned with the confluence of behavioural economics and governmental policy, his prescription of a good dose of neo-Hayekian philosophy primarily argues for the extension of personal responsibility as a means to ensure a form of social equilibrium. Saint-Paul's post-utilitarianism does not see capitalism as a problem (and it is not entirely clear how his theory actually overcomes utilitarianism) but instead, the governmental and legislative programmes that get in the way of the freedom of capital. Futilitarianism is the antithesis of Saint-Paul's post-utilitarianism thesis.
4 In the early twenty-first century, before the 2008 financial crisis, Richard Sennett described what he called "the

spectre of uselessness" that haunted capitalist societies. He identified this spectre as an effect of three developments: global labour supply, automation, and the management of ageing. The global labour supply shifted jobs from high- to low-wage countries, which meant that low-skilled workers lost out in high-wage countries and high-skilled workers performed low-skilled jobs in low-wage countries; automation rendered useless skills that used to be done manually; and the management of ageing meant that while people could work longer, low retirement ages led to them becoming productively useless in later age. He also noted that the public sphere and welfare state had not adapted adequately to this uselessness, which was coupled with a shift in cultural attitudes away from dependency towards self-sufficiency in the late twentieth century – Richard Sennett, *The Culture of the New Capitalism* (New Haven, CT: Yale University Press, 2006), 83–130. While my approach in this book is much more critical of capitalism and is drawn from critical and political theory rather than sociology and ethnography, I am similarly describing what might be called a "spectre of uselessness" at the heart of neoliberal rationality, especially since the 2008 crisis.

5 For more on precarious labour in the university, see, for example, Stephen J. Ball, "Living the Neo-Liberal University," *European Journal of Education* 50, no. 3 (2015): 258–61; Gary Hall, *The Uberfication of the University* (Minneapolis, MN: University of Minnesota Press, 2016); Theresa O'Keefe and Aline Courtois, "'Not One of the Family': Gender and Precarious Work in the Neoliberal University," *Gender, Work and Organization* 26, no. 4 (2019): 463–79; Neil Vallelly, "From the Margins of the Neoliberal University: Notes Toward Nomadic Literary Studies," *Poetics Today* 40, no. 1 (2019): 59–79.

6 Tim Di Muzio and Richard H. Robbins, *Debt as Power* (Manchester: Manchester University Press, 2016).
7 Soshana Zuboff, *The Age of Surveillance Capitalism: The Fight for a Human Future at the New Frontier of Power* (London: Profile Books, 2018).
8 Michel Foucault, "The Subject and the Power," in *Michel Foucault: Beyond Structuralism and Hermeneutics*, eds Herbert Dreyfus and Paul Rainbow (Chicago, IL: The University of Chicago Press, 1982), 220–21.
9 Wendy Brown, *In the Ruins of Neoliberalism: The Rise of Antidemocratic Politics in the West* (New York: Columbia University Press, 2019), 29.
10 *ibid.*, 40.
11 Jamie Peck, Neil Brenner, and Nik Theodore, "Actually Existing Neoliberalism," in *The Sage Handbook of Neoliberalism*, eds Damien Cahill, Melinda Cooper, Martijn Konings, and David Primrose (Thousand Oaks, CA: Sage, 2018), 3–15.
12 William Davies, "Neoliberalism and the Revenge of the 'Social,'" *openDemocracy*, 16 July 2013, emphasis in original, www.opendemocracy.net/en/neoliberalism-and-revenge-of-social.
13 For the debate on neoliberalism and democracy, see, for example, Arthur McEwan, *Neo-Liberalism or Democracy? Economic Strategy, Markets, and Alternatives for the 21st Century* (London: Zed Books, 1999); Lisa Duggan, *The Twilight of Democracy: Neoliberalism, Cultural Politics, and the Attack on Democracy* (New York: Beacon Press, 2004); Mark Purcell, *Recapturing Democracy: Neoliberalisation and the Struggle for Alternative Urban Futures* (London: Routledge, 2008); Jodi Dean, *Democracy and Other Neoliberal Fantasies: Communicative Capitalism and Left Politics* (Durham, NC: Duke University Press, 2009); Henry A. Giroux, *Neoliberalism's War*

on *Higher Education* (Chicago, IL: Haymarket Books, 2014), 1–28; Thomas Biebricher, "Neoliberalism and Democracy," *Constellations* 22, no. 2 (2015): 255–66 and *The Political Theory of Neoliberalism* (Stanford, CA: Stanford University Press, 2019); Wendy Brown, *Undoing the Demos: Neoliberalism's Stealth Revolution* (New York: Zone Books, 2015) and *In the Ruins of Neoliberalism*; Jason Hickel, "Neoliberalism and the End of Democracy," in *The Handbook of Neoliberalism*, eds Simon Springer, Kean Birch, and Julie MacLeavy (London: Routledge, 2016), 142–52; Pierre Dardot and Christian Laval, *Never-Ending Nightmare: The Neoliberal Assault on Democracy*, trans. Gregory Elliot (London: Verso, 2019).

14   William Davies, *The Limits of Neoliberalism: Authority, Sovereignty and the Logic of Competition* (London: Sage, 2014), 4.

15   Friedrich Hayek, *The Road to Serfdom* (London: Routledge, 2001), 37–38.

16   Davies, *Limits of Neoliberalism*, 4, emphasis in original.

17   Quinn Slobodian, *Globalists: The End of Empire and the Birth of Neoliberalism* (Cambridge, MA: Harvard University Press, 2018), 92.

18   Ludwig von Mises, *Human Action: A Treatise on Economics* (Auburn, AL: Ludwig von Mises Institute, 1998), 258.

19   Slobodian, *Globalists*, 93.

20   See McKenzie Wark, *Capital is Dead: Is this Something Worse?* (London: Verso, 2019), 24–28.

21   Kean Birch and Simon Springer, "Peak Neoliberalism? Revisiting and Rethinking the Concept of Neoliberalism," *Ephemera: Theory & Politics in Organization* 19, no. 3 (2019): 476.

22   Quinn Slobodian and Dieter Plehwe, "Introduction," in *Nine Lives of Neoliberalism*, eds Phillip Mirowski, Dieter Plehwe, and Quinn Slobodian (London: Verso, 2020), 3.

23 For the political or class project argument, see, for example, David Harvey, *A Brief History of Neoliberalism* (Oxford: Oxford University Press, 2005); Stephanie Lee Mudge, "What is Neo-Liberalism?" *Socio-Economic Review* 6, no. 4 (2008): 703–31; Johanna Bockman, "The Political Projects of Neoliberalism," *Social Anthropology/Anthropologie Sociale* 20, no. 3 (2012): 310–17; Julien Mercille and Enda Murphy, *Deepening Neoliberalism, Austerity, and Crisis: Europe's Treasure Ireland* (London: Palgrave Macmillan, 2015), 8–31; Neil Davidson, "Neoliberalism as a Class-Based Project," in *The Sage Handbook of Neoliberalism*, eds Damien Cahill, Melinda Cooper, Martijn Konings, and David Primrose (Thousand Oaks, CA: Sage, 2018), 55–68; Elizabeth Humphrys, *How Labour Built Neoliberalism: Australia's Accord, the Labour Movement and the Neoliberal Project* (Leiden: Brill, 2019); and Damien Cahill and Elizabeth Humphrys, "Rethinking the 'Neoliberal Thought Collective' Thesis," *Globalizations* 16, no. 6 (2019): 948–65.

For the economic and political rationality argument, or broadly how neoliberalism shapes social policy, see, for example, Jamie Peck, *Constructions of Neoliberal Reason* (Oxford: Oxford University Press, 2010); Pierre Dardot and Christian Laval, *The New Way of the World: On Neoliberal Society*, trans. Gregory Elliot (London: Verso, 2014) and *Never-Ending Nightmare*; Wendy Brown, *Undoing the Demos* and *In the Ruins of Neoliberalism*; Davies, *The Limits of Neoliberalism* and "The New Neoliberalism," *New Left Review* 101 (2016): 121–34; Melinda Cooper, *Family Values: Between Neoliberalism and the New Social Conservatism* (New York: Zone Books, 2017); Adam Kotsko, *Neoliberalism's Demons: On the Political Theology of Late Capital* (Stanford, CA: Stanford University Press, 2018); William Callison, "Political Deficits: The Dawn of

Neoliberal Rationality and the Eclipse of Critical Theory," PhD diss., University of California, Berkeley, 2019.

For the intellectual history of neoliberalism, see, for example, Juan Gabriel Valdés, *Pinochet's Economists: The Chicago School in Chile* (Cambridge: Cambridge University Press, 1995); Phillip Mirowski and Dieter Plehwe, eds, *The Road from Mont Pèlerin: The Making of the Neoliberal Thought Collective* (Cambridge, MA: Harvard University Press, 2009); Daniel Stedman-Jones, *Masters of the Universe: Hayek, Friedman, and the Birth of Neoliberal Politics* (Princeton, NJ: Princeton University Press, 2012); Phillip Mirowski, *Never Let a Serious Crisis Go to Waste: How Neoliberalism Survived the Financial Meltdown* (London: Verso, 2013); Slobodian, *Globalists*; Biebricher, *The Political Theory of Neoliberalism*; Jessica Whyte, *The Morals of the Market: Human Rights and the Rise of Neoliberalism* (London: Verso, 2019); Mirowski, Plehwe, and Slobodian, eds, *Nine Lives of Neoliberalism*.

24 Dardot and Laval, *Never-Ending Nightmare*, xii, emphasis in original.
25 Wendy Brown, "Who is not a Neoliberal Today?" *Tocqueville* 21, 18 January 2018, emphasis in original, https://tocqueville21.com/interviews/wendy-brown-not-neoliberal-today.
26 Birch and Springer, "Peak Neoliberalism," 473.
27 See the popular work of Nobel Prize-winning economist Joseph E. Stiglitz, "Progressive Capitalism is Not an Oxymoron," *The New York Times*, 19 April 2019, https://nyti.ms/2GpsQoQ and *People, Power, and Profits: Progressive Capitalism for an Age of Discontent* (New York: Penguin, 2019).
28 George Monbiot, "Dare to Declare Capitalism Dead – Before it Takes us all Down with It," *The Guardian*, 25 April

2019, www.theguardian.com/commentisfree/2019/apr/25/capitalism-economic-system-survival-earth.

29 Jason Hickel and Giorgos Kallis, "Is Green Growth Possible?" *New Political Economy* 25, no. 4 (2020): 475.

30 Dardot and Laval, *Never-Ending Nightmare*, 15, emphasis in original.

31 *ibid.*, xx, emphasis in original. See, also, Davies, "The New Neoliberalism."

32 David Kotz, *The Rise and Fall of Neoliberal Capitalism* (Cambridge, MA: Harvard University Press, 2017); Cornel West, "Goodbye, American Neoliberalism: A New Era is Here," *The Guardian*, 17 November 2016, www.theguardian.com/commentisfree/2016/nov/17/american-neoliberalism-cornel-west-2016-election; Nancy Fraser, "The End of Progressive Neoliberalism," *Dissent*, 2 January 2017, www.dissentmagazine.org/online_articles/progressive-neoliberalism-reactionary-populism-nancy-fraser; Ganesh Sitaraman, "The Collapse of Neoliberalism," *The New Republic*, 24 December 2019, https://newrepublic.com/article/155970/collapse-neoliberalism; Jeremy Lent, "Coronavirus Spells the End of the Neoliberal Era. What's Next?" *openDemocracy*, 12 April 2020, www.opendemocracy.net/en/transformation/coronavirus-spells-the-end-of-the-neoliberal-era-whats-next.

33 Jamie Peck, "Zombie Neoliberalism and the Ambidextrous State," *Theoretical Criminology* 14, no. 1 (2010): 104–10; Colin Crouch, *The Strange Non-Death of Neoliberalism* (Cambridge: Polity, 2011); Simon Springer, "No More Room in Hell: Neoliberalism as Living Dead," in *The Sage Handbook of Neoliberalism*, eds Damien Cahill, Melinda Cooper, Martijn Konings, and David Primrose (Thousand Oaks, CA: Sage, 2018), 620–30.

34 Jamie Peck and Nik Theodore, "Still Neoliberalism?" *The South Atlantic Quarterly* 118, no. 2 (2019): 245–65; William Callison and Zachary Manfredi, eds, *Mutant Neoliberalism: Market Rule and Political Rupture* (New York: Fordham University Press, 2019).
35 Callison and Manfredi, "Introduction," in *Mutant Neoliberalism*, 3.
36 *ibid.*, 4.
37 Jason Hickel, *The Divide: A Brief Guide to Global Inequality and Its Solutions* (London: Penguin Random House, 2017).
38 Malcolm Harris, *Kids These Days: Human Capital and the Making of Millennials* (Boston, MA: Little Brown and Co, 2017); Jason C. Sternberg, *The Theft of a Decade: How the Baby Boomers Stole the Millennials' Economic Future* (New York: PublicAffairs, 2019); Keir Milburn, *Generation Left* (Cambridge: Polity, 2019).
39 Joel Stein, "Millennials: The Me Me Me Generation," *Time*, 21 May 2013, https://time.com/247; Tanith Carey, "What's the Problem with Millennials and the Workplace," *The Telegraph*, 10 July 2017, www.telegraph.co.uk/education-and-careers/0/problem-millennials-workplace.
40 Brown, *Ruins of Neoliberalism*, 161–82.
41 Mark Fisher, "Democracy is Joy," *K-Punk* (blog), 12 July 2015, http://k-punk.org/democracy-is-joy.
42 Brown, *Ruins of Neoliberalism*, 171.
43 Rebecca Solnit, "Not Caring is a Political Art Form: On Melania Trump and the Politics of Disconnection," *LitHub*, 22 June 2018, https://lithub.com/rebecca-solnit-not-caring-is-a-political-art-form.
44 Simon Critchley, *Infinitely Demanding: Ethics of Commitment, Politics of Resistance* (London: Verso, 2007), 4–5.

45 Franco "Bifo" Berardi, *Heroes: Mass Murder and Suicide* (London: Verso, 2015); Ronald E. Purser, *McMindfulness: How Mindfulness Became the New Capitalist Spirituality* (London: Repeater Books, 2019).
46 Jia Tolentino, "The Rage of Incels," *The New Yorker*, 15 May 2018, https://www.newyorker.com/culture/cultural-comment/the-rage-of-the-incels; Zack Beauchamp, "Our Incel Problem," *Vox*, 23 April 2019, www.vox.com/the-highlight/2019/4/16/18287446/incel-definition-reddit; Justin Ling, "Incels are Radicalised and Dangerous. But are They Terrorists?" *Foreign Policy*, 2 June 2020, https://foreignpolicy.com/2020/06/02/incels-toronto-attack-terrorism-ideological-violence.

1 The Futilitarian Condition

1 Karl Marx, *Capital: A Critique of Political Economy*, vol. 1, trans. Ben Fowkes (London: Penguin, 1976), 758–59, note 51.
2 *ibid.*, 758.
3 Steven Pinker, *Enlightenment Now: The Case for Reason, Science, Humanism, and Progress* (New York: Penguin, 2018), 98.
4 Ludwig von Mises, *Liberalism: The Classical Tradition*, ed. Bettina Bien Greaves (Indianapolis, IN: Liberty Fund, 2005), 9; Ludwig von Mises, *Economic Freedom and Interventionism: An Anthology of Articles and Essays*, ed. Bettina Bien Greaves (Indianapolis, IN: Liberty Fund, 2007), 50.
5 Pinker, *Enlightenment Now*, 102.
6 *ibid.*, 114.
7 Peter Fleming, *The Worst is Yet to Come: A Post-Capitalist Survival Guide* (London: Repeater Books, 2019), 22.

8 For an excellent critique of Pinker's thought, especially his embracement by the billionaire class, see Jason Hickel, "Progress and its Discontents," *New Internationalist* 520, July–August 2019, https://newint.org/features/2019/07/01/long-read-progress-and-its-discontents. For a critique of Pinker and the "New Optimist" movement more broadly, see Rodrigo Aguilera, *The Glass Half-Empty: Debunking the Myth of Progress in the Twenty-First Century* (London: Repeater Books, 2020).
9 Boris Johnson, "Annual Margaret Thatcher Lecture in Full," *The Telegraph*, 28 November 2013, www.telegraph.co.uk/news/politics/london-mayor-election/mayor-of-london/10480321/Boris-Johnsons-speech-at-the-Margaret-Thatcher-lecture-in-full.html.
10 Jeremy Bentham, *An Introduction to the Principles of Morals and Legislation* (Oxford: Clarendon Press, 1876), 2.
11 For more on Bentham's definition of "happiness," see William Davies, *The Happiness Industry: How Government and Big Business Sold Us Well-Being* (London: Verso, 2015), chapters 1 and 2.
12 Bentham, *The Principles of Morals and Legislation*, 9.
13 *ibid.*, 12–13.
14 *ibid.*, 16.
15 *ibid.*, 23.
16 *ibid.*, 29–32.
17 *ibid.*, 29, note 1.
18 *ibid.*, 3, emphasis in original.
19 Luc Boltanski and Ève Chiapello, *The New Spirit of Capitalism*, trans. Gregory Elliot (London: Verso, 2005), 12.
20 *ibid.*, 13.
21 Jeremy Bentham, *Defence of Usury* (London: Payne and Foss, 1818), 2.

22 For a critique of Bentham's argument in *Defence of Usury*, see Peter Johnson, "Brodbeck on Bentham," *openDemocracy*, 9 October 2009, www.opendemocracy.net/en/brodbeck-on-bentham.
23 Bentham, *Defence of Usury*, 97.
24 Davies, *The Happiness Industry*, 25.
25 Werner Stark, "Jeremy Bentham as an Economist," *The Economic Journal* 56, no. 224 (1946): 583–84.
26 Jeremy Bentham, "Principles of the Civil Code," in *The Works of Jeremy Bentham*, vol. 1, ed. John Bowring (New York: Russell & Russell, 1843), 316.
27 See Davies, *The Happiness Industry*, 43–59.
28 *ibid.*, 50.
29 Gary S. Becker, *The Economic Approach to Human Behaviour* (Chicago, IL: The University of Chicago Press, 1976).
30 John Stuart Mill, *The Subjection of Women* (New York: Henry Holt and Company, 1879), 238.
31 Jonathan Riley, "Utilitarianism and Economic Theory," in *The New Palgrave Dictionary of Economics*, 2nd edn, eds Steven N. Durlauf and Lawrence E. Blume (London: Palgrave Macmillan, 2008), 570.
32 *ibid.*, 573.
33 Henry Sidgwick, *The Methods of Ethics* (London: Macmillan, 1884), vi.
34 *ibid.*, 494.
35 For an introduction to the relationship between utilitarianism and modern economic science, see Riley "Utilitarianism and Economic Theory," 568–76.
36 *ibid.*, 571.
37 *ibid.*, 572.

38 See, for example, Tim Congdon, *Keynes, the Keynesians, and Monetarism* (Cheltenham: Edward Elgar, 2007); Paul Davidson, *John Maynard Keynes* (London: Palgrave Macmillan, 2007); Robert Skidelsky, *Keynes: The Return of the Master* (London: Allen Lane, 2009); Peter Clarke, *The Rise, Fall, and Return of the 20th Century's Most Influential Economist* (London: Bloomsbury, 2012); James Crotty, *Keynes Against Capitalism: His Economic Case for Liberal Socialism* (London: Routledge, 2019); Geoff Mann, *In the Long Run We're All Dead: Keynesianism, Political Economy, and Revolution* (London: Verso, 2019).

39 For a detailed outline of Keynes's anti-utilitarian stance, see Peter V. Mini, "The Anti-Benthamism of J. M. Keynes: Implications for The General Theory," *The American Journal of Economics and Sociology* 50, no. 4 (1991): 453–68; Anna Maria Carabelli and Mario Aldo Cedrini, "The Economic Problem of Happiness: Keynes on Happiness and Economics," *Forum for Social Economics* 40, no. 3 (2011): 335–59.

40 John Maynard Keynes, "My Early Beliefs," in *The Collected Writings of John Maynard Keynes*, vol. 10, eds Elizabeth Johnson and Donald Moggridge (Cambridge: Cambridge University Press, 1978), 445–46.

41 Mini, "The Anti-Benthamism of J. M. Keynes," 456.

42 John Maynard Keynes, "Art and State," in *Collected Writings*, vol. 28, eds Elizabeth Johnson and Donald Moggridge, 342.

43 For a detailed history of the Mont Pèlerin Society, see Phillip Mirowski and Dieter Plehwe, eds, *The Road from Mont Pèlerin: The Making of the Neoliberal Thought Collective* (Cambridge, MA: Harvard University Press, 2009).

44 Mont Pèlerin Society, "Statement of Aims," accessed 23 November 2020, www.montpelerin.org/statement-of-aims.
45 David Harvey, *A Brief History of Neoliberalism* (Oxford: Oxford University Press, 2005), 21. See also, Wendy Brown, *In the Ruins of Neoliberalism: The Rise of Antidemocratic Politics in the West* (New York: Columbia University Press, 2019), 82–87.
46 Campbell Jones points out that state intervention to protect capitalism is not necessarily new to neoliberalism, as "capital has always been accompanied by the capitalist state, to which it turns when it is unable to effect its designs through the 'voluntary' agreement of individuals and enterprises" – Campbell Jones, "Introduction: The Return of Economic Planning," *South Atlantic Quarterly* 119, no. 1 (2020): 3.
47 Friedrich Hayek, *Law, Legislation and Liberty: A New Statement of the Liberal Principles of Justice and Political Economy* (London: Routledge, 1982), 22.
48 *ibid.*, 95.
49 Ludwig von Mises, *Socialism: An Economic and Sociological Analysis*, trans. J. Kahane (New Haven, CT: Yale University Press, 1962).
50 Friedrich Hayek, *The Road to Serfdom* (London: Routledge, 2001), 153.
51 For a thorough examination of the similarities of the philosophies of Hayek and Bentham, see Allison Dube, "Hayek on Bentham," *Utilitas* 2, no. 1 (1991): 71–87. For a critique of Hayek's view on the concept of "society," see Wendy Brown, *In the Ruins of Neoliberalism*, 30–39.
52 Hayek, *The Road to Serfdom*, 63.
53 *ibid.*, 35.
54 *ibid.*, 37.

55 *ibid.*, 38.
56 Friedrich Hayek, *Individualism and Economic Order* (Chicago, IL: The University of Chicago Press, 1948), 6.
57 *ibid.*, 11.
58 C. B. Macpherson, "Individualism," in *The New Palgrave Dictionary of Economics*, 1st edn, eds John Eatwell, Murray Milgate, and Peter Newman (London: Palgrave Macmillan, 1987), 1–5.
59 Bentham, "Essay on Political Tactics," *The Works of Jeremy Bentham*, vol. 2, ed. John Bowring, 301.
60 See Juan Gabriel Valdés, *Pinochet's Economists: The Chicago School in Chile* (Cambridge: Cambridge University Press, 1995).
61 For more on this development in left-wing politics, see Boltanski and Chiapello, *New Spirit of Capitalism*, especially chapter 3; Harvey, *Brief History of Neoliberalism*, chapter 2; Jodi Dean, *Democracy and Other Neoliberal Fantasies: Communicative Capitalism and Left Politics* (Durham, NC: Duke University Press, 2009) and *Crowds and Party* (London: Verso, 2016), chapter 1.
62 Harvey, *Brief History of Neoliberalism*, 41–42.
63 Alain Badiou, *The Communist Hypothesis*, trans. David Macey and Steve Corcoran (London: Verso, 2009), 44.
64 Kristin Ross, *May '68 and Its Afterlives* (Chicago, IL: The University of Chicago Press, 2002).
65 Boltanski and Chiapello, *New Spirit of Capitalism*, 199.
66 Franco "Bifo" Berardi, *Precarious Rhapsody: Semiocapitalism and the Pathologies of the Post-Alpha Generation* (New York: Autonomedia, 2009), 43.
67 Soshana Zuboff, *The Age of Surveillance Capitalism: The Fight for a Human Future at the New Frontier of Power* (London: Profile Books, 2018).

68 Karl Marx, *Grundrisse: Foundations of the Critique of Political Economy*, trans. Martin Nicolaus (London, Penguin, 1973), 650.
69 Wendy Brown, *Undoing the Demos: Neoliberalism's Stealth Revolution* (New York: Zone Books, 2015), 108.
70 Byung-Chul Han, *Psychopolitics: Neoliberalism and New Technologies of Power* (London: Verso, 2017), 7.
71 Mark Fisher, *Capitalist Realism: Is There No Alternative?* (Winchester: Zero Books, 2009).

2 The Rise of *Homo futilitus*

1 Slavoj Žižek, *Like a Thief in Broad Daylight: Power in the Era of Post-Human Capitalism* (London: Allen Lane, 2018).
2 Damien Wilkins, "In Safe Hands with Damien Wilkins," interviewed by Diana Dekker, *Dominion Post*, 18 August 2013, www.stuff.co.nz/dominion-post/9051928/In-safe-hands-with-Damien-Wilkins.
3 Michelle Obama, *Becoming* (New York: Crown, 2018), 332–33.
4 Katie Jeanes, "5 Ways Justin Trudeau's Social Media Game Trumped Other Leaders," Huffington Post, 22 November 2015, www.huffingtonpost.ca/katie-jeanes/justin-trudeau-social-media_b_8362414.html.
5 Shannon Proudfoot, "Selling a PM: The Marketing of Justin Trudeau," *Maclean's*, 11 August 2016, www.macleans.ca/politics/ottawa/marketing-justin-trudeau.
6 Ashifa Kassam, "Is Justin Trudeau Living Up to his Self-Proclaimed Feminist Ideals?" *The Guardian*, 16 March 2017, www.theguardian.com/world/2017/mar/16/justin-trudeau-feminism-scorecard.

7 Khelsilem, "Justin Trudeau Promised to Protect Indigenous Rights. He Lied, Again." *The Guardian*, 19 June 2018, www.theguardian.com/world/commentisfree/2018/jun/19/salish-sea-pipeline-indigenous-salish-sea-canada-trans-mountain.

8 For a thorough account of Trudeau's demise, see Ashifa Kassam, "Justin Trudeau: The Rise and Fall of a Political Brand," *The Guardian*, 22 August 2019, www.theguardian.com/world/2019/aug/22/justin-trudeau-the-rise-and-fall-of-a-political-brand.

9 Leah McLaren, "Justin Trudeau's Disgrace is like Watching a Unicorn get Run Over," *The Guardian*, 1 March 2019, www.theguardian.com/commentisfree/2019/mar/01/justin-trudeau-disgrace-unicorn-political-scandal-canadian.

10 Arwa Mahdawi, "The Furore over the Fish-Eating Vegan Influencer is a Warning to us All," *The Guardian*, 26 March 2019, www.theguardian.com/commentisfree/2019/mar/26/the-furore-over-the-fish-eating-vegan-influencer-is-a-warning-to-us-all.

11 For more on the financialisation of capitalism, see Christian Marazzi, *The Violence of Financial Capitalism*, trans. Kritina Lebedeva (Los Angeles, CA: Semiotext(e), 2009); Costas Lapavistas, *Profiting Without Producing: How Finance Exploits Us All* (London: Verso, 2013); Cédric Durand, *Fictitious Capital: How Finance is Appropriating Our Future*, trans. David Broder (London: Verso, 2017); Grace Blakeley, *Stolen: How to Save the World from Financialisation* (London: Repeater Books, 2019). For a perspective on rentier capitalism grounded in political economy, see Brett Christophers, *Rentier Capitalism: Who Owns the Economy, and Who Pays for It?* (London: Verso, 2020).

12 Tom Peters, "The Brand Called You," *FastCompany*, 31 August 1997, www.fastcompany.com/28905/brand-called-you.
13 *ibid.*
14 Sophie Elmhirst, "'It's Genuine, You Know': Why the Online Influencer Industry is Going 'Authentic,'" *The Guardian*, 5 April 2019, www.theguardian.com/media/2019/apr/05/its-genuine-you-know-why-the-online-influencer-industry-is-going-authentic.
15 Peters, "The Brand Called You."
16 Byung-Chul Han, *Psychopolitics: Neoliberalism and New Technologies of Power*, trans. Erik Butler (London: Verso, 2017), 1, emphasis in original.
17 *ibid.*, 5, emphasis in original.
18 David Harvey, *Spaces of Global Capitalism: Towards a Theory of Uneven Geographical Development* (London: Verso, 2006), 64–68.
19 *ibid.*, 65.
20 Han, *Psychopolitics*, 2, emphasis in original.
21 Quoted in Caroline Castrillon, "Why Personal Branding is More Important than Ever," *Forbes*, 12 February 2019, www.forbes.com/sites/carolinecastrillon/2019/02/12/why-personal-branding-is-more-important-than-ever.
22 Karl Marx and Friedrich Engels, "The German Ideology," in *Collected Works*, vol. 5 (London: Lawrence & Wishart, 2010), 78.
23 Brian Keeley, *Human Capital: How What You Know Shapes Your Life* (Paris: OECD Publishing, 2007), 29.
24 Julia Storberg, "The Evolution of Capital Theory: A Critique of a Theory of Social Capital and Implications for HRD," *Human Resource Development Review* 1, no. 4 (2002): 469.

25 Wendy Brown, *In the Ruins of Neoliberalism: The Rise of Antidemocratic Politics in the West* (New York: Columbia University Press, 2019), 163.
26 See, in particular, Samuel Bowles and Herbert Gintis, "The Problem with Human Capital Theory: A Marxian Critique," *The American Economic Review* 65, no. 2 (1975): 74–82; Michel Foucault, *The Birth of Biopolitics: Lectures at the Collège de France, 1978–79*, trans. Graham Burchell (London: Palgrave Macmillan, 2008), 215–37; Wendy Brown, *Undoing the Demos: Neoliberalism's Stealth Revolution* (New York: Zone Books, 2015); Peter Fleming, *The Death of Homo Economicus: Work, Debt and the Myth of Endless Accumulation* (London: Pluto Press, 2017); Malcolm Harris, *Kids These Days: Human Capital and the Making of Millennials* (Boston, MA: Little, Brown and Co, 2017); Melinda Cooper, "Neoliberalism's Family Values: Welfare, Human Capital, and Kinship," in *Nine Lives of Neoliberalism*, eds Phillip Mirowski, Dieter Plehwe, and Quinn Slobodian (London: Verso, 2020), 95–119.
27 Fleming, *The Death of Homo Economicus*, 98.
28 Foucault, *The Birth of Biopolitics*, 225.
29 *ibid.*, 226.
30 Byung-Chul Han, *The Expulsion of the Other: Society, Perception and Communication Today*, trans. Wieland Hoban (Cambridge: Polity, 2018), 19.
31 *ibid.*, 21.
32 Elmhirst "'It's Genuine, You Know.'"
33 Han, *The Expulsion of the Other*, 19–20, emphasis in original.
34 Brown, *Undoing the Demos*, 37–38.
35 *ibid.*, 42, emphasis in original.
36 Fleming, *Death of Homo Economicus*, 207.

37 For an excellent critique of the absurdity of (self-) entrepreneurialism under neoliberalism, see Anna-Maria Murtola, "Entrepreneurialism *ad absurdum*," in *Against Entrepreneurship: A Critical Examination*, ed. Anders Örtenblad (London: Palgrave Macmillan, 2020), 93–110.
38 William Callison and Zachary Manfredi, "Introduction," in *Mutant Neoliberalism: Market Rule and Political Rupture*, eds William Callison and Zachary Manfredi (New York: Fordham University Press, 2019), 21.
39 Fleming, *Death of Homo Economicus*, 264.
40 *ibid.*, 237.
41 *ibid.*, 143.
42 Peter Fleming, *The Mythology of Work: How Capitalism Persists Despite Itself* (London: Pluto Press, 2015).
43 David Graeber, *Bullshit Jobs: A Theory* (New York: Simon & Schuster, 2018), xvii.
44 David Graeber, "Bullshit Jobs: Why they Exist and Why You Might have One," interview by Sean Illing, *Vox*, 10 October 2018, www.vox.com/2018/5/8/17308744/bullshit-jobs-book-david-graeber-occupy-wall-street-karl-marx.
45 Recent work in social reproduction theory is essential to understanding how production is entirely dependent on social reproduction, especially care work, which is overwhelmingly performed by women and minorities for low or no pay. The Covid-19 pandemic has only accentuated the "essential" nature of the work of social reproduction, and yet economic rescue packages solely focus on "workers" who produce goods or services. See Tithi Bhattacharya, ed., *Social Reproduction Theory: Remapping Class, Recentring Oppression* (London: Pluto Press, 2017); Susan Ferguson, *Women and Work:*

Feminism, Labour, and Social Reproduction (London: Pluto Press, 2019).
46 Fleming, *Death of Homo Economicus*, 140.
47 Charles Fourier, *The Utopian Vision of Charles Fourier: Selected Texts*, trans. Jonathan Beecher and Richard Bienvenu (Boston, MA: Beacon Press, 1971), 148.
48 Max Weber, *The Protestant Ethic and the Spirit of Capitalism*, trans. Talcott Parsons (London: Routledge, 1992).
49 Graeber, *Bullshit Jobs*, xxiii.
50 See Mike Davis, *Planet of Slums* (London: Verso, 2006).
51 Fleming, *Death of Homo Economicus*, 125.
52 *ibid.*, 127.
53 Karl Marx, *Capital: A Critique of Political Economy*, vol. 1, trans. Ben Fowkes (London: Penguin, 1976), 131.
54 Nick Srnicek and Alex Williams, *Inventing the Future: Postcapitalism and a World Without Work* (London: Verso, 2015), 124.
55 Jason Smith, "Preface: Soul on Strike," in Franco "Bifo" Berardi, *The Soul at Work*, trans. Francesca Cadel and Giuseppina Mecchia (Los Angeles, CA: Semiotext(e), 2009), 19.

3 Useless Responsibility

1 For a precise description of the relationship between neoliberalism and the rhetoric of personal responsibility, see Wendy Brown's description of the process of "responsibilisation" in *Undoing the Demos: Neoliberalism's Stealth Revolution* (New York: Zone Books, 2015), 131–34; see, also, Peter Fleming's notion of "ultra-responsible autonomy" in *The Death of Homo Economicus: Work, Debt and the Myth of Endless Accumulation* (London: Pluto Press, 2017), chapter 5.

2 For a critique of cognitive behavioural therapy and mindfulness in the context of contemporary capitalism, see, for example, William Davies, *The Happiness Industry: How Government and Big Business Sold Us Well-Being* (London: Verso, 2015); Anne Mulhall, " 'Mind Yourself': Well-Being and Resilience as Governmentality in Contemporary Ireland," *The Irish Review* 53 (2016): 29–44; Zack Walsh, "Mindfulness Under Neoliberal Governmentality: Critiquing the Operation of Biopower in Corporate Mindfulness and Constructing Queer Alternatives," *Journal of Management, Spirituality, and Religion* 15, no. 2 (2018): 109–22; Ronald E. Purser, *McMindfulness: How Mindfulness Became the New Capitalist Spirituality* (London: Repeater Books, 2019).
3 Mark Fisher, "Why Mental Health is a Political Issue," *The Guardian*, 16 July 2012, www.theguardian.com/commentisfree/2012/jul/16/mental-health-political-issue.
4 Liza Featherstone, "Don't Blame the Babies," *Jacobin*, 15 April 2019, https://jacobinmag.com/2019/04/children-climate-change-family-guilt.
5 Yamiche Alcindor, "Ben Carson Calls Poverty 'A State of Mind,' Igniting a Backlash," *The New York Times*, 25 May 2017, www.nytimes.com/2017/05/25/us/politics/ben-carson-poverty-hud-state-of-mind.html.
6 Andrew Dean, *Ruth, Roger and Me: Debts and Legacies* (Wellington: Bridget Williams Books, 2015); Jane Kelsey, *The New Zealand Experiment: A World Model for Structural Adjustment?* (Wellington: Victoria University Press, 2015).
7 Jennifer Lawn, "Neoliberalism and the Politics of Indigenous Community in the Fiction of Alan Duff and Witi Ihimaera," *Social Semiotics* 21, no. 1 (2011): 85–99, at 91.

8   *ibid.*, 93.
9   Alan Duff, *Once Were Warriors* (London: Vintage, 1995), 166.
10 Simon Barber, "Imagining Beyond Decolonisation," *Counterfutures* 10 (2020): 160–61.
11 For a discussion of how Ngāi Tahu – the principal iwi of Te Waipounamu, Aotearoa New Zealand's South Island – embraced neoliberal economics, see Simon Barber, "In Wakefield's Laboratory: Tangata Whenua into Property/Labour in Te Waipounamu," *Journal of Sociology* 56, no. 2 (2020): 229–46.
12 Barber, "Imagining Beyond Decolonisation," 161.
13 Alan Duff, "An Interview with Alan Duff," interview by Vilsoni Heriniko, *The Contemporary Pacific* 7, no. 2 (1995): 326–344, at 329.
14 *ibid.*, 333.
15 *ibid.*, 336.
16 *ibid.*, 338.
17 Marty Sharpe, "Alan Duff Declares Bankruptcy … in a French Chateau," Stuff NZ, 29 June 2011, www.stuff.co.nz/entertainment/5204766/Alan-Duff-declares-bankruptcy-in-a-French-chateau.
18 Duff, "Interview," 344.
19 Jennifer Lawn and Chris Prentice, "Neoliberal Culture/The Cultures of Neoliberalism," *Sites: A Journal of Social Anthropology and Cultural Studies* 12, no. 1 (2015): 1–29.
20 Duff, *Once Were Warriors*, 182, emphasis in original.
21 Lawn, "Neoliberalism the Politics of Indigenous Community," 92.
22 Several theorists have noted the fact that Clinton and Blair did more to realise the vision of Reagan and Thatcher than subsequent centre-right politicians. See, for example, Michael Meeropol, *Surrender: How*

the Clinton Administration Completed the Reagan Revolution (Ann Arbor, MI: The University of Michigan Press, 1998); Chantal Mouffe, *The Democratic Paradox* (London: Verso, 2000), 108-28; David Harvey, *Spaces of Global Capital: Towards a Theory of Uneven Geographical Development* (London: Verso, 2006), 33; Jodi Dean, *Democracy and Other Neoliberal Fantasies: Communicative Capitalism and Left Politics* (Durham, NC: Duke University Press, 2009), 7; Tariq Ali, *The Extreme Centre: A Warning* (London: Verso, 2015), 6. For a similar development in Australia, see Elizabeth Humphrys, *How Labour Built Neoliberalism: Australia's Accord, the Labour Movement and the Neoliberal Project* (Leiden: Brill, 2019); Damien Cahill and Elizabeth Humphrys, "Rethinking the 'Neoliberal Thought Collective' Thesis," *Globalizations* 16, no. 6 (2019): 948-65. For the same development in Aotearoa New Zealand, see Kelsey, *The New Zealand Experiment*. For a general history of how the Left shaped neoliberalism, see Stephanie L. Mudge, *Leftism Reinvented: Western Parties from Socialism to Neoliberalism* (Cambridge, MA: Harvard University Press, 2018).

23 Nancy Fraser, "Progressive Neoliberalism versus Reactionary Populism: A Choice that Feminists Should Refuse," *Nora - Nordic Journal of Feminist and Gender Research* 24, no. 4 (2016): 281-84; Johanna Brenner and Nancy Fraser, "What is Progressive Neoliberalism? A Debate," *Dissent* 64, no. 2 (2017): 130-40. Nancy Fraser, *The Old is Dying and the New Cannot be Born: From Progressive Neoliberalism to Trump and Beyond* (London: Verso, 2019).

24 Fraser, *The Old is Dying*, 12-13.

25 *ibid.*, 15.

26 Bill Clinton, "Text of President Clinton's Announcement on Welfare Legislation," *The New York Times*, 1 August 1996, https://www.nytimes.com/1996/08/01/us/text-of-president-clinton-s-announcement-on-welfare-legislation.html.

27 Premilla Nadasen notes that "in an era of market worship, those who couldn't demonstrate self-reliance or independence were identified not only as unworthy of assistance, but as a potential threat to the core institutions of American society" – Premilla Nadasen, "How a Democrat Killed Welfare," *Jacobin*, 9 February 2016, www.jacobinmag.com/2016/02/welfare-reform-bill-hillary-clinton-tanf-poverty-dlc.

28 For a comprehensive overview of how the term "dependency" has historically developed in relation to the welfare state in the US, see Nancy Fraser and Linda Gordon, "A Genealogy of Dependency: Tracing a Keyword of the U.S. Welfare State," *Signs* 19, no. 2 (1994): 309–36.

29 Clinton, "Announcement on Welfare Legislation."

30 Jessica Whyte, *The Morals of the Market: Human Rights and the Rise of Neoliberalism* (London: Verso, 2019), 27.

31 Nadasen, "How a Democrat Killed Welfare"; Michelle Alexander, "Why Hilary Clinton Doesn't Deserve the Black Vote," *The Nation*, 10 February 2016, www.thenation.com/article/archive/hillary-clinton-does-not-deserve-black-peoples-votes/; Donna Murch, "The Clintons' War on Drugs: When Black Lives Didn't Matter," *The New Republic*, 10 February 2016, https://newrepublic.com/article/129433/clintons-war-drugs-black-lives-didnt-matter; Keeanga-Yamahtta Taylor, "Why Should We Trust You? Clinton's Big Problem with Young Black Americans," *The Guardian*, 21 October 2016, www.theguardian.com/us-news/2016/oct/21/hillary-clinton-black-millennial-voters.

32 Gary S. Becker, "Unleash the Bill Collectors on Deadbeat Dads," *Bloomberg*, 18 July 1994, www.bloomberg.com/news/articles/1994-07-17/unleash-the-bill-collectors-on-deadbeat-dads.
33 Melinda Cooper, *Family Values: Between Neoliberalism and the New Social Conservatism* (New York: Zone Books, 2017), 71, emphasis in original.
34 *ibid.*, 103.
35 *ibid.*, 62.
36 Tony Blair, "My Vision for Britain," *The Guardian*, 10 November 2002, www.theguardian.com/politics/2002/nov/10/queensspeech2002.tonyblair.
37 Sonja Cecar, *Blatcherism: How Much Thatcherism is in Blairism* (Saarbrücken: Verlag Dr. Müller, 2007); Anthony Barnett, "Open Labour: The Only Way for Corbyn to Replace Blatcherism," *openDemocracy*, 28 September 2015, www.opendemocracy.net/en/opendemocracyuk/open-labour-only-way-for-corbyn-to-replace-blatcherism.
38 Cooper, *Family Values*, 98–109.
39 Perry Anderson, "Ukania Perpetua?" *New Left Review* 125 (2020): 49.
40 Blair, "My Vision for Britain."
41 Jeremy Bentham, *An Introduction to the Principles of Morals and Legislation* (Oxford: Clarendon Press, 1876), 70.
42 Denis Campbell, "People Must Take Responsibility for Own Health, Says Matt Hancock," *The Guardian*, 5 November 2018, www.theguardian.com/society/2018/nov/05/people-must-take-responsibility-for-own-health-says-matt-hancock.
43 Karen McVeigh, "Austerity a Factor in Rising Suicide Rate Among UK Men – Study," *The Guardian*, 12 November 2015, www.theguardian.com/society/2015/nov/12/austerity-a-factor-in-rising-suicide-rate-among-uk-men-study;

Trades Union Congress (TUC), "Child Poverty in Working Households up by 1 Million Children Since 2010," TUC, 7 May 2018, www.tuc.org.uk/news/child-poverty-working-households-1-million-children-2010-says-tuc; Sarah Boseley, "Austerity Blamed for Life Expectancy Stalling for First Time in Century," *The Guardian*, 25 February 2020, www.theguardian.com/society/2020/feb/24/austerity-blamed-for-life-expectancy-stalling-for-first-time-in-century.

44 Rotherham, Doncaster, and South Humber NHS Foundation Trust, "Personal Responsibility Framework SOP," accessed 20 November 2020, www.rdash.nhs.uk/personal-responsibility-framework-sop.

45 Press Association, "Nearly Half of England's Doctors Forced to Find Their Own PPE, Data Shows," *The Guardian*, 3 May 2020, www.theguardian.com/uk-news/2020/may/03/nearly-half-of-british-doctors-forced-to-find-their-own-ppe-new-data-shows.

46 Rosalind Mathieson, "Boris Johnson's Bet on British Common Sense Isn't Paying Off," Bloomberg, 21 October 2020, www.bloomberg.com/news/articles/2020-10-21/covid-pandemic-boris-johnson-s-bet-on-british-common-sense-isn-t-working.

47 For more on this ontological necessity, see my discussion of ontic and ontological relationality in Neil Vallely, "The Relationality of Disappearance," *Angelaki: Journal of the Theoretical Humanities* 24, no. 3 (2019): 38–52.

48 Fleming, *Death of Homo Economicus*, 129–31.

49 A University and College Union (UCU) study in 2016 found that 54% of academic staff in UK universities were on casual contracts – UCU, "Precarious Work in Higher Education: A Snapshot of Insecure Contracts and Institutional

Attitudes," April 2016, www.ucu.org.uk/media/7995/Precarious-work-in-higher-education-a-snapshot-of-insecure-contracts-and-institutional-attitudes-Apr-16/pdf/ucu_precariouscontract_hereport_apr16.pdf.

50 Sinéad Murphy, *Zombie University: Thinking Under Control* (London: Repeater Books, 2017).
51 Brown, *Undoing the Demos*, 110.
52 Isabell Lorey, *States of Insecurity: Government of the Precarious*, trans. Aileen Derieg (London: Verso, 2015), 70.
53 Barack Obama, "Inaugural Address," Obama White House Archives, 21 January 2009, https://obamawhitehouse.archives.gov/blog/2009/01/21/president-barack-obamas-inaugural-address.
54 David Graeber, "A Practical Utopian's Guide to the Coming Collapse," *The Baffler* 22 (2013), https://thebaffler.com/salvos/a-practical-utopians-guide-to-the-coming-collapse.
55 Fraser, *The Old is Dying*, 20.
56 Obama, "Inaugural Address."
57 *ibid*.
58 Ellen Meiksins Wood, *Democracy Against Capitalism: Renewing Historical Materialism* (Cambridge: Cambridge University Press, 1995), 153–67.
59 Max Weber, *The Protestant Ethic and the Spirit of Capitalism*, trans. Talcott Parsons (London: Routledge, 1992), 20.
60 Luc Boltanski and Ève Chiapello, *The New Spirit of Capitalism*, trans. Gregory Elliot (London: Verso, 2005), 10.
61 Brown, *Undoing the Demos*, 26.
62 Andrew Buncombe, "Barack Obama to Make $1.2m from Three Wall Street Speeches," *The Independent*, 18 September 2017, www.independent.co.uk/news/world/americas/us-politics/barack-obama-speeches-fee-wall-street-latest-a7954156.html.
63 Fleming, *Death of Homo Economicus*, 182.

4 Semio-Futility and Symbolic Indigestion

1 Christian Marazzi writes that "at the peak of the 'communication society,' we are paradoxically witnessing a *crisis of communication itself*" – Christian Marazzi, *Capital and Affects: The Politics of the Language Economy*, trans. Giuseppina Mecchia (Los Angeles, CA: Semiotext(e), 2011), 43, emphasis in original.
2 Ludwig Wittgenstein, *Philosophical Investigations*, 4th edn., trans. P. M. S. Hacker and Joachim Schulte (Oxford: Wiley-Blackwell, 2009), 43.
3 Andreas Bernard, *Theory of the Hashtag*, trans. Valentine A. Pakis and Daniel Ross (Cambridge: Polity, 2019).
4 Maurizio Lazzarato, "Immaterial Labour," in *Radical Thought in Italy: A Potential Politics*, eds. Paolo Virno and Michael Hardt (Minneapolis, MN: University of Minnesota Press, 1996), 133–50 and *Signs and Machines: Capitalism and the Production of Subjectivity*, trans. Joshua David Jordan (Los Angeles, CA: Semiotext(e), 2014); Yann Moulier-Boutang, *Cognitive Capitalism*, trans. Ed Emery (Cambridge: Polity, 2011).
5 1 News NZ, "House Prices in Auckland Now 91 per cent Higher than 2007 Peak, Latest Stats Show." TVNZ, 11 January 2017, www.tvnz.co.nz/one-news/new-zealand/house-prices-in-auckland-now-91-per-cent-higher-than-2007-peak-latest-stats-show.
6 Sara Meij, "Older People Forced to Sleep in Car as Housing Crisis Bites," Stuff NZ, 9 August 2018, www.stuff.co.nz/national/106063441/rise-in-homeless-older-generation-predicted-as-housing-crisis-bites.
7 Jacinda Ardern, *I Know This to be True: On Kindness, Empathy, and Strength* (Auckland: Upstart Press, 2020).

8   Simon Bridges, "New National Leader Says There is a Housing Crisis in NZ," interview by Guyon Espiner, RNZ, 28 February 2018, www.radionz.co.nz/news/political/351421/new-national-leader-says-there-is-a-housing-crisis-in-nz.
9   Harry G. Frankfurt, *On Bullshit* (Princeton, NJ: Princeton University Press, 2005).
10 Franco "Bifo" Berardi, *The Uprising: On Poetry and Finance* (Los Angeles, CA: Semiotext(e), 2012), 96.
11 Jean Baudrillard, *Why Hasn't Everything Already Disappeared?*, trans. Chris Turner (London: Seagull Books, 2009).
12 Berardi, *The Uprising*, 17.
13 Jodi Dean, *Crowds and Party* (London: Verso, 2016), 18.
14 Janet Roitman, *Anti-Crisis* (Durham, NC: Duke University Press, 2014), 3–4.
15 *ibid.*, 11.
16 Karl Marx, *Capital: A Critique of Political Economy*, vol. 3, trans. David Fernbach (London: Penguin Books, 1981), 206.
17 For more on neoliberalism's exploitation of crises, see Naomi Klein, *The Shock Doctrine: The Rise of Disaster Capitalism* (Toronto, ON: Random House, 2007); Philip Mirowski, *Never Let a Serious Crisis Go to Waste: How Neoliberalism Survived the Financial Meltdown* (London: Verso, 2013).
18 Pierre Dardot and Christian Laval, *Never-Ending Nightmare: The Neoliberal Assault on Democracy*, trans. Gregory Elliot (London: Verso, 2019), 24.
19 Christian Marazzi, *Capital and Language: From the New Economy to the War Economy*, trans. Gregory Conti (Los Angeles, CA: Semiotext(e), 2008), 30, emphasis in original.
20 Berardi, *The Uprising*, 17–18.

21 *ibid.*, 29.
22 John Urry, "The Complexities of the Global," *Theory, Culture & Society* 22, no. 5 (2005): 237.
23 Jodi Dean, *Democracy and Other Neoliberal Fantasies: Communicative Capitalism and Left Politics* (Durham, NC: Duke University Press, 2009), 24.
24 Berardi, *The Uprising*, 15. See, also, Eugene Thacker, "Networks, Swarms, Multitudes (Part Two)," *CTheory*, 18 May 2004, https://journals.uvic.ca/index.php/ctheory/article/view/14541/5388; Byung-Chul Han, *In the Swarm: Digital Prospects*, trans. Erik Butler (Cambridge, MA: MIT Press, 2017).
25 Berardi, *The Uprising*, 15.
26 Marazzi, *Capital and Affects*, 72.
27 *ibid.*, 73.
28 Byung-Chul Han, *The Expulsion of the Other: Society, Perception and Communication Today*, trans. Wieland Hoban (Cambridge: Polity, 2018), 37, emphasis in original.
29 Bernard, *Theory of the Hashtag*.
30 Han, *Expulsion of the Other*, 53, emphasis in original.
31 See Gayatri Chakravorty Spivak, "A Borderless World?" *Conflicting Humanities*, eds Rosi Braidotti and Paul Gilroy (London: Bloomsbury, 2016), 47–60; Neil Vallelly, "From the Margins of the Neoliberal University: Notes Towards Nomadic Literary Studies," *Poetics Today* 40, no. 1 (2019): 59–79.
32 Reece Jones, *Violent Borders: Refugees and the Right to Move* (London: Verso, 2016), 5.
33 Han, *Expulsion of the Other*, 65.
34 *ibid.*, 72–74, emphasis in original.

35 Simone Drichel, "Introduction: Reframing Vulnerability: 'So Obviously the Problem...'?" *Substance* 42, no. 3 (2013): 5.
36 Simone Drichel, "Towards a 'Radical Acceptance of Vulnerability': Postcolonialism and Deconstruction," *Substance* 42, no. 3 (2013): 53.
37 Han, *Expulsion of the Other*, 33, emphasis in original.
38 Franco "Bifo" Berardi, *Futurability: The Age of Impotence and the Horizon of Possibility* (London: Verso, 2017), 28.
39 Dean, *Crowds and Party*, 57.
40 Zoë Corbyn, "Get Ahead in Silicon Valley: Replace Real Food with Liquid Meals," *The Guardian*, 11 July 2015, www.theguardian.com/technology/2015/jul/11/hack-yourself-upgrade-diet-meals-beaker.
41 Gilaad Kaplan et al., "Worldwide Incidence and Prevalence of Inflammatory Bowel Disease in the 21st Century: A Systematic Review of Population-based Studies," *The Lancet* 390, no. 10114 (2017): 2768–79; Eberhard Standl et al., "The Global Epidemics of Diabetes in the 21st Century: Current Situation and Perspectives," *European Journal of Preventive Cardiology* 26, no. 2 (2019): 7–14.
42 Carl Zimmer, "Germs in Your Gut Are Talking to Your Brain. Scientists Want to Know What They're Saying," *The New York Times*, 28 January 2019, www.nytimes.com/2019/01/28/health/microbiome-brain-behavior-dementia.html.
43 Han, *Expulsion of the Other*, 77, emphasis in original.
44 McKenzie Wark, *Capital is Dead: Is this Something Worse?* (London: Verso, 2019), 45. See also, *A Hacker Manifesto* (Cambridge, MA: Harvard University Press, 2004).
45 Wark, *Capital is Dead*, 48.
46 *ibid.*, 169.

5 The Politics of Futility

1. Madeline Conway, "Obama: 'You get the Politicians you Deserve,'" *Politico*, 5 September 2017, www.politico.com/story/2017/05/09/obama-you-get-the-politicians-you-deserve-238150.
2. Obama continued a long tradition of using democracy to protect corporate interests. See Alex Carey, *Taking the Risk Out of Democracy: Corporate Propaganda versus Freedom and Liberty* (Champaign, IL: University of Illinois Press, 1996); Carl Boggs, *Phantom Democracy: Corporate Interests and Political Power in America* (New York: Palgrave Macmillan, 2011); Martin Gilens and Benjamin I. Page, "Testing Theories of American Politics: Elites, Interest Groups, and Average Citizens," *Perspectives on Politics* 12, no. 3 (2014): 564–81.
3. Benjamin Day, "Why Obamacare Didn't Work," *Jacobin*, 16 September 2016, www.jacobinmag.com/2016/09/obamacre-aca-aetna-public-option-clinton-trump.
4. Wendy Brown, *Undoing the Demos: Neoliberalism's Stealth Revolution* (New York: Zone Books, 2015), 168.
5. Cornel West, "Pity the Sad Legacy of Barack Obama," *The Guardian*, 9 January 2017, www.theguardian.com/commentisfree/2017/jan/09/barack-obama-legacy-presidency.
6. Emily Apter, *Unexceptional Politics: On Obstruction, Impasse, and the Impolitic* (London: Verso, 2018), 4.
7. *ibid.*, 10.
8. *ibid.*, 1.
9. William Davies, "Who Am I Prepared to Kill?" *London Review of Books* 42, no. 15 (2020): 3.
10. *ibid.*

11 Orge Castellano, "Why 'Buycotting' is the New Form of Political Activism: How Ethical Consumption Could Make or Break Your Business," Medium, 26 June 2018, https://orge.medium.com/why-buycott-is-the-new-form-of-political-activism-a85a746756e3.
12 Monroe Friedman, "A Positive Approach to Organised Consumer Action: The 'Buycott' as an Alternative to the Boycott," *Journal of Consumer Policy* 19, no. 4 (1996): 448.
13 Jason Hickel and Arsalan Khan, "The Culture of Capitalism and the Crisis of Critique," *Anthropological Quarterly* 85, no. 1 (2012): 223.
14 Pierre Bourdieu, "The Forms of Capital," in *Handbook of Theory and Research for the Sociology of Education*, ed. John Richardson (Westport, CT: Greenwood, 1986), 241–258, at 242.
15 *ibid.*, 248–49.
16 *ibid.*, 251.
17 James Coleman, "Social Capital in the Creation of Human Capital," *American Journal of Sociology* 94 (1988): S95–S120; Thomas H. Sander and Robert D. Putnam, "Rebuilding the Stock of Social Capital," *School Administrator* 56, no. 8 (1999): 28–33; Francis Fukuyama, "Social Capital and Civil Society," International Monetary Fund (IMF) Working Paper (April 2000): 1–18.
18 Robert D. Putnam, *Bowling Alone: The Collapse and Revival of American Community* (New York: Simon & Schuster, 2000), 19.
19 Robert D. Putnam. "*E Pluribus Unum*: Diversity and Community in the Twenty-First Century, the 2006 Johan Skytte Prize Lecture," *Scandinavian Political Studies* 30, no. 2 (2007): 137–74.
20 Fukuyama, "Social Capital and Civil Society," 15.

21 Kenneth J. Arrow, "Observations on Social Capital," in *Social Capital: A Multifaceted Perspective*, eds Partha Dasgupta and Ismail Serageldin (Washington, DC: World Bank 1999), 3–6; Samuel Bowles, "Social Capital and Community Governance," *Focus: Newsletter for the Institute for Research on Poverty* 20, no. 3 (1999): 6–10; Lindon J. Robinson, A. Allan Schmid, and Marcelo E. Siles, "Is Social Capital Really Capital?" *Review of Social Economy* 60, no. 1 (2002): 1–21.

22 Mark Fisher, *Capitalist Realism: Is There No Alternative?* (Winchester: Zero Books, 2009), 8.

23 Castellano, "Why 'Buycotting' is the New Form of Political Activism."

24 Green America, "Mission Statement," accessed 25 October 2020, https://greenamerica.org/our-mission.

25 Green America, "What Does it Mean to Vote with your Dollar?" Green America (blog), accessed 25 October 2020, https://greenamerica.org/blog/what-does-it-mean-vote-your-dollar.

26 *ibid*.

27 Nicole Aschoff, *The New Prophets of Capital* (London: Verso, 2015), chapter 2.

28 Ndongo Samba Sylla, "Fairtrade is an Unjust Movement that Serves the Rich," *The Guardian*, 5 September 2014, www.theguardian.com/global-development/2014/sep/05/fairtrade-unjust-movement-serves-rich; see, also, Ndongo Samba Sylla, *The Fair Trade Scandal: Marketing Poverty to Benefit the Rich* (London: Pluto Press, 2014).

29 Green America, "Vote with your Dollar."

30 Ludwig von Mises, *Socialism: An Economic and Sociological Analysis*, trans. J. Kahane (New Haven, CT: Yale University Press, 1962), 21.

31 Aschoff, *New Prophets of Capital*, 53.

32 Jodi Dean, *Democracy and Other Neoliberal Fantasies: Communicative Capitalism and Left Politics* (Durham, NC: Duke University Press, 2009), 11.
33 Jodi Dean, *Crowds and Party* (London: Verso, 2016), 256.
34 Tim Di Muzio, *Carbon Capitalism: Energy, Social Reproduction, and World Order* (London: Rowman & Littlefield, 2015).
35 Fisher, *Capitalist Realism*, 66, emphasis in original.
36 Liza Featherstone, "Don't Blame the Babies," *Jacobin*, 15 April 2019, www.jacobinmag.com/2019/04/children-climate-change-family-guilt.
37 See United Nations, Department of Economic and Social Affairs, Population Division, "World Fertility and Family Planning 2020: Highlights" (New York: United Nations, 2020), 1–35.
38 Featherstone, "Don't Blame the Babies."
39 Extinction Rebellion UK (@XRebellionUK), Twitter post, 2 September 2020, https://twitter.com/XRebellionUK/status/1300794775138906114?s=20.
40 Quoted in Mark Montegriffo, "Yes, 'Socialism or Extinction' is Exactly the Choice We Face," *Jacobin*, 9 April 2020, www.jacobinmag.com/2020/09/extinction-rebellion-socialism-capitalism.
41 Peter Fleming, *The Death of Homo Economicus: Work, Debt and the Myth of Endless Accumulation* (London: Pluto Press, 2017), 176.
42 Dean, *Crowds and Party*, 3–4, emphasis in original.
43 David Harvey, *Spaces of Global Capitalism: Towards a Theory of Uneven Geographical Development* (London: Verso, 2006), 51.
44 Milton Friedman and Rose D. Friedman, *Two Lucky People: Memoirs* (Chicago, IL: University of Chicago Press, 1998), 605.

45 Jessica Whyte, *The Morals of the Market: Human Rights and the Rise of Neoliberalism* (London: Verso, 2019), 28–30.
46 Keir Milburn, *Generation Left* (Cambridge: Polity, 2019).
47 Grace Blakeley, *Stolen: How to Save the World from Financialisation* (London: Repeater Books, 2019), 217.
48 Dean, *Crowds and Party*, 71–72.

6   Futilitarianism in the Age of Covid-19

1 Donald J. Trump (@realDonaldTrump), Twitter post, 23 March 2020, https://twitter.com/realDonaldTrump/status/1241935285916782593.
2 Steve Hilton (@NextRevFNC), Twitter video, 23 March 2020, https://twitter.com/NextRevFNC/status/1241914037476175872.
3 Toby Helm, "Austerity to Blame for 130,000 'Preventable' UK Deaths – Report," *The Guardian*, 1 June 2019, www.theguardian.com/politics/2019/jun/01/perfect-storm-austerity-behind-130000-deaths-uk-ippr-report.
4 Hilton (@NextRevFNC), Twitter video.
5 For an overview of the potential financial impact of the pandemic, see Jack Foster, "The Corona Crash," *Economic and Social Research Aotearoa* 16 (April 2020): 1–7; Grace Blakeley, *The Corona Crash: How the Pandemic Will Change Capitalism* (London: Verso, 2020).
6 William Davies, "The New Neoliberalism," *New Left Review* 101 (2016): 121–34.
7 Pierre Dardot and Christian Laval, *Never-Ending Nightmare: The Neoliberal Assault on Democracy*, trans. Gregory Elliot (London: Verso, 2019), xx, emphasis in original.

8 Phillip Inman, "Rightwing Thinktanks Call Time on Age of Austerity," *The Guardian*, 16 May 2020, www.theguardian.com/politics/2020/may/16/thatcherite-thinktanks-back-increase-public-spending-in-lockdown.
9 Jonathan Wolff, "Making the World Safe for Utilitarianism," *Royal Institute of Philosophy* 58 (2006): 2.
10 William Davies, *The Happiness Industry: How Government and Big Business Sold Us Well-Being* (London: Verso, 2015), 17.
11 Wolff, "Making the World," 2.
12 Hilton (@NextRevFNC), Twitter video.
13 Quoted in Toby Helm, Emma Graham-Harrison, and Robin McKie, "How Did Britain Get Its Coronavirus Response So Wrong?" *The Guardian*, 19 April 2020, www.theguardian.com/world/2020/apr/18/how-did-britain-get-its-response-to-coronavirus-so-wrong.
14 Tim Chipman and Caroline Wheeler, "Coronavirus: Ten Days that Shook Britain – and Changed the Nation Forever," *The Times*, 22 March 2020, www.thetimes.co.uk/article/coronavirus-ten-days-that-shook-britain-and-changed-the-nation-for-ever-spz6sc9vb.
15 Gareth Morgan (@garethmorgannz), Twitter post, 13 April 2020, https://twitter.com/garethmorgannz/status/1249586995858264070.
16 Duncan Maskell, "Melbourne Uni Chief Says Victoria Must Address Difficult Ethical Questions," interview by Chip Le Grand, *The Age*, 19 September 2020, www.smh.com.au/national/melbourne-uni-chief-says-victoria-must-address-difficult-ethical-questions-20200919-p55x82.html.
17 Quinn Slobodian and Dieter Plehwe, "Introduction," in *Nine Lives of Neoliberalism*, eds Phillip Mirowski, Dieter Plehwe, and Quinn Slobodian (London: Verso, 2020), 11.

18 My narrative here is indebted to David Dayen, "How the Fed Bailed Out the Investor Class without Spending a Cent," *The American Prospect*, 27 May 2020, https://prospect.org/coronavirus/how-fed-bailed-out-the-investor-class-corporate-america.
19 Federal Reserve, "Federal Reserve Announces Extensive Measures to Support the Economy," Press Release, 23 March 2020.
20 United States Senate, "Coronavirus Aid, Relief, and Economic Security Act," Bill no. 3548, 2nd Session, 19 March 2020.
21 Robert Brenner, "Escalating Plunder," *New Left Review* 123 (2020): 10.
22 *ibid.*, 7
23 *ibid.*, 13.
24 *ibid.*, 17.
25 Amit Seru and Luigi Zingales, "Save Capitalism from the CARES Act," *The Wall Street Journal*, 30 March 2020, www.wsj.com/articles/save-capitalism-from-the-cares-act-11585608917.
26 Patrick W. Watson, "Coronavirus Socialism," *Forbes*, 13 April 2020, www.forbes.com/sites/patrickwwatson/2020/04/13/coronavirus-socialism.
27 Sameer Butt, "As Former Wall Street Trader, I Was Horrified by the CARES Act. Here's What Should Have Been in Trump's Stimulus Package," *The Independent*, 8 April 2020, www.independent.co.uk/voices/trump-coronavirus-stimulus-package-cares-act-congress-a9456311.html.
28 Bianca Austin et al., "Billionaire Wealth vs. Community Health: Protecting Essential Workers from Pandemic Profiteers," Institute for Policy Studies Report (November 2020): 4–7.

29 Jonathan Ponciano, "Jeff Bezos Becomes the First Person Ever Worth $200 Billion," *Forbes*, 26 August 2020, www.forbes.com/sites/jonathanponciano/2020/08/26/worlds-richest-billionaire-jeff-bezos-first-200-billion/#41c61f0d4db7.

30 Rupert Neate, "Billionaires' Wealth Rises to $10.2 Trillion amid Covid Crisis," *The Guardian*, 7 October 2020, www.theguardian.com/business/2020/oct/07/Covid-19-crisis-boosts-the-fortunes-of-worlds-billionaires.

31 Australian Government, Department of Education, Skills and Employment, "Job-Ready Graduate Package," accessed 3 November 2020, www.dese.gov.au/job-ready.

32 Paul Karp, "Australian University Fees to Double for Some Arts Courses, But Fall for Stem Subjects," *The Guardian*, 18 October 2020, www.theguardian.com/australia-news/2020/jun/19/australian-university-fees-arts-stem-science-maths-nursing-teaching-humanities.

33 Dan Tehan, "Minister for Education Dan Tehan National Press Club Address," Speech, 19 June 2020, https://ministers.dese.gov.au/tehan/minister-education-dan-tehan-national-press-club-address.

34 Daniel Bessner, "House of Cards: Can the American University be Saved?" *The Nation*, 8 September 2020, www.thenation.com/article/society/gig-academy-meritocracy-trap-universities-crisis.

35 Boris Johnson, "We Will Not Need Another National Lockdown," interview by Edward Malnick, *The Sunday Telegraph*, 19 July 2020, www.telegraph.co.uk/politics/2020/07/18/boris-johnson-exclusive-interview-will-not-need-another-national.

36 Peggy McGlone, "Trump Budget Again Calls for the Elimination of Federal Arts Agencies," *The Washington*

Post, 11 February 2020, www.washingtonpost.com/entertainment/trump-budget-again-calls-for-the-elimination-of-federal-arts-agencies/2020/02/10/8b9e8df2-4c4f-11ea-bf44-f5043eb3918a_story.html.
37 Rosi Braidotti, "The Contested Posthumanities," in *Conflicting Humanities*, eds Rosi Braidotti and Paul Gilroy (London: Bloomsbury, 2016), 11.
38 William Davies, "How the Humanities Became the New Enemy Within," *The Guardian*, 28 February 2020, www.theguardian.com/commentisfree/2020/feb/28/humanities-british-government-culture.
39 For the origins of the term "racial capitalism," see Cedric J. Robinson, *Black Marxism: The Making of the Black Radical Tradition* (London: Zed Books, 1983).
40 Lyra Walsh Fuchs, "The Rise of Telehealth," *Dissent*, 2 September 2020, www.dissentmagazine.org/online_articles/the-rise-of-telehealth.
41 Dan Diamond, Adam Cancryn, and Rachel Roubin, "Trump Signs Order Aimed at Boosting Rural Health Care, Telehealth," *Politico*, 8 March 2020, www.politico.com/news/2020/08/03/trump-executive-order-rural-health-care-telehealth-390947.

Conclusion: The Becoming-Common of the Futilitariat

1 Isabell Lorey, *State of Insecurity: Government of the Precarious*, trans. Aileen Derieg (London: Verso, 2015), 12, emphasis in original.
2 *ibid.*, 19–20.
3 *ibid.*, 2.
4 Precarias a la deriva, "Adrift through the Circuits of Feminised Precarious Work," *Feminist Review* 77 (2004):

157-61 and "A Very Careful Strike – Four Hypotheses," *The Commoner* (Spring 2006): 33-45; Julia Tirler, "Precarias a la deriva," *Krisis: Journal for Contemporary Philosophy* 2 (2018): 129-30.
5 Guy Standing, *The Precariat: The New Dangerous Class* (London: Bloomsbury, 2011) and *A Precariat Charter: From Denizens to Citizens* (London: Bloomsbury, 2014); Matthew Johnson, ed., *Precariat: Labour, Work, and Politics* (London: Routledge, 2015).
6 I make a similar argument about relationality, but in the context of "disappearance," in Neil Vallelly, "The Relationality of Disappearance," *Angelaki: Journal of the Theoretical Humanities* 24, no. 3 (2019): 38-52.
7 Lorey, *State of Insecurity*, 15, emphasis added.
8 Pierre Dardot and Christian Laval, *Common: On Revolution in the 21st Century*, trans. Matthew MacLellan (London: Bloomsbury, 2019), 28, emphasis in original.
9 See Michael Hardt and Antonio Negri, *Empire* (Cambridge, MA: Harvard University Press, 2000) and *Multitude: War and Democracy in the Age of Empire* (New York: Penguin, 2004).
10 Standing, *Precariat*, 4.

Index

Adam Smith Institute, 153
Allende, Salvador, 46
Amazon, 62, 162, 164
Anderson, Perry, 90
anticapitalism, 12–13, 16, 27, 48, 145–6
anti-natalism, 80, 142–5
antipathy, 28–9
anxiety, 121–4
Aotearoa New Zealand, 6, 53, 81–4, 107–9, 157–8, 206n11, 207n22
Apple, 56
Apter, Emily, 129–30, 139
Ardern, Jacinda, 157
asceticism, 28
Aschoff, Nicole, 140–1
austerity, 13, 70, 92, 130, 151–3, 159–60, 170, 180, 182
Australia, 6, 21, 161, 165–6, 170, 207n22
authenticity, 67–8, 77

Badiou, Alain, 47
Barber, Simon, 83, 206n11
Baudrillard, Jean, 106, 110
Becker, Gary, 36, 64, 67, 88
becoming-common, 22, 177–83
Bentham, Jeremy, 2, 23–31, 33–7, 39, 41, 43, 45–6, 49, 91, 153–4, 171, 179
Berardi, Franco 'Bifo', 49, 106, 109–10, 113–6, 122
Bezos, Jeff, 62, 164
Biden, Joe, 128
Birch, Kean and Simon Springer, 11–2
Black Lives Matter, 169, 183
Blair, Tony, 86, 89–91, 95, 97–8, 103, 206n22

Blakeley, Grace, 148–9
"Blatcherism," 90
Boltanski, Luc and Ève Chiapello, 31–3, 47–8
borders, 17, 29, 117–20, 137
Bourdieu, Pierre, 135–7
Braidotti, Rosi, 167
"Brand Called You, The" (Peters), 58–64
Brenner, Robert, 162–3
Bresner, Daniel, 166
Brexit, 131, 151, 181
Bridges, Simon, 107–9, 112
Brown, Wendy, 7, 12, 17, 50, 58, 65, 68–9, 95, 204n1
"bullshit jobs," 72–3
Burke, Edward, 43–4
Butler, Judith, 173
Butt, Sameer, 164
buycotting, 2, 133–5, 138–9, 142, 146, 149, 177

Callison, William and Zachary Manfredi, 14, 70
Cameron, David, 151, 166
capitalism
    colonisation and, 84–6
    communication and, 106, 110, 112–3, 124
    crisis of, 111–2
    exploitation and, 15
    freedom and, 49–50, 92, 102–3
    futility and, 4, 183
    green growth and, 13
    neoliberalism and, 12–14, 47–8, 58, 71, 96–8, 175–6, 180–1
    politics and, 129–30, 141–2, 144, 146–9

capitalism (*cont.*)
  progressive capitalism and, 13
  rentier, 75, 180, 182
  spirit of, 48, 98–101
  utilitarianism and, 2–3, 19, 24–7, 31–6, 51, 71, 171–2, 179
  work and, 71–6, 102
capitalist realism, 51, 138
carbon footprint, 143–4
Carson, Ben, 80
Centre for Policy Studies, 26, 153
Chicago School of Economics, 6, 36, 46, 88
Chile, 16, 46, 183
climate change, 13, 16, 52, 56, 79–80, 111, 142–5, 177–8, 180
climate emergency, 112–3
Clinton, Bill, 86–91, 95, 97–9, 103, 206n22
Clinton, Hillary, 132
cognitive behavioural therapy (CBT), 80, 205n2
cognitive capitalism, 106
colonialism, 26, 29, 39, 85, 131, 145, 169
colonisation, 81–6, 131, 143
common good, the, 1, 3, 8, 32, 180
communication, 18, 20, 59, 76, 94, 105–6, 109–10, 113–25, 177
community, 27, 30, 41, 43, 46, 62–4, 68, 77, 85, 120, 134, 136, 157
competition, 3, 5, 7–8, 10, 18, 42, 44–5, 49, 56, 57–9, 62–4, 69–70, 77, 88, 100–2, 109, 132, 148, 152, 176, 178–9, 182
consumer activism, 133–42, 178
consumerism, 6, 21, 47, 60, 133–4, 179
consumers 62–3, 67, 115, 133–5, 139, 141
Cooper, Melinda, 88–90
Coronavirus Aid, Relief, and Economic Security Act (CARES), 21, 161–4, 170
cost-benefit analysis, 9, 154–61, 180
Covid-19 pandemic, 14–15, 21, 48, 73, 92–3, 111–2, 130, 148, 151–72, 182
crisis
  overuse of term, 109–14
Critchley, Simon, 17
Cummings, Dominic, 156–9

Dardot, Pierre and Christian Laval, 12–14, 111, 153, 180
data, 6, 25, 38, 51, 74, 115, 154, 181
Davies, William, 7–8, 34, 36, 130–1, 152, 154, 168–9
Dean, Jodi, 12, 110, 115, 141–2, 146, 149–50, 181
debt, 3, 5, 16, 65, 70, 100, 107, 148, 163, 166, 183
decolonisation, 147
democracy, 8, 10, 12, 17, 19, 69, 97, 128, 136, 187n13
dependency, 20, 86–93, 208n28
Descartes, René, 43
digestion, 123–4
Drichel, Simone, 120–1
Duff, Alan, 81–6, 102–3

economic science, 24, 27, 31–3, 36–40
Edgeworth, Francis, 38–9
education, 16, 55, 65, 80–1, 94–5, 101, 148, 160, 165–70
Elmhirst, Sophie, 68
English, Bill, 108
entrepreneurialism, 7, 42, 63, 70–1, 84, 87, 97, 203n27
"entrepreneur of the self" (Foucault), 62, 67–8
environment, the, *see* climate change
equality, 35, 37, 56, 69, 80, 87, 96, 100, 147, 159
ethical consumerism, 6, 21, 133–142
Extinction Rebellion, 145

Index

Fairtrade, 140
familial responsibility, 88–9
Featherstone, Liza, 144–5
Federal Reserve, 162–3
felicific calculus, 29–30, 39–40
financialisation, 5–6, 13, 58, 75–6, 180, 182, 200n11
Fisher, Mark, 12, 17, 138, 143
Fleming, Peter, 25, 58, 66, 71, 73, 75, 102, 145–6, 204n1
fossil fuels, 3, 80, 143, 145
Foucault, Michel, 58, 66–7
Fourier, Charles, 74
Fraser, Nancy, 86–7, 97
freedom
 government and, 33
 Hayek on, 45–6
 human capital and, 68
 human rights and, 147–8
 Marx on, 49–50, 62–3
 neoliberalism and, 12, 42, 49–50, 77, 147
 of capital, 92, 185n3
 of the individual, 34–5, 51, 100, 147
 of the market, 34, 96–7
 personal responsibility and, 102–3
 self-branding and, 62–3
 utilitarianism and, 34–5, 37
Friedman, Milton, 50, 147
Friedman, Monroe, 133–4
Fukuyama, Francis, 137
futilitarian condition, the, 19, 26–7, 57, 68, 71, 77, 179
 definition of, 3–5, 26–7
 neoliberalism and, 11–13, 26–7, 46–52
 university and, 4–5
futilitarianism, 3, 16, 21, 27, 51–2, 132, 144, 150, 161, 178–9, 183
futilitarian spirit of capitalism, the, 98–102
futilitariat, the, 22, 181–3

futility, *see also* uselessness
 capitalism and, 3–4, 12–13, 19, 58, 71–4
 experience of, 5, 19, 21–2, 51, 63, 68, 70, 95, 149–50, 173, 182
 language and, 105–6; *see also* semio-futility
 neoliberalism and, 6, 10–2, 15–7, 19, 22, 72–3, 149–50, 155, 171, 182
 nihilism and, 17–18
 politics of, 21, 127–50
 precarity and, 176–8
 university and, 94–5
 work and, 71–7

"gaplessness," 116–20
Geneva School of neoliberalism, 9
gig economy, 101
Global Financial Crisis (2008), the, 7, 13, 69–70, 96–8, 110, 152, 162, 167
Gove, Michael, 108
government, 2, 12, 14, 17, 20–1, 33–6, 44, 46–8, 67, 79, 81, 83–4, 91–5, 100–3, 108, 111, 128, 137, 140–1, 143, 147, 149, 151–4, 156–7, 159–61, 165–7, 170–2, 175
Graeber, David, 12, 72–4, 96
Great Depression, the, 9, 13, 19, 27
greatest-happiness principle, the, 26, 49, 79
Green America, 139–42
Guattari, Félix, 106
gut-brain axis, 124

Han, Byung-Chul, 50, 61–2, 67–8, 117–21, 124, 173
Hancock, Matt, 91–2
happiness, 1–2, 24, 28–9, 34, 38, 46, 49, 60, 76, 80, 91, 154, 159, 179
Harvey, David, 42, 47, 61, 146–7
hashtag (#), 106, 117–8

Hayek, Friedrich, 8, 19, 27, 40, 42–6, 50
healthcare, 16, 80–1, 91, 128, 136, 160, 170
herd immunity, 156–7
Hickel, Jason and Arsalan Khan, 134–5
Hickel, Jason and Giorgos Kallis, 13
Hilton, Steve, 151–5, 158–60, 172
Hobbes, Thomas, 43
Homo economicus, 19, 41, 58, 66–71, 77
Homo futilitus, 11, 20, 58, 68–77
housing crisis (Aotearoa NZ), 107–8
human capital, 10, 19, 57, 64–70, 76, 136, 138, 176, 202n26
humanities, 4, 164–9
human rights, 79, 146–8
Hume, David, 43
hyperbole, 109
hyper-complexity, 114–6

immaterial labour, 106
Incel community, 18
indigestion, 122–4; *see also* symbolic indigestion
individual, the, 6, 30, 32, 34–5, 37, 40–5, 48, 50, 64–8, 89–90, 122, 141, 143–4, 147–50
individualism, 8, 18, 32, 41, 44–8, 51, 58, 70, 88, 132, 143, 146, 153
inequality, 10, 16, 25–6, 49, 51, 77, 79, 83, 97, 111, 174
influencer, 59–60, 68
influencer power, 59–60
Institute for Policy Studies, 164
Institute of Economic Affairs and Policy Exchange, 153
International Institute of Modern Letters (IIML), 53–5
intervention, state, 7, 33, 35, 43, 45, 156, 185n3

Jevons, William Stanley, 36
Job-Ready Graduates Package, 162–8
Johnson, Boris, 25–6, 93, 131, 156, 158, 166
Jones Campbell, 197n46
Jones, Reece, 119

Key, John, 108
Keynes, John Maynard, 27, 40–6, 75, 196n38
Keynesianism, 9, 13, 19, 27, 40, 42, 46
KFC, 54–5

labour, *see* work
language, *see* communication
Lawn, Jennifer, 82, 85
Left, the, 7, 46, 48, 86, 88, 90, 96–7, 109, 127–8
Levinas, Emmanuel, 120–1
liberalism, 11, 17, 33, 37, 43, 66, 179
liberty, *see* freedom
listening, 119–25
Locke, John, 43–4
Lorey, Isabell, 96, 173–8

Macpherson, C. B., 45
Manhire, Bill, 53–4
Māori
    Duff on, 84–5
    economic deprivation, 82–3
    Mātauranga, 85
    Pākehā and, 83–5
    working class struggle and, 83
Marazzi, Christian, 113, 116–7, 212n1
market, the 9, 25, 34–5, 40–1, 45, 49–50, 85, 88, 93, 96–7, 134, 138, 140, 147, 181
Marx, Karl
    on Bentham, 23–4
    on community, 41, 62–3
    on crisis, 11
    on freedom, 49–50, 62–3
    on useless labour, 75
    on utility, 1

Index

Marxism, 11, 102, 181
Maskell, Duncan, 158–60
May 1968, 47–8
McLaren, Leah, 57
Me Inc., 59–60
Mendes, Chico, 145
Mendoza, Yovana, 57
Mill, John Stuart, 27, 37, 39, 49, 64
millennials, 16–7, 148, 166
mindfulness, 17, 18, 205n2
Mini, Peter V., 41
money, 2–3, 33–4, 41, 76, 97, 106, 110, 114, 118, 133, 140, 155
Mont Pèlerin Society (MPS), 6, 42, 147, 196n43
morality, 2, 12, 24, 29, 31, 38, 155
Morgan, Gareth, 157–8, 172
Murtola, Anna-Maria, 203n37

National Health Service (NHS), 92
neocapital, 64
neoclassical economics, 1, 19, 27, 36, 38–42, 66
neoliberal capitalism, 4–6, 14–15, 21, 27, 71, 173, 176
neoliberal economics, 1, 27, 30, 36, 69, 85, 97, 107, 153, 183
neoliberalism
  approaches to, 11–2
  as a political project, 10–11, 61
  autonomy and, 49–51
  capitalism and, 3, 6, 12–14, 47–8, 58, 71, 96–8, 175–6, 180–1
  competition and, 5, 44, 59, 178
  consumption and, 134–5
  Covid-19 pandemic and, 161, 169–72
  crisis and, 13–14, 111–2, 213n17
  death of, 14–15, 152, 161
  definitions of, 6–13
  democracy and, 8, 10, 12, 97, 187n3, 216n2
  digestion and, 123–4
  education and, 65
  entrepreneurialism and, 70–1
  everyday life and, 5–6, 16, 19, 123, 177
  Foucault on, 66–7
  freedom and, 12, 42, 49–50, 77, 147
  futilitarian condition and, 11–13, 26–7, 46–52
  futility and, 6, 10–12, 15–17, 19, 22, 72–3, 149–50, 155, 171, 182
  Global Financial Crisis (2008) and, 13–14, 96–8, 152–3
  history of, 9, 11, 19, 46–7, 190n22
  human capital and, 57, 65, 70, 101
  humanities and, 164–9
  human rights and, 146–8
  in Aotearoa New Zealand, 81–5
  inequality and, 24–5
  language and, 113, 116
  mutant metaphor and, 14–15
  "new neoliberalism" (Dardot and Laval) and, 13–14
  personal responsibility and, 79, 85, 88–9, 92, 102, 143
  precarity and, 175–7
  progress and, 25
  progressive neoliberalism and, 86–7, 95, 97, 99
  subjectivity and, 12, 60–2, 65–7, 143–4, 176
  the social and, 6–8, 16, 135
  the state and, 7–10, 42–3, 47
  university and, 4–5, 15, 65, 94–5, 101, 160, 165–6, 168, 176
  utilitarianism and, 21, 26, 31, 48–9, 51–2, 152–6, 171–2
  utility and, 48–9, 175
  utility maximisation and, 5, 48, 72, 171, 179
  work and, 15, 20, 47–8, 71–7, 101–2, 121, 160, 171, 176–8
  zombie metaphor and, 14
neoliberal rationality, 6–7, 11–12, 14–15, 21, 144, 146, 149, 173, 176, 189n22

New Democrats, the, 7; *see also* Bill Clinton
New Labour, 7, 86; *see also* Tony Blair
New Right, the, 6, 10, 86, 90–1, 93
nihilism, 17–18
Nike, 56, 59

Obama, Barack, 96–101, 103, 127–8, 150
Obama, Michelle, 55
Obamacare (Affordable Care Act), 127
Occupy Wall Street, 146, 181
Once Were Warriors (Duff), 81–7, 103
opportunity
 personal responsibility and, 89–94

paranoia, 62–4, 93
personal protective equipment (PPE), 93
personal responsibility, 5, 7, 14, 20, 79–103, 132, 142–3, 170, 173
"Personal Responsibility and Work Opportunity Reconciliation Act, The," 87
Peters, Tom, 58–63, 69
PHARMAC, 157
Pinker, Steven, 25–6, 32, 38
Pinochet, Augusto, 46
Plato, 157
political disillusionment, 130–3
political pretence, 132
political rationality, *see* neoliberal rationality
political, the, 8, 15, 21, 129, 132, 134, 174
Precarias a la deriva, 176
precariat, the, 4–5, 95, 176, 181–2
precariousness, 173–7, 182
precarity, 3, 5, 49–50, 96, 117, 122, 173–8, 181–2
privatisation, 13, 80, 92, 182
progressive capitalism, 13, 190n26

progressive neoliberalism, 86–7, 95, 99
projects
 versus subjects, 61
Proudfoot, Shannon, 56
Putnam, Robert D., 136–7

rational choice theory, 36, 40
Raybould, Jody-Wilson, 57
Reagan, Ronald, 79, 90, 98
recycling, 3, 80
refugees, 51, 110–1, 118, 178, 180
Ricardo, David, 35–6
Riley, Jonathan, 38–9
Rogernomics, 81
Roitman, Janet, 110–1
Ross, Kristin, 47
Rousseau, Jean-Jacques, 43

Saint-Paul, Gilles, 185n3
self-branding, 6, 19, 55, 57–64, 66, 77, 171
self-destruction, 101–3
self-help, 79, 81–5, 103, 170
self-interest, 34, 38, 41, 66, 70–1
self-reliance, 7, 148
self, the, 10, 117, 119–21, 125
semio-capitalism, 106
semio-futility, 11, 20–1, 106, 109–17, 122, 124, 126, 170
semio-inflation, 109
Sennett, Richard, 4, 185–6n4
Sidgwick, Henry, 27, 37–9
Silicon Valley, 123
Slobodian, Quinn, 9–10
Slobodian, Quinn and Dieter Plehwe, 11, 161
Smith, Adam, 32–3, 44, 64
Smith, Jason, 76
social capital, 135–8
social democracy, 9, 19, 43, 89, 147
social media, 5, 55, 59, 130
social reproduction, 73, 136, 203n45

Index

social, the
   Bentham on, 30–1
   Hayek on, 43–5
   Keynes on, 41
   neoliberalism and, 6–8, 16, 135–6
   precarity and, 174
   the individual and, 6
   utilitarian views on, 32–7
social welfare, 36, 38, 81, 87, 95
Srnicek, Nick and Alex Williams, 76
Stadler, Josef, 164
Standing, Guy, 181–2
Stark, Werner, 35
state, the, 7–10, 35, 42–3, 46–7, 58, 65, 69, 80, 88–90, 100–1, 111, 117, 137, 141, 149, 156, 175
surveillance capitalism, 49
swarm, the, 114–6, 214n24
Sylla, Ndongo Samba, 140
symbolic disorder, 116–7
symbolic indigestion, 11, 20, 121–6
sympathy, 28–9

technology, 5, 16, 20, 33, 38, 74–7, 105, 110, 115–7, 125
Tehan, Dan, 165–6
telehealth, 170
Thatcher, Margaret, 7, 90, 98
Trudeau, Justin, 55–7
Trump, Donald, 14, 132
Trump, Melania, 17
Twitter, 131, 145, 157

university, 4–5, 15, 65, 94–5, 101, 160, 165–6, 168, 176, 186n5
University of Melbourne, 158
Urry, John, 114
use value, 5, 106, 113–4
useless labour, 58, 71–7; *see also* "bullshit jobs"
uselessness, 3–4, 167–8; *see also* futility
utilitarianism, 1–3, 16, 23–8
   Benthamite, 24, 28–31, 33–5, 40–1, 43, 45, 91, 179
   capitalism and, 2, 19, 26, 51–2, 172, 179
   colonialism and, 26
   Covid-19 pandemic and, 156–60
   crisis of, 171–2
   definition of, 2, 24–5
   economic science and, 24, 31–2, 36–40
   futilitarianism and, 3, 16, 178
   Hayek on, 43–6
   herd immunity and, 156
   Homo economicus and, 66
   Keynes on, 40–2, 46
   neoliberalism and, 21, 26, 31, 48–9, 51–2, 152–6, 171–2
   the futilitarian condition and, 48–9
   the social and, 32–7
utility
   definitions of, 1–3, 23–24, 28
   language and, 106, 114
   maximisation, 1–4, 8, 10, 24, 26–7, 28, 33–4, 36, 46, 48, 66, 71–2, 80–1, 94, 100, 126, 161, 171–2, 179
   neoliberalism and, 48–9, 175
   social, 58, 73, 77, 95
   the principle of, 27–31, 33–4, 36, 40–1, 153
   work and, 71–3

Victoria University of Wellington, 54
von Mises, Ludwig, 9, 25, 43, 141
voting with your dollar, 21, 139–43, 149
vulnerability, 119–21, 124

Waitangi Tribunal, 81–2
Wark, McKenzie, 125
Weber, Max, 74, 99–100
Whyte, Jessica, 88, 147
Wiles, Souxsie, 157–8

Wilkins, Damien, 53–4
Wittgenstein, Ludwig, 106
Wolff, Jonathan, 153–5
Wood, Ellen Meiksins, 99
work
    anxiety and, 121–2
    care, 160
    casualisation of, 3, 13
    Covid-19 pandemic and, 155
    ethic, 62, 65, 92, 99, 159
    happiness and, 49, 74, 76
    in the university, 4–5, 94–5, 185n5
    millennials and, 17, 148
    neoliberalism and, 15, 20, 47–8, 71–7, 101–2, 121, 160, 171, 176–8
    personal responsibility and, 87–8, 94–5
    symbolic indigestion and, 124
    technology and, 74–7
    useless labour and, 71–7

Žižek, Slavoj, 53